Endorse

What better way to find a light at the end of a dark tunnel than by following those who know the way out. Christian author, Becky Toews, uses inspirational stories to guide readers to find a deeper walk with God. Now, you can ignite your passion for serving, following, and loving Jesus through the thematic readings in *Keep Your Lamp Burning*. The readings will inspire you to reflect on Scriptures, delight in personal life stories, and apply the solid spiritual principles in your everyday life. Enjoy!

Joanne T. Williams
Sr. Technical Writer

I am grateful for the opportunity to endorse this new work by my favorite contemporary Christian author. I've read her previous books many times and continue to appreciate them.

When reading this new manuscript, the ideas presented for me to chew on in just the first devotion made me want to stop there and meditate for days. I hated moving on! Becky's thoughts are relatable, giving us glimpses into her personal life and experiences. They are sometimes poignant, other times laugh out loud funny. She is so well read, she brings us treasures old and new. She challenges us to live lives that reflect our master and encourages us to see ourselves through God's eyes. I hope you enjoy this latest offering of Becky's and find it valuable for your daily walk with the Lord. And if you haven't read her previous works, grab them too!

Meredith Parente
Director, Magee Project, Pittsburgh

When I happened upon Becky Toews first book, *Virgin Snow,* I was struck by the wisdom and spiritual insight that she brought to her writing. Her follow up devotional, *Between the Lampposts*, was a treasure for God seekers desiring a closer relationship with The Lord. And now, *Keep Your Lamp Burning,* comes at a time when we are all feeling the weariness of a world that is changing and full of uncertainty. This devotional brings clarity to the darkness and her engaging style will help readers keep their eyes focused on Him, lamps full of oil, looking for His coming. I am always so inspired by Becky's books that I buy multiple copies to give to my friends and their response is always the same. "Thank you for the spiritual insight and hope that I got from this book."

Debra Tunney
YWAM Philadelphia

Reading *Keep Your Lamp Burning,* I felt immersed in a bubble of love that drew me into a sense of peace that can only be found in Jesus. Living in a world with so much pain, Becky's writing reminds me of my purpose to love.

Patty Eastep
Executive Director
Anchor Lancaster

Becky's deep and personal relationship with God is evident as she takes you on a spiritual journey in her book, *Keep Your Lamp Burning.* Not only is she able to articulate the truth of God's Word, she is able to capture the essence of His heart as well.

Nancy Graybill
Wife, Mother, Grandmother
Ministry Team, Praise Fellowship
Reading PA

Keep Your Lamp Burning

Devotions to Help You Reflect God's Love, Our Faith, and Purpose

Becky Toews

Name: Becky Toews
Title: Keep Your Lamp Burning: Devotions to Help You Reflect God's Love, Our Faith, and Purpose/ By Becky Toews
Identifiers:
ISBN: 978-1-953114-97-6
Subjects: 1. Religion/Devotional
2. Religion/Christian Living/Inspirational
3. Religion/Christian Living/General

Cover design: Robin Black

Published by EA Books Publishing, a division of
Living Parables of Central Florida, Inc. a 501c3
EABooksPublishing.com

To Tobin, Mason, and Quinn

Grandpa Creech dedicated his last book to his grandchildren. I thought it fitting to do the same. May you always shine your light for Jesus.

CONTENTS

"Then the kingdom of heaven will be like ten virgins who took their lamps and went to meet the bridegroom. Five of them were foolish, and five were wise. For when the foolish took their lamps, they took no oil with them, but the wise took flasks of oil with their lamps. As the bridegroom was delayed, they all became drowsy and slept. But at midnight there was a cry, 'Here is the bridegroom! Come out to meet him.' Then all those virgins rose and trimmed their lamps. And the foolish said to the wise, 'Give us some of your oil, for our lamps are going out.' But the wise answered, saying, 'Since there will not be enough for us and for you, go rather to the dealers and buy for yourselves.' And while they were going to buy, the bridegroom came, and those who were ready went in with him to the marriage feast, and the door was shut. Afterward the other virgins came also, saying, 'Lord, lord, open to us.' But he answered, 'Truly, I say to you, I do not know you.' Watch therefore, for you know neither the day nor the hour.'" Matthew 25:1–13

Introduction

The story of the wise and foolish virgins is a sobering passage from the gospel of Matthew. Like the women in the parable, we started our journey carrying lamps radiant with life. But for whatever reason, we find the oil in our lamps running low. Many of us feel depleted and weary. The darkness of a world rife with anger, division, and conflict has drained us of love, of faith, of hope. We're encountering new definitions of right and wrong. Once acknowledged virtues of self-sacrifice, truth, courage, and humility are viewed as *passé*. Maybe we didn't understand that life in a fallen world would never be easy. We didn't realize following Christ meant we had to keep replenishing the life sustaining oil. Like the five foolish women, we let our limited understanding dictate our decision-making. And midnight approaches.

I don't know why five of the ten virgins in Jesus' parable ran out of oil. Maybe they mistakenly thought they had enough to get by. Maybe they simply got tired of waiting for promises to be fulfilled. Or maybe they forgot their purpose. They had one assignment—watch for the bridegroom—and they blew it. Whatever the reason, their negligence caused them to lose everything.

In addressing these five, the Lord says they can't come to the wedding feast because he doesn't know them. Now isn't that interesting? Had they known him, their lamps would have been full and flowing with oil. It makes me think the consequences of their neglect was also the cause.

Nothing is more important in life than knowing and being known by God. It's what gives meaning to every hour of every day in our lives. It's what we're here for. It's what keeps our lamps burning.

So how's your oil supply?

If we hope to keep our lamps burning, it's vital to replenish the oil by cultivating our relationship with the Lord. We can't let busyness or lesser affections or complacency divert us from what truly makes life worth living.

So how do we—you and I—do that?

It begins with remembering God has given each of us a light to shine. No matter how old or young we are, no matter our position or status, whether we live on Pennsylvania Avenue or in a hut in Zimbabwe, God has designed us to shine his light. Does it matter? It matters more than we dare to hope. It matters in this life because it radiates God's love and prepares all the earth for the "marriage feast" Jesus spoke about.

The oil provides the glow of gratitude and praise, holiness, truth, and faith. We replenish it with humility, dependence on God, mercy, grace, and persistence. God calls us to shine the light into our culture, into mundane life, into disappointment and doubt. We shine this light in the face of fear and find confident trust. We shine the light when we see his gifts of goodness and discover happiness. We shine the light in our celebrations and turn stale traditions into new wine.

These are the things I want to unpack in *Keep Your Lamp Burning.* I've written it in a devotional format, similar to *Between the Lamp Posts: 365 Devotions for God-Seekers.* Only this time I've used a thematic approach to organize the devotionals. I pray you will find encouragement in these pages to keep your wick trimmed and your oil filled to the brim. The days fall too uncertainly and the time approaches when it will no longer be day. May we be ready and watchful.

Part One

Who Can Shine and to Whom?

CHAPTER ONE

Followers of Jesus Shine Worth into Wandering Hearts

"With God there are no little people."

Francis Schaeffer

—*No Little People*

Feelings of low self-esteem have spawned numerous multi-million-dollar businesses on successful strategies for helping people find their worth. Topics like the necessity of self-care and self-love can be helpful, but all too often they divert us from the true and lasting source of meaning. God created us in his image to shine in the world, each with individual facets of his likeness. No matter our age, our gender, or social status, we don't have to wander from relationship to relationship or job to job to find our worth. There will always be people who can do things better than we do. But no one can be a better you than you. God wants you to discover the tremendous value he places on his highest form of creation. Then let your light shine!

Leftovers

*And when they had eaten their fill, he told his disciples, "Gather up the leftover fragments, that nothing may be lost." —*John 6:12

Jesus had access to all the bread and fish in the world. He had just taken five loaves of bread and two small fish and turned them into enough to feed five thousand people. And if that wasn't enough, a surplus of twelve basketfuls remained. Does that strike anyone else's curiosity? Why would Jesus be concerned about not wasting food? About leftovers?

Jesus demonstrated the importance of stewardship in everything he did, whether it involved food, resources, time, or talents. He didn't waste one minute of his call. He used all the resources around him to help the disciples understand basic truths. Mustard seeds, fishing nets, and leaven bread became lessons about the kingdom of God (Matthew 13). A poor widow who put all she had in the temple treasury became an illustration of what true devotion to God looks like (Luke 21:1–4). He used a prodigal son to offer a picture of the Father heart of God (Luke 15:11–32).

In a world filled with people who suffer as outcasts, losers, and underdogs, Jesus calls them friends. For him, there are no "leftover" people. He sees potential even in those whose poor choices have left them wasting away. That's why Jesus never gave the people in his life anything but his full attention. No drifting eyes to the crowd when he was engaged in a conversation. No wandering mind about where he was going to sleep that night when someone asked him a question or presented a need. He was fully present.

I think he wants us to steward life the way he did.

We've all heard the phrase, "A mind is a terrible thing to waste." But so is love that breaks down walls. So is kindness that turns away wrath. So is hope that frees people from despair. And faith that can move mountains. If you are a follower of Christ, you have access to all these things. He has made them available to you for a purpose. Don't neglect them.

You don't want to get to the end of your life and see all your potential stacked in a heap of leftovers. Neither do I.

Stewarding Your Sphere

As each has received a gift, use it to serve one another, as good stewards of God's varied grace. —1 Peter 4:10

We all have one. But each differs in size and scope. They can be broad or narrow. As varied as eleven thousand followers on Instagram to six people sitting around the kitchen table. Scripture encourages us to use whatever gift we have within them. What are they?

Our spheres of influence.

We don't have the resources to respond to every request that lands in our mailbox or inbox. If we had to pray for all the needs in the world, we would never get off our knees. But we do have a circle of family, friends, co-workers, and neighbors. They include the people who belong in our spheres of influence. Spheres we are called to steward.

We don't always recognize the importance of our spheres, so we often miss seeing the difference we can make. We consider the movers and shakers of the world limited to the rich and powerful, the politicians, the celebrities, and CEOs. But we ought never overlook our part. Stewarding our spheres is not about success; it's about faithfulness.

It's about serving others in the "various forms" of God's grace.

I recently read the report of an eighty-eight-year-old woman who has been waving to schoolchildren from her window every day for the last twelve years. When word spread, she was moving to an assisted-living home, over four hundred children gathered in her front yard to wave goodbye. They held signs and blew kisses to let her know how much her simple act of kindness had meant to them.

I know a woman who sends cards to people in need of encouragement, some of whom she knows, and some she's never met. She's faithfully been at it for over forty-five years.

Bob Goff writes in *Everybody Always*[1] how he likes to drive to his local In-N-Out and buy about twenty hamburgers. Then he goes to the city and randomly distributes them. It inspired me so much that I bought some fruit snacks and bags of trail mix. Now when I see someone on the side of the road asking for food, I'm prepared to help, even if in a small way.

Jesus expects us to steward our spheres. So, what are we waiting for? Let's get out there and make an impact.

No Little People

Greet those workers in the Lord, Tryphaena and Tryphosa. Greet the beloved Persis, who has worked hard in the Lord. Greet Rufus, chosen in the Lord; also his mother, who has been a mother to me as well. Greet Asyncritus, Phlegon, Hermes, Patrobas, Hermas, and the brothers who are with them. Greet Philologus, Julia, Nereus and his sister, and Olympas, and all the saints who are with them. —Romans 16:12–15

Is there any other religion besides Christianity that heralds individuals? Any other holy book like the Bible? It counts a poor widow gathering enough sticks to make a "last meal" for her son (1 Kings 17:9–16) as significant to God's plan as the disciples on whom Jesus would build the Church.

Christianity makes the outrageous declaration that every single person on earth has the opportunity to participate with God in writing history. Different roles, yes. Different positions. Different lifestyles. And different centuries. But we each have the potential to experience lives filled to the brim with significance and purpose.

In the twenty-seven verses of Romans 16, Paul mentions thirty-five different individuals by name. I couldn't help but wonder why. Most of them aren't mentioned elsewhere either in Scripture or the annals of history. Some are commended for risking their lives for the gospel, others simply for their hard work or hospitality. If you believe all Scripture is inspired by God (2 Timothy 3:16) as I do, then you know God has a reason for including each name.

I'm convinced he wants us to know how important we are...you, me, every single person in his creation. He doesn't look on some people as "big" and others as "small." Our significance doesn't come from a résumé of good works but from him whose image we bear.

In 2003, theologian Francis Schaeffer published the book, *No Little People*. It contains sixteen sermons that rebut the idea many of us conclude that our lives don't much matter. I thought of that title as I read the names in Romans 16. Tryphena and Patrobus really existed. As faithful followers of Christ they were anything but "little." My goodness, they lived over two thousand years ago and we're still reading their names!

So take heart! The same is true with you Stephanie, Janice, Gloria, Tim, Ken . . . Because with God there are no little people!

Pass It On

So even to old age and gray hairs,
O God, do not forsake me,
until I proclaim your might to another generation,
your power to all those to come. —Psalm 71:18

I love the *Pass It On* billboards along the road. Like the picture of Jackie Robinson with the words "Here's to you Mr. Robinson" that encourages people to pass on *Character.* Or the photo of Mr. Rodgers and the words "Won't you be my neighbor?" admonishing us to pass on *Friendship.* And one of my favorites shows Kermit the Frog with the words "Eats flies. Dates a pig. Hollywood star." *Live Your Dreams."*

I think we sometimes get trapped into thinking we have nothing of value to pass on to those in the next generation. We don't live on a big estate filled with priceless heirlooms. We haven't won acclaim for writing a best seller or had buildings named after us. But the intangible things in life prove to be far more valuable than the tangible.

Have you read the children's book, *Ordinary Mary's Extraordinary Deed?*[2] It's about an ordinary girl who picked blueberries and gave them to an elderly neighbor. The neighbor, in turn, made ordinary blueberry muffins and gave them to five people, setting off a chain reaction that eventually impacted the whole world. The book's message rang clear: kindness can be a pretty powerful entity to pass on.

The other day my husband planted forty Fraser fir trees on our property. Since he's seventy-four years old, he most likely will never see them fully mature. But he labored in planting those seedlings because he wanted to pass on something of beauty to a future generation.

Most scholars attribute Psalm 71 to King David, written in his old age. In that psalm he asks God to give him strength to *pass on* the most precious asset he had experienced in life. He wanted to declare the power and might of God to the next generation.

I don't know *how* God wants you to affect your surroundings, but I know he *does*. He has gifted you with more than you realize. Maybe it's compassion or courage or confidence. One thing is certain, if you know Jesus, he wants you to let others in on his goodness and grace.

So whatever it is, my friend, *pass it on*! Even when you're old and gray!

Therefore I Am

See what kind of love the Father has given to us, that we should be called children of God; and so we are. The reason why the world does not know us is that it did not know him. —1 John 3:1

"I think; therefore I am." These words captured 17th century French philosopher Rene Descartes's conclusion that he could no longer doubt his existence because he was the one doing the doubting. We've come a long way in discovering our identity since the days of Descartes. Here are some variations I found on Amazon's book list (with my added commentary).

- *I Tweet; Therefore I Am.* Never underestimate the power of social media to shake up one's identity.
- *I Feel; Therefore I Am.* Our feelings determine reality, rather than reality determining our feelings. What?
- *I Sketch; Therefore I Am.* If my identity fell to how well I could draw, well, I never existed.
- *I Drive; Therefore I Am.* So, what happens if you fail your driver's test?
- *I Surf; Therefore I Am.* Too bad for all us who live in the Midwest.
- *I Shop; Therefore I Am.* Only in America!

But a new source of affirming our existence has popped up that should be taken seriously: *I'm a victim; therefore I am.* We're becoming a victimization culture. Victims are the new heroes. The ones with the loudest voices. My heart goes out to all different kinds of people who have been victimized. But we do them no favor when we encourage them to let their identity be shaped by the injustices and hurts they've experienced.

Because I was raised in Appalachia, I grew up with a bit of a poverty complex. *I'm poor; therefore I am.* But my financial status comprised only a small segment of my identity. I had to release that small segment if I hoped to discover the other parts of what made me who I am.

As believers, our identity is not found in wounded pasts. Neither is it found in our accomplishments. And definitely not in what other people think. God says we are his children. We are the offspring of his lavish love. What greater affirmation of our existence do we need? Knowing we belong to him makes all the difference. So, let's celebrate the truth. *I'm his child; therefore I am.*

"Invisible" People

She gave this name to the LORD who spoke to her: "You are the God who sees me," for she said, "I have now seen the One who sees me."
—Genesis 16:13 (NIV)

She was a slave, a pregnant slave, whose unborn child was fathered by the husband of her mistress. To make matters worse, the liaison had been engineered by her barren mistress in a desperate attempt to obtain a child for herself. But it didn't go as planned. Once the slave girl became pregnant, her mistress began mistreating her, forcing her to flee into the desert. Alone, miserable, isolated from all human compassion, Hagar felt invisible. And she probably was to most people.

But she wasn't invisible to God. Not only did he see her, he spoke words of comfort and gave her a vision for the little one in her womb. In grateful response, she called him *El Roi*— "the God who sees me."

The God who saw Hagar is the same God who sees us. And it's no wonder. He made us! He knows everything about us. The psalmist declares in Psalm 139 such knowledge is too wonderful for him to grasp. "The God who sees" wants us to know we're not invisible. Not alone. Not without hope.

My son received the diagnosis of Type 1 diabetes a few years after graduating from college. This life-altering news came as a shock to all of us. Suddenly, he was thrust into a whirlwind of eliminating sweets, counting carbs, and constantly monitoring his blood sugar. When he called from Nashville to tell us the news, we at first thought he was calling to thank us for the transfer of money into his checking account. Earlier that week, my husband had deposited money for him from an unexpected inheritance. It was enough to completely pay off his school debt. He hadn't seen it yet, but the timing could not have been more perfect. On the same day he got some of the worst news of his life, he got some of the best. Although the money was monumental, it in and of itself didn't counterbalance the bad news. The timely deposit made him realize God *saw him* at that crucial moment and would be with him in days to come.

No matter what you might be experiencing right now, look for the "one who sees you." You will never be invisible to him.

It Is Who We Are

Beloved, we are God's children now, and what we will be has not yet appeared; but we know that when he appears we shall be like him, because we shall see him as he is. —1 John 3:2

"Politics is what we do. It's not who we are."[3] I love that quote from the late Barbara Bush. It expresses what I believe to be profound wisdom: Life is not about what we do; it's about who we are becoming. Although her family found great success in "what they did," she understood good character meant far more than any accomplishment, even if that accomplishment included having the prestigious position of leading the whole free world.

As followers of Christ, we should know this. Jesus focused far more on building virtue, than on constructing résumés. He taught us to be kind and generous, faithful and forgiving. He encouraged us to have childlike faith, unquenchable hope, and unbreakable love. In fact, he said our greatest aspiration should be to love God and people with all our heart, soul, and mind (Matthew 22:37).

Our successes don't define us. Neither do our failures. After all, they're only temporary. A culture that makes heroes in a day can also destroy them in a minute. We can enjoy our accomplishments and learn from our mistakes, but not set up shop in their shadows. We have bigger fish to fry.

Scripture says those who follow Christ are children of God. Who we are has not yet been revealed. But who we are becoming has. We are becoming like Jesus Christ. We are becoming love. All that masquerades as our identity is being tempered with what we have been created for all along.

So although I might teach as a professor, might sell a few books as an author, and might serve in the church in a variety of capacities, these things that I do don't define me. They simply, but wonderfully, give me opportunity to express who God says I am.

Friend, make no mistake. First and foremost, you are God's child. As his representative on the earth, you have the privilege of revealing to every person he puts on your path what he's like. You are a VIP. Yep, that's who you are!

Kids and Slides and *Chikin*

Jesus said, "Let the little children come to me and do not hinder them, for to such belongs the kingdom of heaven." —Matthew 19:14

Every person created in the image of God has significance, no matter the size.

A few years ago, my husband and I traveled to Rhode Island to babysit our two grandsons for the weekend. We assured our daughter and son-in-law we would be fine. What could go wrong with a rowdy three-year-old whose one-year-old brother tries everything he can to keep up?

Snow lingered on the ground so playing outside was a nonstarter. By Saturday afternoon we figured we needed to find a place to release some pent-up energy. What better place than the indoor playground at Chick-Fil-A? *Eat Mor Chikin w*as calling our name.

My husband got our food while I went straight to the play area with the boys since an adult had to be present. An enclosed slide—the kind where you can't see where you're going because it bends—turned out to be the big attraction. To get to the top, you had to climb up a set of steps. Tobin was in his glory. He raced up, slid down, raced up, slid down. Little Mason, however, got to the top of the slide and froze. He was afraid to go around a bend he couldn't see, especially downhill. Who could blame him?

So, with all my grandma agility, I hiked up the steps and made it over to the top of the slide. He started to go down but somehow managed to turn on his tummy and hold out his hands for me to grasp. As I grabbed his hands, we both started down the slide on our stomachs. But Tobin knew exactly what to do. He grabbed hold of my ankles and the three of us landed in a pile at the bottom of the slide. The whole way down Tobin yelled, "I saved Grandma!"

I actually think Chick-Fil-A should have at least given us free sandwiches. We provided entertainment for the whole restaurant.

Sometimes it's good to get into children's shoes. Jesus welcomed children. When others rebuked the kids for getting in the way, he freely offered them affection and attention. He showed us little people are just as important as the big ones. So, although you might prefer a board game to sliding boards, let's not neglect those whom Jesus says belong to his kingdom.

Stay in Your Lane

I know how to be brought low, and I know how to abound. In any and every circumstance, I have learned the secret of facing plenty and hunger, abundance and need. I can do all things through him who strengthens me. —Philippians 4:12–13

So, what is this "secret" Paul refers to in his letter to the Philippians? If you're like me, you sometimes experience days when your sense of contentment seems to fly right out the window. You scroll through the internet and discover everyone else on social media seems happier than you. Their family ties are stronger. They experience more success in work, in weight loss, in how many friends they have. For goodness' sake, their food even looks better than yours!

Few things fuel discontentment more than comparing ourselves to others. If we hope to learn Paul's secret, we have to resist the temptation to assess our situations in regard to other people. Paul never wasted time on wondering why his life was filled with beatings, stonings, and shipwrecks while other believers suffered less. Or why he was sent to the Gentiles rather than the Jews. Or why he spent years confined in prison—writing—rather than being "in the arena." As far as we know, he had no idea that people would still be reading those writings two thousand years later.

Paul's contentment rested in simply *doing* his part. As long as he knew he was right smack dab in the middle of God's will, nothing else mattered. It deflected every arrow of discontentment shot his way.

It will do the same for us.

Nothing lifts the weight of discontentment from me more than reassessing my position. Am I, as far as I know, where God wants me to be? Am I doing what he wants me to be doing? We each have a unique mixture of assignments, experiences, failures, and successes comprising who we are. We shine the light of Christ in different ways into different areas of darkness.

Contrary to popular opinion, we don't have to "have it all" or "do it all" to be content. We just need *to stay in our lane.* Nothing else brings the satisfaction of a meaningful life. Nothing enables our light to shine with radiance.

What Say You?

He said to them, "But who do you say that I am?" —Matthew 16:15

By the time Lauren Daigle's phenomenal song, "You Say," went triple platinum, it became clear a lot of folks were looking for the answer to who God says we are. *Are we really loved? Do we truly belong? Are we still accepted when we mess up?* I believe we can answer those questions with a resounding yes only when we know the answer to an even more profound question:

Who do we say God is?

Do we recognize him as the author of life, strength, beauty, and of every good thing that exists? If he has authority over all he created, then do we believe he is stronger than any enemy we face? Such knowledge should give us the confidence we need to overcome internal foes like insecurity and pride and external threats like pandemics and wars.

Do we believe he is a God of compassion? My goodness, he created compassion! But do we see his love individually directed to every single person on the planet . . . the poor as well as rich, the newborn as well as the octogenarian, the disenfranchised as well as the privileged? And when he says he works all things together for good to those who love him, do we realize it includes us?

In the last days of Jesus' ministry on the earth, he asked Peter that most profound of questions. The disciples had just told Jesus who other people thought he was. Now, the question landed directly on Peter's lap. Who did he, Peter, say Jesus was?

Peter did not realize it at the moment, but his bold response—"You are the Messiah, the Son of the living God"—determined his own identity as well. Jesus replied, "Blessed are you, Simon Bar-Jonah! For flesh and blood has not revealed this to you, but my Father who is in heaven. And I tell you, you are Peter, and on this rock I will build my church, and the gates of hell shall not prevail against it" (Matthew 16:17–18). Peter's perception of Jesus opened the door to believe what Jesus said about him. He believed he was who Jesus said he was. *The Rock.*

Jesus still asks each of us, "Who do you say I am?" Our answer could not be more significant. It determines our destiny.

So friend, "What say you?"

Not a Cookie-Cutter God

But Jesus . . . knew all people and needed no one to bear witness about man, for he himself knew what was in man. —John 2:24–25

The term cookie-cutter indicates a lack of originality; everything looks the same, patterned. We don't like to think of ourselves as just a part of the crowd, do we? Don't we want to be viewed as originals, as there's-no-one-else-like-us individuals? I believe there's a reason for this longing: it's how God made us. Our Creator God is not in the cookie-cutter, one-size-fits-all business.

For example, look how Jesus called his disciples. Andrew was one of the first to be chosen. He had been a disciple of John the Baptist, but when John pointed Jesus out as the Lamb of God, Andrew followed. Immediately, Andrew found his brother Simon and brought him to Jesus. Jesus looked at Simon and saw him beyond his present, impetuous, unstable self. He prophetically called him *Peter* the "rock." And Peter followed.

The next day Jesus called Philip. Philip quickly found his buddy, Nathanael, and told him they had discovered the long-awaited Messiah. When Nathanael met Jesus, Jesus addressed him prophetically also, declaring, "Behold, an Israelite indeed, in whom there is no deceit!" And how did Nathanael respond at having this stranger (a Nazarite, no less), read his mail? "Rabbi, you are the son of God! You are the King of Israel!" (John 1:47, 49).

So, did Jesus love Peter and Nathanael more than he did the other disciples whom he called in a less supernatural way? I don't think so. Not for a minute. Jesus knew his first followers better than they knew themselves. He understood their differences. He would orchestrate circumstances to uniquely expose their prejudices, address their unbelief, and challenge their concepts of servanthood. They did not lose their personalities; they gained purified ones.

When we say yes to this great adventure of following Christ, he will treat us differently than he does every other person. His love for us as individuals compels him to arrange situations that uniquely help us discover anything within our hearts that hinders us from becoming like him. The One who created us knows what we need. He loves you and me enough to help us discover and become the one-of-a-kind he created us to be. Nothing cookie-cutter about it!

"Maulk Chunk" No More

He who has an ear, let him hear what the Spirit says to the churches. To the one who conquers I will give some of the hidden manna, and I will give him a white stone, with a new name written on the stone that no one knows except the one who receives it." —Revelation 2:17

"Who are you?"

Most of us answer that question with our name. We could be in a crowded room having an intense conversation, but someone says our name and we turn toward the source. Never underestimate the power of a name. But, of course, *who we are* encompasses far more than nomenclature. Some folks spend their whole lives searching for their true identity.

So what's in a name?

Take the town of Maulk Chunk. You've probably never heard of it. I hadn't either until my husband and I recently visited it in northeastern Pennsylvania. It was a thriving community in the early 20th century when coal mining flourished. But as the industry died, the town started to spiral downward. Eventually, as part of an effort to revitalize and attract business, the town fathers renamed Maulk Chunk after the famous Olympian athlete, Jim Thorpe.

Interestingly, Jim Thorpe was born on an Indian reservation in Oklahoma. He had never lived in Maulk Chunk, nor had any connection to the community! But Thorpe's body is buried in the now flourishing town, alongside a memorial in his honor.

There's nothing new about name changes. Celebrities do it all the time in attempts to make themselves more attractive to audiences. I grew up in southern Ohio where our claim to fame resided in being the birthplace of cowboy/actor Roy Rogers. His birth name: Leonard Sly. Audrey Hepburn was born Edda Kathleen van Heemstra Hepburn-Ruston and Robert Allen Zimmerman famously changed his name to Bob Dylan.

I don't know how surprised the folks of Maulk Chunk or Bob Dylan were when they experienced the impact of a name change. But one thing is certain. The new name promised to faithful followers of Christ far surpasses anything we could imagine.

That new name reflects victory over our old nature. It bears the fingerprint of our Creator and pulsates with life-giving purpose. It's what makes us unique individuals, giving us the assurance that *who we are* matters. And like the picturesque town of Jim Thorpe, it's something beautiful.

Don't forget it, my fellow seeker.

Don't Bury the Lead

The Word became flesh and blood, and moved into the neighborhood. We saw the glory with our own eyes, the one-of-a-kind glory, like Father, like Son, Generous inside and out, true from start to finish. —John 1:14 (MSG)

Why are you a Christian? One of the assignments I give my public speaking students requires them to give a six-minute speech explaining why they believe in Christ. After listening to one and a half hours of speeches, I sometimes feel like I've been to church! It's refreshing to hear college students give clear explanations for their faith. They know the purpose of their speech and they deliver. They keep the main thing the main thing.

The most effective speeches don't "bury the lead."

"Burying the lead" occurs when reporters begin with relatively unimportant information and relegate the most important information for later. By the time the main point is reached, the audience has long since tuned out.

Admittedly, it's fairly easy to keep the main thing the main thing in a six-minute speech, but I've been asking myself how often I bury the lead in living out my faith. Sometimes I let concerns consume my story. I fret about the country. The Church. Family. Friends. The lead should be: "In spite of everything going on in the world, Becky chooses to keep trusting in the Lord with all her heart." Instead, the lead gets buried under an avalanche of me trying to figure things out.

Jesus never buried the lead. He kept his focus on why he came to the earth, and never strayed from reflecting a life bursting at the seams with grace and truth (as author Mark Buchanan describes). He wants us to do the same, and not let worry, unforgiveness, cowardice, or apathy usurp our headline.

We live in a world where every weakness, flaw, and faux pas becomes front page, above-the-fold news. It's into this atmosphere Jesus sends us to show his "one-of-a-kind" glory. He wants the fullness of his grace and truth to be our lead, from start to finish.

Friend, I don't know what in your life might be threatening to bury your lead. But don't let it. You have a purpose to fill as long as you're on the earth. Make no mistake. The world is waiting to hear some good news.

CHAPTER TWO

We Shine Faithfulness to the Fickle

"Faithfulness in little things is a big thing."

—Chrysostom

I'm afraid we've become a fickle society. We shift loyalties as often as the latest fashions. If our work, our church, or a relationship disappoints us, the trend seems to point toward moving on to the next job, church, or spouse. Although circumstances at times require change, I wonder if we are losing the virtue of faithfulness: that ability to remain steadfast in affection or allegiance when times get tough. Especially when it comes to Jesus. When Christ returns to the earth, he will be called Faithful and True. He can't be unfaithful. Even if we are faithless toward him, he will remain faithful to us because he can't deny who he is (2 Timothy 2:12).

So, it's no surprise he calls his children to shine the light of faithfulness. First and foremost, he calls us to be faithful in following his laws and keeping in step with the Holy Spirit as we follow his nudges. We're to be faithful in how we work, how we listen, and how we repent. Faithful in always putting his plan above our own. Faithful in shining his light to the fickle.

Why All the Shall Nots?

The rules of the LORD are true,
and righteous altogether.
More to be desired are they than gold,
even much fine gold;
sweeter also than honey
and drippings of the honeycomb.
Moreover, by them is your servant warned;
in keeping them there is great reward. —Psalm 19:9–11

Every responsible parent sets boundaries. No running in the street. No picking the neighbor's flowers (or your nose). You may not call someone fat. You can't watch TV until after your homework is done. Usually, behind every rule stands a reasonable explanation. Most of us try to explain why, but we soon realize that a child's obedience shouldn't rest on whether or not they understand the rule. We want them to learn how to both trust and obey.

No matter how much we appreciate order, most of us—whether children or adults—have an aversion to rules. And we often carry over our dislike for rules to disliking the rule-giver. Since God reigns as the ultimate rule-maker, when one of his rules conflicts with our desires, we pull away from him, missing the motivation behind the mandate. We want what we want.

But as Tim Keller notes, "God is not just a cosmic rule-keeper who smites the disobedient and showers blessings on the obedient."[4] He purposes his laws and rules for our good. In the Old Testament, all 613 Mosaic commands were given to protect and carry us until the laws were fulfilled in Jesus. That's a lot of thou-shall-nots, but each one originates from a God of love.

There are a lot of commands in the New Testament as well. They, too, serve the high end of helping us fulfill the reason God put us here in his universe. We may not see the need to forgive or sacrifice for others or tell the truth, but God does. Some people accuse Christians of focusing too much on rules pertaining to sexuality, but there's a reason why every epistle in the New Testament addresses it. Maybe our Creator knows something we don't.

The psalmist describes God's commands as more precious than gold, as sweeter than honey. Keeping them leads us to the most rewarding, fulfilled life we could imagine. Oh, how I hope you see the thou-shall-nots for what they really are … a reflection of his deep love.

May we be faithful in keeping them.

Nudges: Don't Ignore Them

And they said, "Cornelius . . . was directed by a holy angel to send for you to come to his house and to hear what you have to say." —Acts 10:22

Nudges? Yeah, you know, those little inklings you get to do something. They can be somewhat easy, or they can take you way out of your comfort zone. No matter whether they come as quiet urgings or a heart-pounding prod, promptings of the Holy Spirit should never be ignored

The other day I was walking around our block when I passed a woman in our neighborhood. I knew her daughter had just given birth to a preemie, and I stopped to ask how things were going. She described how incredible it was that the baby had made it and was slowly making progress in the NIC unit.

After we parted, I started praying for the family when I got the distinct impression this baby's life was a *miracle* and that God was going to use her birth to do a spiritual work in the mother. This was followed by a second nudge: "Tell the grandmother." *But, Lord, I hardly know her. She'll think I'm crazy. I don't even know if her daughter knows you. . . . Okay, Lord. If this is from you, let me see her again before I get to the top of my driveway.* Wouldn't you know, as I turned the corner fifteen minutes later, guess who was coming toward me!

I wasn't even tempted to rationalize my way out of it. My request of *if this is you, Lord* had been answered clearly. So, I stopped her again and told her what I'd felt. She didn't look at me like I was a religious fanatic. I spoke. She listened. Then we went our own ways.

Responding to the nudges of the Lord doesn't always feel comfortable or easy. And flashing lights indicating their future impact are usually absent. I'm glad Cornelius followed the directive to ask the apostle Peter to come to his house. I'm glad Peter was willing to stretch far from his comfort zone to respond. Otherwise, the door to the gospel may not have been opened to Gentiles like you and me today.

Friend, be faithful in following the nudges of the Holy Spirit. You never know the ripples you might set into action.

Do the Work

*David also said to Solomon his son, "Be strong and courageous, and do the work." —*1 Chronicles 28:20 (NIV)

One of the most common opportunities to express faithfulness displays itself in the work we do.

Do you know God has work for you to do? Whether the "paid" kind of work or voluntary, if you're still breathing, your assignments have not been completed. Who knows but that your very best accomplishment still lies ahead?

I'm afraid our country is forgetting the value of work. *Help Wanted, Position Openings,* and *Apply Now* signs have reproduced in the landscape more than Sheetz, Wawas, and Starbucks combined. And it's painful to hear how the shortage of workers has stretched those who do have jobs almost beyond capability.

Work offers countless benefits. The most obvious, of course, arrives with the paycheck. The first "paycheck" job my kids had growing up entailed working on a tomato farm. They picked tomatoes, packed watermelons, and basically did whatever their boss assigned. The work was hot, hard, and dirty. But they were quite happy when payday came.

Although making money provided them the motivation for work, the tomato farm offered so much more than cash. It taught them the value of diligence, discipline, and finding satisfaction through productivity. Life lessons that have carried them through their adult careers. And not just careers.

Whether high-paying or non-paying, work shapes us into responsible human beings. People others can depend upon. People who can be trusted to persevere when faced with difficulty. People who walk in faithfulness. So, although our work does not define us, it aids us in becoming who God intends us to be.

When Solomon became king of Israel, David commissioned him to build the temple. Since God took worship seriously, the task was formidable. It had to be built precisely in every aspect, from the length and width of the dimensions to the quantities of gold and silver used in its furnishings. After all the instructions, David exhorted Solomon to be strong and courageous, and *do the work*.

I believe the world would be in better shape if we took the same counsel. Cultivate a strong work ethic. Whether we're called to serve meals at a rescue mission, clean the house, or run a business, may we give God glory. Give him glory as we faithfully *do the work*.

Do Your Own Thing?

In those days there was no king in Israel. Everyone did what was right in his own eyes. —Judges 21:25

I love the Bible and read it every day. But I have to admit, when my reading cycle lands on Judges, I become a reluctant reader. The book records, arguably, the most sordid chapter in Israel's history. Kind of a Judeo-Christian version of *The Lord of the Flies*.

The Bible doesn't pull any punches in describing the behavior of God's people. The same ones who vowed to serve God faithfully turned to pagan worship on a regular basis. They condoned vile acts, including the abduction of virgin women to provide wives for one of their tribes— a tribe that had almost been annihilated when they refused to surrender the men responsible for gang-raping a woman to her death. The last verse in the book of Judges succinctly gives the reason for Israel's rampant immorality. There was no king, so everyone did what they wanted to do.

In other words, everyone did their own thing instead of God's thing. And the results proved devastating. No matter how much we romanticize rugged individualism, there's nothing beautiful or noble about stomping all over God's plan in order to achieve our goals. Israel learned this the hard way. And it's the same for us.

The mantra of "do your own thing" is more deadly than we think. Our hearts can be incredibly deceitful.

I recently discovered an old diary I had kept from 1966. I honestly didn't know if I wanted to peek into my seventeen-year-old self, but I took the plunge. I started reliving all the ups and downs of a highly emotional senior in high school. My desire to have a closer walk with God was juxtaposed to the drama of a possessive boyfriend who clearly had no interest in him. At that point, I didn't recognize the conflict. I seemed content to pursue dating a guy who was all wrong for me, because in my mind, it fit. Had I continued to rely on my heart to lead, the results would have been disastrous.

But God graciously steered me toward his Lordship. Disaster averted.

Inherent danger lies in the choice to do our own thing without regard to God. Trust me, no matter how many times the culture entices you to be unfaithful, resist its lethal call. Let God be your King.

Landfill or Recyclable?

Let all bitterness and wrath and anger and clamor and slander be put away from you, along with all malice. —Ephesians 4:31

So, what do trash cans have to do with my spiritual life?

We have new trash cans on our college campus. They contain two different receptacles: one for *landfill* and one for *mixed recyclables*. Landfill items, of course, have no further use. They're destined for burial or burning. Kind of like those areas in my fallen nature that litter the landscape of my soul. Unredeemable items like bitterness, anger, slander, and malice. If I hope to grow in Christ, I need to deposit them in the landfill along with any justification for keeping them.

But what about the bin for recyclables?

I like the idea of "mixed recyclables." It makes me think of all those areas in my life I turn over to God. All those areas I want him to recycle and use for his glory instead of my own. Like a few mornings ago.

I was driving to school, asking God to use me in my Public Speaking class. By the time I pulled into the college driveway, I heard a quiet nudge, *Tell them about your faith journey.* We were finishing up their speeches on "Why I Am a Christian," so, it wasn't completely out of context, but . . . *Okay, Lord, if this is you, give me the open door.*

He did, and I walked through it.

It's really not *my* class anyway. He gave me this class for a few brief weeks. For His glory. His plan. His purpose. He can recycle it into whatever he wants. But I first have to dump my agenda in the recycle bin.

Giving God glory in all we do doesn't mean we slip Christianese into a conversation or slap a Scripture on our art. As Scripture encourages, it's about whether we use our words and deeds to further ourselves or to further his kingdom (Colossians 3:17).

So why not be faithful in giving everything to God? Why not listen to his voice and do whatever he tells us to do? As we respond to him, he not only helps us get rid of our trash, he will transform even the mundane into a glorious mixed recyclable.

Do It Anyway

And the king stood in his place and made a covenant before the LORD, to walk after the LORD and to keep his commandments and his testimonies and his statutes, with all his heart and all his soul, to perform the words of the covenant that were written in this book. —2 Chronicles 34:31

Disheartened. Discouraged. Demoralized. Any of those sentiments describe you? Do you ever feel like throwing in the towel? How can we stay faithful to the call when we feel mentally and emotionally paralyzed?

King Josiah inspires me. If anyone might feel justified in giving up, it would be him. In spite of all his efforts, sure destruction was coming to his beloved country. He had led Judah through numerous reforms since his assent to the throne. Reforms like repairing the temple. In the midst of the construction, Hilkiah the priest discovered the Book of the Law. As Josiah read about Israel's covenant with God, he tore his robes in distress. He knew the people had broken the covenant. They were goners. The prophetess, Huldah, confirmed Josiah's assessment. She told him all the curses for unfaithfulness were, indeed, coming to pass.

So, how did Josiah respond to such dire news? You might think he would be so distraught he would throw up his hands and quit. But quitting was not in his repertoire. Doing the right thing was.

He called all the people together and renewed the covenant. He charged them to obey every word of the Law. Nowhere does Scripture indicate he did this to somehow appease God, to get him to change his mind. He simply purposed that in the time they had left as a nation, the people of Judah would do the right thing no matter what.

And so must we. Whether we feel our family is falling apart or our country is going down the tubes, our challenge as believers remains. No matter the cost. No matter what others do. No matter what we think the outcome will be. We must do the right thing anyway.

Speak the truth as long as we have breath. Walk in love as long as we have a beating heart. Resist the temptation to throw in the towel. Make every day count for God. To whatever extent we can, we must faithfully do the right thing. Always.

Leprosy of the Soul

Therefore the leprosy of Naaman shall cling to you and to your descendants forever. So he went out from his presence a leper, like snow.
—2 Kings 5:27

Are you familiar with the Farmers Insurance commercial? "We know a thing or two because we've seen a thing or two."

As Elisha's servant, Gehazi was a man who had "seen a thing or two." He witnessed the power of God working through Elisha on numerous occasions, from restoring life to the Shunammite woman's dead son, to the supernatural feeding of one hundred men with only twenty loaves of bread. Gehazi saw the Aramean soldier, Naaman, miraculously healed of leprosy. He also watched Elisha refuse gifts offered by Naaman in response to his healing. Elisha did not want Naaman to be confused as to the source of his healing. He wanted Naaman to recognize Israel's God as the only true God in the world. And he did!

This didn't sit well with Gehazi. He convinced himself Naaman, "the Syrian" should pay something for his cure. So, he ran after Naaman and lied, saying Elisha had sent him to collect a bag of silver and some clothing. Then he took it and hid it in his house. But he couldn't hide his actions from Elisha. My goodness, Elisha was a prophet! Gehazi really thought he could get away with his deception? Such is the power of rationalization.

Gehazi didn't care that his greed might weaken Naaman's perception of God. He was contaminated with the world's way of thinking. As a result, Elisha declared Naaman's leprosy would now cling to Gehazi and his descendants forever. The consequences of his actions revealed his problem ran more than skin deep. Gehazi was afflicted with leprosy of the soul.

Leprosy of the soul can happen today. It creeps in whenever we rationalize our sin in order to get *what we want.* We become so consumed with our desires, we no longer care how our actions might reflect on the God we serve. It eventually isolates us, not only from God, but from other people.

No matter how seasoned our faith walk, just because we've "seen a thing or two," doesn't mean we know everything. Like Gehazi, we can succumb to faithlessness and come up with reasons to sin. Let's always be on guard against greed and selfishness—against anything (or two) that could cause leprosy of the soul to cling to us.

Good Listeners

And Samuel grew, and the LORD was with him and let none of his words fall to the ground. —1 Samuel 3:19

At the end of each day when my six-year-old grandson gets home from school, his mom asks the most consequential of questions, "Were you a good listener today?" He's learning his answer determines how the rest of his day will go.

Listening is important. Especially listening to God. And like with my grandson, our response to God's directives brings profound consequences. Every follower of Christ should desire to hear him speak.

But listening to God can be tricky. Scripture says we "know in part and prophesy in part" (1 Corinthians 13:9). None of us have the whole picture. But isn't it better to strive for the *part* than shelve the idea that God wants to speak to his children? We are human, and sometimes we mishear. But that's not reason enough to dismiss one of life's richest opportunities.

When the Lord first spoke to Samuel as a young boy, he didn't recognize his voice. It took some instruction from Eli to help him learn how to listen. But eventually he got it. And did he ever! The book of 1 Samuel describes his precision in relaying what he heard from the Lord. Not one of his prophesies failed to happen. Samuel proved to be a listening prophet extraordinaire.

Today, hearing God speak is not confined to "prophets." Each of us who have the Holy Spirit living within have access to his voice. We can all become good listeners. So, how do we develop that pattern?

I think we begin the same way Samuel did. We cry, "Speak, for your servant hears" (1 Samuel 3:10). We approach each day with a heart to hear. And we resist all the clamor around us that seeks to drown out his voice. It takes intention. Some days my mind keeps circling back to grief. Or worries. Or even shopping lists. Those are the days when I have to confess, like my grandson, that I haven't been a good listener.

Samuel learned how to listen. And so can we. God faithfully offers us another day, another opportunity, to say, "Speak, Lord, for your servant hears."

Oh What A Beautiful Morning!

If we live by the Spirit, let us also keep in step with the Spirit. —Galatians 5:25

The classic Rodgers and Hammerstein song, "Oh What a Beautiful Morning," ran through my mind as I started on my daily walk. I had veered off my typical morning routine, lingering longer than usual in my devotions before walking. As the song came to mind, I veered off the lyrics as well: "I got a wonderful feeling, Jesus is guiding my way."

That proved to be truer than I knew.

I was concerned for one of my neighbors. Although I almost never see him on my walk, this morning he "happened" to be in his yard. I knew it was no accident. The Lord had set it up for me to offer him both encouragement and prayer. I would have missed it if I had not altered my routine.

I like planning my days. Following a routine actually helps me become more efficient. But adhering to the rules I set for myself should never be so rigid that I miss those quiet leadings—leadings instigated by the Holy Spirit—to shift gears. There's nothing quite as exhilarating as when God interjects himself right into my plans and offers me the opportunity to trade my agenda for his.

Picasso once famously remarked that if we learn the rules like a pro, we can break them like an artist. He was saying we need to learn how to color within the lines before our wild creativity takes us over the edge. Immersing ourselves in the basics gives us the freedom to fly.

I think keeping in step with the Spirit is kind of like that. After being grounded in their faith, Paul exhorted the Galatians to keep walking in the freedom of the Holy Spirit. He didn't want them to return to solely living life as a set of rules. Keeping in step with the Spirit would protect them from legalism and open the door to lives filled with more fruitfulness than they could imagine.

So, the next time you sense a leading from the Holy Spirit, follow it! Don't get stuck in your own agenda. I promise many *beautiful mornings* and *beautiful days* await when you faithfully keep in step with the Spirit.

It Wasn't Dental Floss

But with me it is a very small thing that I should be judged by you or by any human court. In fact, I do not even judge myself. . . . It is the Lord who judges me. —1 Corinthians 4:3–4

Be faithful to who God created you to be.

I asked my students to give an impromptu speech using something they carried with them as a prompt. One student presented a small white box. As he began his introduction, he said, "Everyone knows what this is. If you don't know, you would have to be living under a rock!" He went on to explain the usefulness of his wireless earbuds.

After he finished, I responded, "I'm crawling out from under my rock. I thought it was dental floss!" The class laughed at my self-admitted ignorance. I did too. So much for having a cool image! Sure, I care about what my students think of me, but my dinosaur status seemed too good not to share.

It's way too easy for many of us to get caught up in what other people think. *Do they like me? Do they think I'm incompetent? Or boring? Am I measuring up?* When we feel insecure about the answer to these questions, we're tempted to put on masks—and I'm not talking about

N95s. We feel compelled to cover up our inadequacies, presenting ourselves as something we're not. Consequently, there are a lot of unhappy people on the planet confused about who they really are. No wonder suicide rates are soaring.

Paul took a completely different approach. He said it didn't really matter to him how people judged him, even folks who had the authority to put him in jail or kill him. He viewed others' evaluations as insignificant and limited compared to the only One that mattered. The only One able to see the whole picture, both the inside and outside of a man. Paul valued God's judgment above all else, and it set him free to be who he was meant to be, even if he made mistakes along the way.

How about you? Do you value what other people think of you more than what God thinks? Resist the temptation to let others' judgments define you. Instead, depend on the One who created you. It's not a big deal to mistake earbuds for dental floss, but it's a very big deal to dismiss God's judgment. Shine the light of faithfulness.

CHAPTER THREE

We Shine the Way Home to the Lost

"One road leads home and a thousand roads lead into the wilderness."

C.S. Lewis — *Pilgrim's Regress*

Despite reports the Church is in decline, some theologians like Tim Keller believe the Church is actually on the upswing. That's good news. News that reawakens my hope for those who have lost their way. It encourages me not to so quickly write off those whose resistance to the gospel seems to be embedded in concrete. It moves me to keep praying for those whose wandering has led them on roads far from grace. And it challenges me to never hesitate in shining the light of love and truth. Scripture tells us the feet of those who bring good news are blessed (Isaiah 52:7). Blessed, because they shine to those who are lost. They steer them to what they're really looking for—the way home.

How Desperate Are You?

And when they could not get near him because of the crowd, they removed the roof above him, and when they had made an opening, they let down the bed on which the paralytic lay. And when Jesus saw their *faith, he said to the paralytic, "Son, your sins are forgiven." —*Mark 2:4–5

How desperate are you to bring people to Jesus? It's a question I've been asking myself lately. I realize I'm far from the kind of desperation the four friends of the paralyzed man displayed.

Now those men were desperate. They believed Jesus could heal their friend, so they lifted him up and carried him to the home where Jesus was teaching. But when they arrived, the massive crowd blocked them from any chance of getting him to Jesus. Undeterred, they dug a hole in the roof of the house! They lowered their friend before Jesus, and Jesus responded to their faith. The paralytic left that house with new legs and a forgiven soul.

But what if the friends hadn't taken the time or exerted the energy to carry their friend to Jesus? What if they let themselves think Jesus couldn't do the impossible? What if they feared looking stupid in front of other people? What if they were afraid of giving their friend false hope?

Thankfully, those faithful friends succumbed to none of the above. They believed. They acted. They witnessed a miracle.

Jesus is the answer for every person in the world—no matter what the circumstance. No one falls outside his love or ability to rescue. I forget that sometimes. I'm reluctant to talk about Jesus to those who seem to "have it all together" and display no need for him. But as Francis Schaeffer often said, God designed us to fit in the world he created. We experience a tension when we resist his plan—no exceptions. No amount of success, money, or self-indulgence will satisfy the purpose God stamped on us when we were created.

On the other hand, I can view some people as "too far gone," too hardened to ever acknowledge their need for Jesus. They have so identified with their sin, it seems like nothing could ever break through. I overlook the *impossibility factor*—with God all things are possible.

Let's not be intimidated by outward appearances. Let's respond to God's heart for people. Let's become desperate to bring them to Jesus.

You Just Never Know

I will seek the lost, and I will bring back the strayed, and I will bind up the injured, and I will strengthen the weak. —Ezekiel 34:16

Sometimes looking at the past gives us hope for the future. That's what happened to me while reading my Grandpa Creech's diary from 1958.

The pages reflect Grandpa's concern for my parents. Their marital problems were increasing. Neither of them walked with God and sadly, my dad had a rebellious streak a mile long. Grandpa's entries: *Lord, take care of the trouble in that little house. Lord, help them stay together.* And when Dad moved back in, Grandpa wrote: *I'm giving God all the honor.* But their reconciliation proved to be short-lived. My parents divorced and my mother became a single mom, raising my brother and me alone.

I can only imagine the anguish Grandpa must have experienced. As a country pastor, he knew all about man's sinful nature. Yet he didn't expect his own son to become a prodigal. I'm sure he agonized over how the divorce would impact my brother and me, as well as my mom. But you just never know . . .

Thirty-two years later, on a Sunday morning, Grandpa would be sitting in his living room with Grandma when my dad would walk in, kneel before them with tears streaming down his face, and say the words Grandpa had been waiting to hear his whole life. "Dad, I got saved this morning."

In the next twenty-five years of his life, my dad became a powerful witness for Christ. And not only that, my mom became a Christian, and my brother and I both came to love Jesus with all our hearts. In 1958, Grandpa didn't realize God was already working redemption. You just never know . . .

In Ezekiel 34, God declares himself to be the shepherd of his sheep. He promises to seek the lost and bring back the strayed, bind the injured, and strengthen the weak. God doesn't give up on his sheep. No matter how broken, how distant, how rebellious. If God doesn't write them off due to bad behavior, we shouldn't either.

Maybe some of you are struggling with wavering children, grandchildren, friends. Maybe you think your prayers aren't making a difference because you don't *see* any change. Please don't stop hoping. Don't stop loving. Don't stop praying. Because you just never know.

All We Are Saying . . .

So you should rather turn to forgive and comfort him, or he may be overwhelmed by excessive sorrow. —2 Corinthians 2:7

How do we respond to weak believers? Do we throw them under the bus or extend an olive branch?

The song, "All We Are Saying," from the musical *Hair* has been running through my mind lately. Not because I'm feeling nostalgic for the '60s. I'm thinking about it in a slightly different context: people who dismiss God because they think they know about (or think they've tried) Christianity and found it wanting. They had a bad church experience and feel they've been there, done that. As a result, they close themselves to any possibility their experience could be different. To them, I am saying, "Give the church a chance."

I know people who fit that category. "For although they knew God, they did not honor him as God or give thanks to him, but they became futile in their thinking, and their foolish hearts were darkened" (Romans 1:21). They didn't thank God because they didn't recognize what he was doing in their lives. So, their picture of him became incomplete and distorted. They gravitated to sin and self-indulgence to replace the God they rejected. The process of knowing—really knowing—God became tragically interrupted.

So how do we respond? How can we shine light into darkened hearts?

Christianity is about more than crime and punishment, sin and consequences. It goes further. It holds hope for repentance and with repentance comes forgiveness. Paul encouraged the Church to be gentle with fellow believers caught in sin. He exhorted them to confront the sin (that's the mark of true love), but after the brother or sister repents, the church ought to offer comfort, forgiveness, and reaffirmation. To the Church, Paul was saying, "Give grace a chance."

When we let ourselves be permeated with the grace of God, we can pierce the darkness of an injured heart. There is no conceivable situation the grace of God can't cover. If you, like me, are grieving over loved ones who are drifting from the truth, take heart. Let God's love and grace fill you with renewed hope as you pray they would hear what we are saying and, "Give God a chance."

Losing Jesus

There is a way that seems right to a man, but its end is the way to death.
—Proverbs 14:12

Is anything worth losing Jesus?

I've been reading *The Dusty Ones: Why Wandering Deepens Your Faith* by A.J. Swoboda.[5] In one of the chapters, "Losing Jesus," Swoboda writes how even Mary and Joseph lost Jesus at one point. You're probably familiar with the story of when twelve-year-old Jesus stayed behind in Jerusalem while his parents began the journey home. As soon as they realized Jesus was missing, they asked their relatives if any of them had seen him (Luke 2:41-46).

Swoboda encourages all those who feel like they're losing touch with Jesus to do what Mary and Joseph did. Talk about it with people who recognize what he looks like. Missing person flyers won't help if we take them to folks who have no knowledge or experience of his presence.

I know a young woman who began struggling with her faith. Instead of asking for help from people who *know* Jesus, she turned to an Internet of strangers—people who knew neither her nor Jesus. They reinforced her doubts, leading her to a way that "seems right" but leads to death.

How differently her story might have been had she asked people who know what Jesus looks like to help her. People who would direct her back to where she last saw him.

But deception and compromise often hide in "ways that seems right."

The writer of Hebrews exhorts us to encourage one another *daily* so we don't become "hardened by the deceitfulness of sin" (Hebrews 3:13). For at the very heart of sin lies deception. It lures us into thinking things about God that aren't true. It's the oldest trick in Satan's playbook, beginning with Eve. Once we compromise our perceptions about God, our hearts will start to harden until truth becomes relegated to what "seems right" to our dulled sensitivities.

Losing Jesus. Two of the most heart-wrenching words I can think of. If you feel like you're losing Jesus, don't delay. Return to the place where you last saw him. Go to folks who know what he looks like to help you in your search.

Don't fall for a "way that seems right."

Lost and Found

And when Jesus came to the place, he looked up and said to him, "Zacchaeus, hurry and come down, for I must stay at your house today." — Luke 19:5

Sunday School songs about the wee little man who climbed a sycamore tree to see Jesus don't do Zacchaeus justice. Luke 19 presents a less sanitized version than the melody crooned by preschoolers. Zacchaeus checked in about a step above lepers in the ranks of Jewish society.

Not only was Zacchaeus a tax collector, but a *chief* tax collector—a chief tax collector who had grown wealthy on the backs of his people. His profession of collecting taxes from the Jews and depositing them in the coffers of the despised Romans designated him as a turncoat and cheat. Scripture describes his height as short; in the eyes of his kinsmen, he stood as a pigmy in moral stature. Although Zacchaeus' money offered him all the benefits of the "good life," he lived in lonely isolation. The smirks and sneers of his neighbors followed him home after a long hard day of embezzlement.

We don't know how much Zacchaeus knew about Jesus. But we do know it was probably more than curiosity that drove him to scale that sycamore tree to get a glance of him. Nor do we know how long he sat perched on those branches, waiting, searching like a raven for someone to drop a morsel of kindness into his lost, starving soul. But we do know life for this pariah was about to turn upside down.

Jesus pushed through the sea of greedy selfishness that hid Zacchaeus and offered him a way out. His words, "I must stay at your house today," proved to be more than a morsel. And Zacchaeus responded in the only way he knew how. He would give half of all his possessions to the poor and pay back anyone he cheated four times over!

Zacchaeus' story makes me wonder how many lost people are sitting in unlikely places waiting to get a glimpse of Jesus. There's a crowd of hurts, wounds, and disappointments blocking him from their view. But they desperately want to be found. Maybe Jesus is asking you and me to stop, look, and invite them to come see him. And just maybe, as it did with Zacchaeus, salvation will come to their house.

And the lost will be found.

What About Those Prodigals

For this my son was dead, and is alive again; he was lost, and is found.
—Luke 15:24

Prodigals. They can be found in every spectrum of Christianity. They flee from religious establishment congregations as well as free-in-the-spirit flocks. Kids raised on the *Donut Man, Veggie Tales,* and Jesus festivals start looking for something sexier than John 3:16. They leave behind heartbroken parents bombarded with a barrage of unanswered questions like, "What went wrong?"

Maybe you know some of those prodigals. Their disdain of moral restrictions leads them as far away from *church* as they can manage. They find it hard to identify with the Jesus of the Bible and prefer a Jesus they form in their own image. A Jesus who winks at sin until he recedes into the shadows of irrelevancy. They become so distant from the truth that they forget what it looks like. They're similar to people who think they know France because they eat croissants and crepes.

Maybe you can identify with those parents standing on the front porch watching, waiting, hoping to see that once familiar figure heading down the driveway again. You've run the gambit of grief, guilt, and regret. Anger and disappointment have tried to snuff out your little light. Yet stubborn hope keeps resurfacing in your prayers. Somewhere deep in your heart you know the story isn't over. Yet it's a struggle to hold on.

If that's you, remember the father in Luke 15. He didn't let his son's rejection of him and all he held dear deplete him of what he knew to be true. He wasn't the man his son mischaracterized him to be. But a man of grace, love, and second chances. This father remained steady, ready for the day when his son had enough of pigpen living.

So what about those prodigals? You may know them as sons or daughters, brothers or sisters, nieces or nephews, maybe friends, maybe even a spouse. I believe Jesus told the parable in Luke 15 to encourage us to never give up. The tie between the father and his prodigal son appeared to be irrevocably severed. The son was *dead lost.*

But only for a while.

Maybe we should be viewing our prodigals through temporary lenses. Trust the Father who loves them far more than we do to see them through their process. Until they are *alive again, found.* Then get ready for the celebration!

What a Reversal!

And when he was in distress, he entreated the favor of the LORD his God and humbled himself greatly before the God of his fathers. He prayed to him, and God was moved by his entreaty and heard his plea and brought him again to Jerusalem into his kingdom. Then Manasseh knew that the LORD was God. —2 Chronicles 33:12–13

Are there people you see as being so corrupt and godless that they stand outside the circle of any hope? I must confess . . . I do. But reading the story of Manasseh makes me think again.

Manasseh reigns as one the worst kings to ever rule over Judah. He built altars to Baal and sacred poles to Asherah. He established the worship of pagan gods right in the temple of the Lord and sacrificed his sons in homage to them. He practiced divination and witchcraft and consulted mediums and sorcerers. Manasseh was bad. Really, really, bad.

As a result of his apostasy, God allowed Assyrian troops to invade the nation. They captured Manasseh and with a hook in his nose, drug him off to Babylon. At this point in the story, I'm cheering, *Yay, God! You are bringing down on this bastion of evil exactly what he deserves!* Ah, but that's not the way God saw it.

From his dank, dark prison, Manasseh cried out to God. He had reached the bottom, and the bottom caused him to look up. His humility touched the heart of God. Manasseh was released from captivity and returned to Jerusalem. There he bore fruit in keeping with his repentance. In his remaining years, he sought to repair all the damage he had done and restore Judah to the worship of the God of a thousand redemptions.

If that's not a reversal, I don't know what is! It makes me want to throw away all my judgments and repent of my lack of faith. I don't want to box *anyone* in. No matter how scarlet their sins. No matter whether they live in my sphere or strut on the national stage. If Manasseh can turn around, maybe all those folks I deem *hopeless* can too.

Friend, if there are people in your life whom you feel could never come to the truth, take heart. Don't stop praying for their redemption. Maybe they might someday, like Manasseh, humble themselves greatly before God. You never know when another great reversal is on the way!

Water Everywhere but Not a Drop to Drink?

On the last day of the feast, the great day, Jesus stood up and cried out, "If anyone thirsts, let him come to me and drink. Whoever believes in me, as the Scripture has said, 'Out of his heart will flow rivers of living water.'" —John 7:37–38

How frustrating to know the supply of water is near with no means of accessing it.

We experienced an electrical outage last summer. After about three hours the electricity was restored, much to our delight. But one caveat interrupted our relief. We had no running water! Evidently, the outage damaged the foot valve in our pump. Although we had plenty of water in the well, the pipes remained dry. Unfortunately, this happened on a Saturday night, meaning no plumbers were available until after the weekend.

So we made do. My husband lowered buckets to draw up enough water from the well to flush the toilets. And I boiled enough to wash dishes. We were stocked with bottled water for drinking, and my sister-in-law offered us their shower. It actually triggered sweet memories of camping vacations! But I have to say   we were ready when the water started flowing through the pipes again.

No one disputes the necessity of water. H_2O makes life possible. But it does us little good if we can't get to it.

The same with *living* water.

I wonder how Jesus felt as he looked over the crowded temple courts on the last day of the Feast of Tabernacles. It was the day when the priests read from Isaiah 12:3: "With joy you will draw water from the wells of salvation." Jesus, in declaring himself to be the source of living water, revealed the way to that well. Those who believed in him, in his death and resurrection, would have access to RIVERS of nonending waters . . . nonending waters of life.

As followers of Jesus, the Holy Spirit bubbles up within us like an artesian well. We have 24/7 accessibility. But many don't. Their souls are parched. They've been wandering in the desert a long time, looking for a well. Or perhaps they've become stranded on a ship surrounded by undrinkable sea-water.

Maybe it's time for us to repair some faulty foot valves in our spiritual lives to make the living water more accessible. Lead the thirsty to Jesus who offers water, water everywhere . . .with plenty to drink!

Leveling the Playing Field

Therefore lift your drooping hands and strengthen your weak knees, and make straight paths for your feet, so that what is lame may not be put out of joint but rather be healed. —Hebrews 12:12–13

At times we may not realize how much our choices, as believers, effect the world God calls us to impact. We have the opportunity to leave trails that actually heal our fellow travelers. Or we can disregard our influence and create potholes that cause those coming behind us to stumble.

The writer of Hebrews encourages believers to make level paths in order to help the lame coming after them. And who are those *lame*? They might include the person you used to go to church with, but who has strayed off the path. Could be that sister whose faith is faltering because she just found out her husband is having an affair. Maybe the one who thinks he's messed up so badly that God couldn't possibly love him.

So how do we make a difference?

If we hope to leave level paths, it begins with our own commitment to discipline. No one likes to be disciplined, but without discipline we don't learn self-control and without self-control it's impossible to resist sin. Don't fall for the lie that your sin only affects you. David's sin with Bathsheba left a devastating mark not only on his family but the whole nation of Israel for generations. It all began with David's failure to exercise self-control.

Drooping hands are hands that probably aren't lifted up in praise very often. They stay crossed in body language that says, *I won't praise you till I see you.* Hands raised in praise are hands surrendered to reach up in faith to a God they choose to trust even when they don't understand what he's doing. They make level paths.

And those weak knees? My guess is they don't get a lot of exercise bending in prayer. They would rather depend on themselves to get where they want to go. Prayer might mean waiting for answers, and these knees stay far too busy to take the time to kneel. Consequently, they never grow strong enough to prepare the road for anyone who might be looking to them for direction.

Life in a fallen world is hard. But as followers of Christ we can level the playing field for those who come after us. As we cultivate these disciplines, those who seek more than what the world has to offer will be able to see "we've left the light on" for them. A light that leads them home.

Part Two

Why Does It Matter?

CHAPTER FOUR

It Brings Love into Isolation

"The ultimate goal of love is connection."

Jamie George
——*Poets and Saints*

Love comes from God because God is love. He extends his love into our lives of separation and loneliness with the charge to help others see the vast ocean spreading in front of them. An ocean that testifies to his disposition toward those made in his likeness. He works through each of us to show the world what his love looks like. It looks like sacrifice and intimacy, a lot like kindness and goodness. It expresses itself in the sweetness of friendship and in the beauty of the body of Christ. Nothing defines us as followers of Jesus more than love. And what in life could matter more than showing the world what it looks like?

For God So Loved the World

For God so loved the world. —John 3:16

We are told words have power. Some words step right into the darkness and alter the trajectory of life.

When Nicodemus slipped in to see Jesus in the dead of night, he found the sun at noonday. He came with honest questions. "Who are you? How can a man be born a second time?" Although he was a teacher, he found himself woefully inadequate to answer the big questions, or as someone has said, "the questions behind the questions." His brief encounter with Jesus, however, left the world with words that have become the source of hope for billions and billions of people over the centuries. Words that explain the why, what, and how behind everything. For God so loved the world . . .

Nicodemus looked for a candle to light the confusion in his mind. He discovered something more powerful than the brightest laser beam in the universe. An inextinguishable light directing him to the source of truth. The source of hope. The source of peace. For God so loved the world . . .

I don't know about you, but sometimes I feel world-weary. It can be pretty ugly at times. I hate seeing all that is good and pure and lovely mocked. I want to distance myself from people who find pleasure in bashing my faith. I grieve over children being turned into sex slaves, over injustice trumping justice, and deception masquerading as truth. I'm sure it saddens Jesus too. But instead of withdrawing from the surge of darkness, he runs straight into it, offering redemption. For God so loved the world . . .

It's the kind of love I want to cultivate. Recently a television celebrity ridiculed people who believe they "hear God." She called them mentally ill. Nothing new in our present culture, but this time, I didn't react the same as I have in the past with sighs and moans of disgust. Instead, I prayed she would hear God speak to her (and join the rest of us mentally ill ones). I don't know whether my prayers affected her, but they did affect me. Rather than building resentment toward this person I disagreed with, I experienced a new compassion. A compassion made possible due to one unshakeable fact. For God so loved the world . . .

Is God Mindful of Us?

What is man that you are mindful of him, and the son of man that you care for him? —Psalm 8:4

As I left the house for my daily two-mile walk, I knew it could start raining any minute. The forecast predicted a 60 percent chance, and the looming clouds seemed to agree. But I made it around my block. Right as I was opening the back door, it started to sprinkle. By the time I got to my desk, it was pouring. I had asked the Lord to hold off the rain— and he did. He knows how much those morning walks mean to me. They have become my sanctuary of prayer. Could I have suited up in rain gear and walked in the rain? Of course. Could I have simply prayed somewhere else in the house? Certainly. But this morning, God wanted me to know he was with me, caring for me, meeting me right where I was.

The Bible has answers. As Christians, we believe it contains the answers to all of life's most pressing mysteries: Where did we come from? How do we find love? Is there meaning to my life? But lately I've been thinking about the many questions asked in the Bible. Questions posed by God, by psalmists, by Jesus. These questions contain a treasure chest of insights about the God we love. One especially came to mind as I watched the tardy rain fall that morning.

In Psalm 8, David asks God "what is man that you are mindful of him, and the son of man that you care for him?" David expresses his awe at the majesty of God's creation. In light of his splendor and majesty, David wonders why he would pay attention to puny man. Why would he put us fallen creatures in charge of his glorious creation?

Why would he hold off the rain for me? Thoughts of God's greatness should bring us all to our knees. But if we focus only on his incomprehensible magnitude and miss the personal side, I'm afraid we forfeit the relationship he longs to have with us. He will meet each of us right where we are to communicate how much he cares.

Friend, don't ever think God is not mindful of you. Scripture voices the question so we could be sure of the answer.

The Power of Sacrifice

Greater love has no one than this, that someone lay down his life for his friends. —John 15:13

At times it's hard to wrap our minds around the kind of sacrifice Jesus made to save us. Some people spend their whole lives trying to figure it out, refusing to believe what they can't understand. Others get it; they fall on their knees and cry "Holy." And a few folks experience sacrifice up close and personal. Like John Stout, one of my Public Speaking students.

John told our class a gripping story from his days in the Marine Corp. His platoon had been deployed to Afghanistan. As he described the men in his unit, he focused on one guy in particular—Lance Corporal Timothy Poole. He said Poole stood out from the rest of the squad. A quiet person, he never went out drinking with them and usually kept to himself. Come to find out, Poole was a Christian. This led to more than a little mocking and ridicule from his fellow soldiers.

John's platoon had not lost a man since they arrived in Kandahar, but that was about to change. As they moved through the treacherous Taliban landscape, Poole inadvertently knelt on a hidden IED device and was killed immediately.

Months later when the Marines gathered for Poole's memorial service, his father shared a few words. As he looked over the men in his son's platoon, he told them about one of the last conversations he had with his son. Poole told his father he was asking God that if anyone in his platoon had to lose his life, it would be him. He knew he was the only one ready to meet God.

The Lord answered Poole's prayer. Not one other man in their company died.

My student didn't become a Christian until years later. But when he did, his mind went back to Lance Corporal Timothy Poole. This fellow soldier was willing to sacrifice his own life for a group of men who rejected him and made fun of his faith.

Jesus said there is no greater love than to lay down one's life for a friend. He knew it because he lived it. And he exhorts his followers to do the same. It's the kind of love that leaves a mark on the world. A mark on me, on you, even on war weary soldiers.

How Do I Love Thee?

Anyone who does not love does not know God, because God is love. — 1 John 4:8

"How do I love thee? Let me count the ways." Words from this sonnet written by Elizabeth Barrett Browning for her husband popped into my head this morning. Love. Who but a God of love could think up such an outlandish, exquisite, sublime entity?

God gives us love so strong that in marriage it transforms two separate beings—a man and woman—into one (Mark 10:8). Marital love differs from every other love on earth in its uniqueness, completeness, and opportunity for lifelong companionship. Who knew that the guy who picked me up hitchhiking almost fifty years ago would end up being my dearest companion in life's travels? God knew. He must have been smiling that day on the outskirts of the Grand Canyon as I stood with my thumb out.

And how about that tenacious love mothers and fathers have for their children. Who knew when I gave birth to my kids it would usher me into a beautiful dying to my own (often) self-centered agenda and expand my capacity for affection like nothing I'd ever experienced? God knew. And I think he's still smiling, as I'm still releasing them.

The greatest joys in my life come in one form of love or another. Through the love I experience for my extended family and friends, but also through the pleasantries I discover in what I see, hear, touch, smell, and taste. Through the satisfaction I find in my work. In creativity. In beauty. Even in my sorrows.

None of this would be possible without the love of God. Scripture tells us God is love. When we love, we get a glimpse of him. "No one has ever seen God; if we love one another, God abides in us and his love is perfected in us" (1 John 4:12).

So, "How do I love thee?"

I can only begin to count the ways because you, Lord, have given me so much. I love you because you made me. Because you offered me a second birth. I love you because you bring good out of my messes and aren't scared off by my petty, selfish relapses. I love you because of the cross. Because of eternal life.

How about you? Are you counting the ways you love the lover of your soul?

Love Me Tender

Jesus had compassion on them. —Matthew 20:34 (NIV)

In 1956, Elvis Presley recorded his most iconic hit, "Love Me Tender." Funny I would recall those lyrics as I think of broken people still wondering if anyone loves them. Are we reflecting the compassion of Jesus?

Tenderheartedness has staying power. The memory of my Grandpa Creech standing at his picture window after family gatherings, waving a teary goodbye as we went our separate ways, remains a poignant symbol of what tenderheartedness looks like. And not without consequence—his tenderness unmistakably directed me to a heavenly Father watching over me with the same compassion. And it's probably why I run to the front of our house for one last wave goodbye when our kids drive out the lane.

Even secularists recognize the power of tenderheartedness. As writer Henry James noted, there are three important things in human life: "The first is to be kind. The second is to be kind. And the third is to be kind."[6] A soft look or word can transform a hurting soul. Yet tenderhearted kindness doesn't seem to be the virtue of choice in today's world of wary cynicism.

Jesus exuded a tender heart. The gospels portray his compassion toward a widow who had just lost her only son (Luke 7:12–13). He felt pity for the crowds who followed him three days without food (Mark 8:2). Compassion moved him to touch the eyes of blind men, heal the sores of lepers and weep over the "harassed and helpless" people of Judea (Matthew 9:36). And when he stood over Jerusalem, he lamented over their unwillingness to find shelter beneath his wings (Matthew 23:27).

A lot of things have changed over the years, but the longing of every human being to receive tender loving kindness isn't one of them. Just as my grandpa's tender heart led me to the very source of kindness, so Jesus wants to use our tender hearts to touch the wounds of hurting people. Bruised and hardened people who are watching hope drain from their souls like leaking buckets.

What an opportunity we have to show them how Jesus loves them tender, and he always will.

Like A Cat 5 Hurricane

If anyone comes to me and does not hate his own father and mother and wife and children and brothers and sisters, yes, and even his own life, he cannot be my disciple. —Luke 14:26

Some of Jesus' teachings land on our hearts like a Cat 5 hurricane. They rip off the roofs and demolish the walls of our carefully constructed viewpoints. If we take his words seriously—words like those found in Luke 14:26—we should expect irreparable damage to our self-centered lifestyles.

Everything in life pales in comparison with loving the God who wants our whole heart. All our achievements, our good deeds, our nearest and dearest relationships. Maybe that's why Jesus put it in such drastic terms. He wanted us to get it. Only love for God has the power to help us release the burdens we put on other things and other people to satisfy our needs. In fact, Tim Keller writes "If you love anything in this world more than God, you will crush that object under the weight of your expectations."[7]

Most of us know we should love God more than anything. The challenge from this passage in Luke makes us question *how much more*? Jesus says in comparison to loving God, our love for those closest to us should seem like hatred. I don't know about you, but that shakes my paradigm.

Loving God puts everything else in perspective. *Everything.* The intensity with which we love God actually gives us the framework to love people more, even lay down our lives for them, because our egos demand nothing in return.

I don't want to dismiss Jesus' words as mere hyperbole. So, I've been digging into them. I've realized every time I have an overreaction to someone's behavior or to a circumstance out of my control, it most often stems from assigning too much importance to the person or the situation. Only when I step back and recall what's of most importance—God's love—do I find peace.

I recently saw an advertisement for an AOL app: "Stay on top of what your care about most." I'm taking that to heart. Not by making plans for a new phone app, but by prioritizing loving God more and more, with all my heart, mind, strength, and soul.

Let's not shrink back from those Cat 5 words of Jesus. They bring life.

On the Street Where You Live

LORD, I love the house where you live, the place where your glory dwells. —Psalm 26:8 (NIV)

Loving God draws us to loving his people.

A while back we had the opportunity to see yet another production of *My Fair Lady.* I enjoyed listening to "I Could Have Danced All Night," "Wouldn't It Be Loverly," and "I've Grown Accustomed to Her Face." But you know the song that moved me most? "On the Street

Where You Live." Sung by love-struck Freddie, he finds blissful contentment simply hanging outside Eliza Doolittle's doorstep.

It reminded me of our daughter's freshman year of college. I remember walking around the Grove City campus on our first parents' weekend. I wanted to soak up every street, sidewalk, and footpath of her new residence. True confession: while on my isolated morning jaunt, I actually belted out the lyrics to "On the Street Where You Live." Yep, it was the epitome of mom-sappiness.

David writes in Psalm 26 about a place that has captured his affection. He loves the temple because the temple is the street where the Lord lives. The place where he can enter God's presence, God's glory. I can only imagine how his heart must have started racing as he approached the temple steps. Anticipation greater than an American soldier kissing the ground after returning from foreign battle, greater than Freddie's infatuation with Eliza, greater than a mom longing to connect with her daughter. "I was glad when they said unto me, let us go into the house of the LORD!" David declares (Psalm 122:1, KJV).

It appears American church membership and attendance has dropped sharply in the last two decades. Clearly, a majority of people don't share David's enthusiasm for "the house where [God] lives." Of course, we know God doesn't dwell in houses or man-made structures. But Scripture warns us not to forsake the gathering of the saints. Something supernatural happens whenever two or three come together in the name of Jesus.

He promises to be present (Matthew 18:20).

Let's not overlook such outrageous potential, whether it happens on a Sunday morning, Thursday night, or Monday afternoon. The Holy Spirit wants to be right in the middle of us. And that, friend, is pure dynamite! I think it's time we shed our mediocre expectations of church and start anticipating.

Start loving the street where he lives.

What Love Helps Us See

And this is my prayer: that your love may abound more and more in knowledge and depth of insight, so that you may be able to discern what is best. —Philippians 1:9–10 (NIV)

Think those little grudges we bury toward people aren't that significant? Bought into the lie that when Jesus commanded us to love other people, he exempted us from *certain* people? Beware! Refusing to love other people not only hardens our hearts, it also muddles our minds and poisons our perceptions.

I've been thinking about how different people can hear the same words and view the same actions but come up with completely different perceptions. Do you know if we have a negative mindset toward someone, that negativity acts like a cloud cover over our discernment? That's what the apostle Paul says. He prayed the Philippians would abound in love *so that* they would be able to discern clearly. And he knew what he was talking about.

Further, in the letter he writes about those who are preaching Christ out of envy and selfish ambition. They want to cause trouble for him, but he refuses to condemn them. Instead, he rejoices that Christ is being preached! (See Philippians 1:15–18.) Paul didn't allow himself to get caught up in their petty insecurities. This Christ-follower loved, and because he loved, he could discern their motives without passing judgment. He set an example for them—and us—to emulate.

This plays out clearly on the national stage. I'm not trying to make a political statement—hatred knows no party affiliation—but some of the most outlandish statements about political leaders come, I believe, from those who seethe with hatred toward the other side. They don't realize how they've allowed their anger to actually distort their perceptions. Haters hate even more when they refuse to consider any viewpoint but their own.

On a more personal level, some of us have experienced being the brunt of someone's hatred. It doesn't feel good, but if we hope to remain faithful to the gospel, we have to ask Jesus for help in choosing love.

Never entertain the spirit of offense, not even for a moment. Forgive. Let the Lord deepen your capacity for his great love so you can discern the truth.

Let love help you see.

Lean On Me

A new command I give you: Love one another. As I have loved you, so you must love one another. By this everyone will know that you are my disciples, if you love one another. —John 13:34–35 (NIV)

Did you know that the shortest sentences are usually the most powerful? *I love you. We're pregnant. I'm sorry.* The briefest verse in all Scripture comes from John 11:35, "Jesus wept." It was recorded when Jesus went to the tomb where Lazarus was laid. Martha and Mary's grief over their brother's untimely death touched Jesus deeply. He did not hide his tears. Those two words speak volumes about Jesus' compassion.

Maybe that's why it's written that way. Its brevity makes it the ideal Scripture for little kids to memorize. Perhaps God wanted children to know first and foremost, he is a God who cares for them when they're sad or lonely or disappointed. And maybe he wants us big people to know that too.

When we love, we paint a picture of God. I witnessed a lot of those pictures during the coronavirus crisis. I'm sure you did too.

A man sits outside the window of a nursing home reading to his elderly father because they can no longer be in close proximity. Firefighters in New York line the street outside the hospital to cheer on weary healthcare workers with sirens, horns, and applause. A grandfather walks four miles a day to see his new baby granddaughter . . . through a glass door. These stories mirror the compassion of God. And they bring me to tears.

It all reminded me of soul singer Bill Wither's iconic song, "Lean On Me." It's what we humans are here for. To be for one another a reached-out hand, a weight-bearing shoulder, an empathetic heart. Oh, there will always be those who exploit crises. During the pandemic, some folks hoarded toilet paper and surgical masks in order to make a buck. Politicians were quick to point fingers of blame. But don't let any of these actions dampen your compassion. Jesus said our love would direct the world toward him.

So paint a picture of God's love. Say to your family, friends, and neighbors these three short powerful words: *Lean on me.*

No Strings Attached

Freely you have received; freely give. —Matthew 10:8 (NIV)

No Strings Attached. That's the name of the ministry the ladies in our church embarked upon a few years ago. We made trays of goodies for local librarians and the police department. We gave out water bottles at a Fourth of July parade and handed out scotch tape to shoppers at Christmas. Our desire was to show the love of Christ through kindness. We didn't even identify the name of our church lest someone mistake our motives. We simply included a note to the recipients telling them God loved them.

We live in a culture that has become increasingly skeptical, so much so that it's easy to think acts of kindness come with some ulterior motive. And if we're honest, we sometimes fall into the same mindset. Have you ever given someone a gift and not received the expected thank you? Or maybe you've invested hours, days, even years in a person who rejects everything you've tried to impart? We can find ourselves asking, *Why am I doing this?*

That's a good question to ask ourselves. Are we giving to get back or are we giving to reflect the generous nature of the Lord?

When Jesus sent out his disciples, he instructed them to preach the good news of the kingdom, heal the sick, raise the dead, and cast out demons. They were to give without any expectation of return. They had received freely from Jesus and now they were to give freely. Their job was not to build their résumés or guilt trip people into responding. If their message was accepted—good. If not, they were to move on (Matthew 10:14). No strings.

I think some people just need to be freed from the false thinking that everything comes with a price. It's our job as followers of Christ to show them what love without strings looks like. Although we remain fallen vessels who could never purely reveal the love of God, he has deposited in each of us a deep reservoir. A reservoir of love that cost us nothing. But cost him everything.

So, let's keep pouring out that love wherever and whenever. Let's not expect anything in return. Just a smile from a Father who delights in seeing his children do what he does. No strings attached.

What Every Person Needs

Satisfy us in the morning with your steadfast love . . . establish the work of our hands upon us; yes, establish the work of our hands! —Psalm 90:14, 17

My friend, Frank Ferrari, liked to say everyone in the world is searching for two things: to know someone loves them and that their life has purpose. Moses would agree. In Psalm 90 he asks the Lord to show Israel his unfailing love and establish the work of their hands. He prayed for God's mercy to show up in the midst of their human frailty. They were worthy of neither love nor a sense of purpose, but Moses asked. And God answered. He's still answering.

It may be disguised in a number of ways, but I believe these two longings lie at the core of each of us. It's the way God created us. He made us to be loved. He made us to have meaning. Once we realize it in our own lives, we can't help but want everyone else to discover it for themselves. That was the case with my friend.

Frank lived what he preached. He would strike up conversations with complete strangers to communicate God's love. He reached out to people others deemed unreachable. Nowhere was the work of Frank's hands more "established" than in Nicaragua where he relayed his message to orphanages, schools, and churches. He obeyed God's call to the end. The massive stroke that took Frank's life occurred while he was serving in Nicaragua. His mission of bringing love and hope to the poor, abandoned, and seeking was completed.

Frank's message that no one is unloved or worthless rings true in the heart of every believer. Those who think their failures disqualify them from receiving anything from God have an incomplete view of him. Of course they don't deserve his love and purpose, but who does? Not me. Not you. But when we come to him with humble, repentant hearts, we find we can pray the same way Moses did—asking God to grant us love and purpose.

I don't know where you might be right now. But I pray no matter what your circumstance, God will satisfy you today with his unfailing love and establish the work of your hands.

S.O.S.

And his banner over me was love. —Song of Solomon 2:4

I have read and studied the Song of Solomon many times over the years. In fact, at one point, my Bible automatically fell open to its pages because I referenced it so much. Recently, I've been rereading it, and for the first time I noticed the abbreviation for the book: *S.O.S.* I couldn't help but think what an appropriate acronym.

We all recognize *S.O.S.* as a call of distress. Those in trouble send the signal and hope help is on the way. But what about those cries that emanate from our souls? What about our spiritual *S.O.S.s*?

The Song of Solomon describes the love between Solomon and his bride, but it extends much deeper in depicting the love between Christ and his bride, the Church. The love of God is the answer to our *S.O.S.*

Really. No stronger force in the universe exists than the love of God. It burns so fiercely that a gazillion tons of water can't quench it; floods can't drown it (Song of Solomon 8:6–7). Paul says not death, nor life, not angels, rulers nor anything in creation can separate us from God's love (Romans 8:38-39). No matter what threatens us, we can prevail through the relentless power of God's love.

Like a banner waving over us, his love declares victory in all our circumstances. The more we grasp God's love, the more clearly we see life. We *know* because he loves us, he will use every failure, every mistake, every disappointment, for a higher purpose. The bride came up from the wilderness leaning on her lover (Song of Solomon 8:5). The tests she encountered in the desert purified her and increased her dependence on him. It's the same with us. God will take our hard things and turn them into something beautiful.

So I've been asking God to reveal more of his love, not only to me but

To my friend battling cancer . . . *S.O.S.*

To another burdened with past sins and mistakes . . . *S.O.S*

To more than one I know overwhelmed with work and responsibilities . . . *S.O.S.*

And to you who, like me, want to be more rooted and grounded in his love . . . *S.O.S.*

It's hard to read the Song of Solomon without concluding God is crazy about us. I hope you realize that. I hope the banner flying over your heart signals his love.

CHAPTER FIVE

It Prepares Us for Eternity

"Heaven is meant to be our *fixation*—our Big Fix. It's to be our deep secret, like being in love, where just the thought of it carries us through menial chores or imparts to us courage in the face of danger. We fix on it, and it fixes us."

Mark Buchanan
—*Things Unseen*

Although we twenty-first century people tend to be obsessed with the here and now, I believe our lives would be filled with more joy, peace, and contentment if we broadened our perspective. When we view each day in the light of eternity, we realize all we experience serves as a piece of a bigger picture. A picture crystalized in the death and resurrection of Jesus Christ. One that encompasses, for believers, redemption, purpose, and destiny. It teaches us how to grieve our losses and hold our wins lightly. And not of least importance, fixing our eyes on heaven reminds us about the importance of keeping oil in our lamps, lest we run dry and miss the Party.

Misty Lives

Yet you do not know what tomorrow will bring. What is your life? For you are a mist that appears for a little time and then vanishes. —James 4:14

Two acquaintances of ours died unexpectedly one summer, leaving behind families totally unprepared for life without them. Although I didn't know these men well, their deaths saddened me. The close proximity of their passing—within a month of each other—served as a stark reminder of life's brevity.

The book of James asks, "What is your life?" It reminds us we're here today and gone tomorrow. Even if we live to be a hundred, I'm guessing we'll still feel like we've barely begun the first scene of the first act. I don't know about you, but realizing my life is "but a mist" challenges me to make the most of the mist while I still can.

It also humbles me. James cautions us not to take our days for granted. We should approach each one as a gift given, an opportunity not to squander. Each day we can choose to either push ahead with our own agenda or ask God what he has in store.

My late father-in-law knew this well. When faced with difficult situations, he used to always say we need "to be grateful and make the most with what we've got." And he should know. He came to this country as a young German immigrant in the early 1900s. His family was poor, but they worked hard and trusted God to help them adapt. Rather than grumbling, they faced their uncertainties with a profound thankfulness for the "mist that appears for a little time."

The two men who died this summer were solid believers in Christ. They appeared for a little while and then vanished. But they vanished only from our natural eyes. Although their time on earth came to an end, as C. S. Lewis writes, death is but the beginning of the real story. When followers of Christ die, they begin "Chapter One of the Great Story, which no one on earth has read: which goes on forever: in which every chapter is better than the one before"[8]

Friend, we don't know what tomorrow holds. So, let's make the most of each day. We only have one chance to be all God wants us to be. Let's embrace this gift of life. This misty life.

Injustice Undone

Prompted by her mother, she said, "Give me the head of John the Baptist here on a platter." —Matthew 14:8

Injustice isn't supposed to happen. God never created the world to be rife with it. He loves justice. All his works are just; not even a trace of injustice can be found in him. He stands as the perfect balance of love and justice. (Psalm 101:1). Injustice is man's doing. And there's a lot of folks "doing injustice" these days. It's downright depressing.

When I witness injustice, I'm like a moth headed to a flame. I find it hard to pull away from its draw. In situations where I can do nothing to stop it, I sit and stew until it almost becomes an obsession. It locks me into the moment and makes me forget God created the world to display *justice.* Injustice reflects an aberration.

The Bible reports numerous accounts of injustice. One of the most disheartening occurs in Matthew 14, which describes how John the Baptist became one of its victims. Angry with John's confrontation of her and Herod, her husband, Herodias exacted revenge by calling for John's head to be presented on a platter. John courageously told the truth, and for this, the sword of injustice took his life.

So how should we respond when injustice wins? Or seems to win?

Although John's death was detestable, in the end, neither Herod nor Herodias won. The man who said, "He must increase, but I must decrease" knew the time would come when Jesus would take over the work. John the Baptist completed his purpose on the earth. His beheading ushered in the beginning of the end of injustice's power.

The God of justice turns the most devious of plans into redemption. When Jesus uttered those three magnificent words on the cross—"It is finished"—the greatest injustice in the world stopped dead in its tracks.

Although it didn't look like victory at the time, three days later the empty tomb proclaimed loudly and clearly the undeniable cry of victory. Injustice would never again be the final word.

Today, when facing injustice, we don't have to let it consume us. Instead, we can choose to trust in the God who loves justice and who loves people. Take heart, friend. A day is coming when every wrong will be made right.

Every injustice undone.

Not the End

Jesus said to her, "I am the resurrection and the life. Whoever believes in me, though he die, yet shall he live, and everyone who lives and believes in me shall never die. Do you believe this?" —John 11:25–26

A long-time friend died in a horrendous car wreck not long ago. The last time I talked to him I had no idea I would never see him again. Or the next time I saw his dear wife, that she would be a widow. I've been grieving.

Grieving, but not as those who have no hope (1 Thessalonians 4:13). I know it's not the end.

Dale hung tight to his faith through all he experienced in life. He made a lot of mistakes, missing the mark on more than one occasion. But through it all he continued to believe he was bought with the blood of Christ. A blood so powerful and pure it carried him beyond life's boundaries to a better place.

Now Dale is meeting his Redeemer face-to-face.

Jesus hated death. It deeply disturbed him when his friend Lazarus died. He wept because he knew mankind was created for so much more. So much more than the consequences of sin and its resulting pain and sorrow. The fall of man brought the curse of death to the earth. But the story doesn't end there.

What could be more irreversible than the finality of death? Yet into this stark reality Jesus brings astounding assurance. Resounding assurance. Blessed assurance: Those who believe in him will never die. Here lies the hope of every believer. This life is but a shadow of the one to come. Our short span on earth, whether marked by beauty or ashes, healing or brokenness, comfort or confusion, culminates in the victory cry echoing from the cross. When Jesus shouts, "It is *finished*," it opens up the *beginning* for all of us who follow him.

So although I still grieve for my friend, I find a smile through the tears because he's discovered for himself the place where every single one of our failures disappears and the man he was created to be ascends.

Just As He Said

He is not here, for he has risen, as he said. Come, see the place where he lay. —Matthew 28:6

I was listening to a TED Talk one time and the presenter opened with, "The person on your left is a liar. The person on your right is a liar. The person sitting in your seat is a liar. We are all liars!"[9] I like to use it as an example of an effective attention-getter for my public speaking students. At least until the audience starts throwing tomatoes!

I don't know about you, but I'm having trouble these days knowing who to believe. Faithfulness. Integrity. "Speaking the truth even when it hurts." All these have become sparse commodities. But it's really nothing new. Even the psalmist lamented hundreds of years ago, "All men are liars" (Psalm 116:11 NIV). As humans, we all have a sin problem—a sin problem that sometimes results in us not keeping our word.

The significance of knowing there is One who always kept his word, who never fudged the truth, or broke a promise, can't be overstated. Even when the claims he made sounded outrageous, Jesus always followed through. He did exactly what he said he would do.

- Jesus prophesied Jerusalem would be overrun and the Temple destroyed (Matthew 24). It happened just as he said.
- Jesus told Peter he was the rock upon which he would build his Church (Matthew 16:18). It happened just as he said.

- Jesus told the woman who'd been bleeding twelve years that her faith had healed her (Matthew 9:20–22). It happened just as he said.

Out of the many evidences of Jesus' unwavering veracity, one declaration draws us to the most important thing Jesus ever promised:

- "From that time Jesus began to show his disciples that he must go to Jerusalem and suffer many things from the elders and chief priests and scribes, and be killed, and on the third day be raised" (Matthew 16:21). It all happened just as he said.

Jesus kept his word in spades. Not even death could stop him from doing what he said he would do! He rose from the dead, and he said all who believe in him would too. That remains true even if the person sitting next to us is a liar!

If Your Right Eye....

If your right eye causes you to sin, tear it out and throw it away. For it is better that you lose one of your members than that your whole body be thrown into hell. —Matthew 5:29

Living in the light of eternity can also be viewed from the consequences of not choosing to follow God.

My husband and I had the opportunity to see *The Great Divorce,* a play based on the book by C.S. Lewis. The title comes as a counter to a poem written by William Blake called *The Marriage of Heaven and Hell.* Lewis believed in no uncertain terms there could never be a union between good and evil. *The Great Divorce* depicts the great chasm between good and evil, heaven and hell.

In the story, passengers on an allegorical train have the opportunity to leave the *greyness* of hell/purgatory and enter the outskirts of heaven. But they all have particular attachments keeping them from paradise. An artist clings to his creativity; a mother obsesses over her son. One woman thinks her husband can't survive without her control. They may want heaven, but they want it on their terms. And if they can't have their own pet sins thrown in, forget it.

I think there are a lot of attempts these days to marry heaven and hell. Many fear if we don't embrace the culture, the culture won't embrace us. So, we invite the world to be our partner in determining right from wrong. The world assures us there's no harm in sneaking a little immorality, a little greed, a little pride into heaven. But we can't. Jesus makes it clear. If we hope to enter heaven, we must deal drastically with sin. Cut it off!

Maybe it's a good time to examine whether we've been justifying behaviors that just can't fit through the narrow gate. Have we been sipping on a deadly cocktail of good with a shot of compromise? God gives us the profound honor of choosing our own destiny. But it's on his terms, not ours.

Lewis wrote in *The Great Divorce,* "If we insist on keeping Hell (or even earth) we shall not see Heaven: If we accept Heaven we shall not be able to retain even the smallest and most intimate souvenirs of Hell."[10]

Friend, don't be afraid to cut off *anything* that causes you to stumble. Heaven will be more than worth it.

Unimaginable Perks

For the wages of sin is death, but the free gift of God is eternal life in Christ Jesus our Lord. —Romans 6:23

Perks. Those extra benefits to a salary or position that makes one's work sweeter. Perks can range from in-store discounts to college tuition reimbursement to onsite amenities like car washes, haircuts, wellness centers, and spas. My daughter-in-law is a blogger whose perks have provided beautiful clothing, makeup, free vacation lodging, even dog food! I know someone who works a second job at a coffee shop, not for the salary, but for the health care perk. Turns out, 57 percent of job seekers consider perks a major factor in choosing a vocation.

But perks aren't limited to the job market.

Scripture says "the wages of sin is death." This "salary" carries its own perks. Those occupied by sin can look forward to having their lives marked with shame (Romans 6:21). They get to become slaves to impurity and wickedness (Romans 6:16). They don't have to wrestle with the truth because they reach the point of no longer being able to discern truth from lies (2 Thessalonians 2:11). And as an extra bonus, they're provided with a wide path on their way to destruction (Matthew 7:13).

Thankfully, none of these perks are available to those who believe in Christ. In fact, he cancelled those "wages" completely.

For Christians, theirs is the *gift* of eternal life. It's the perk of all perks. It includes freedom from the enslavement of sin and a ticket to holiness (Romans 6:22). Amenities like "love, joy, peace, forbearance, kindness, goodness, faithfulness, gentleness and self-control" come with the benefits package. Our beneficiary promises us the power to forgive, the ability to hope, and the security of knowing our loving Father. A life of meaning and purpose becomes available the minute we say yes to his Lordship.

Of course, there's a price tag on all these benefits. Romans 6 makes it clear the death and resurrection of Jesus Christ has secured this life of unlimited perks. It's pretty simple. Accepting his sacrifice means we die to the old life and embrace the new one. The one found in him. The eternal one.

It's good to be reminded from time to time of the vast array of undeserved benefits we have as children of God. Why don't we take a moment to thank him again for a life of unimaginable perks?

East of Eden No More

He drove out the man, and at the east of the garden of Eden he placed the cherubim and a flaming sword that turned every way to guard the way to the tree of life. —Genesis 3:24

In 1940, Winston Churchill famously remarked that "Never in the field of human conflict was so much owed by so many to so few." He was referring to the sacrifices made by the Royal Air Force fighting against the Nazis in the Battle of Britain.

I thought of his words the other day when reading about the fall of man in Genesis 3—only with a twist. "Never in the field of human history have so few caused so much pain to so many." Adam and Eve affected the whole human race when they succumbed to Satan's temptation in the garden.

Doubt, fear, and self-interest replaced the sweet communion once enjoyed between God and his creation. The first family's rebellion against God created a divide so deep, that no matter how hard we might strive, our human effort could never bridge the gap. Their fatal bite of the forbidden fruit caused all future generations to live east of Eden. Until . . . Jesus.

Another time. Another garden. But this time Satan was the one to fall.

- Eve's doubt: "Did God actually say? " (Genesis 3:1) stands in sharp contrast to the Lord's ruthless trust: "shall I not drink the cup the Father has given me?" (John 18:11).

- Fear caused Adam and Eve to hide from God: "I heard the sound of you in the garden . . . and I hid myself" (Genesis 3:10). Jesus met fear straight on. "Then Jesus, knowing all that would happen to him, came forward and said to them, 'Whom do you seek?' . . . 'I am he'" (John 18:4–5).

- Self-interest motivated Eve: "When the woman saw that the tree was good for food . . . she took of its fruit and ate" (Genesis3:6). Reverent submission motivated Jesus: "not my will, but yours, be done" (Luke 22:42).

The Garden of Gethsemane prepared the way for Resurrection Sunday. It reopened the path leading to the Tree of Life. Now every man, every woman, has opportunity to walk in God's presence for eternity.

Do you know you're no longer stuck east of Eden? Are you living in the profound reality of what Jesus accomplished?

Never in the field of human existence has one man sacrificed so much for so many. We owe him everything.

Torn Curtain

And Jesus cried out again with a loud voice and yielded up his spirit. And behold, the curtain of the temple was torn in two, from top to bottom. And the earth shook, and the rocks were split. —Matthew 27:50-51

I've been thinking about torn curtains.

The setting takes place during the Cold War. In Alfred Hitchcock's 1966 thriller, *Torn Curtain*, a US physicist feigns defection into East Germany in order to steal nuclear secrets from the Soviets. To do this, he has to penetrate the "Iron Curtain," retrieve the files he needs, then breach the unforgiving barrier again in order to return home. Hence the name, *Torn Curtain*.

The Iron Curtain was a metaphor for the barrier separating the free world from Communist oppression. This drape of total government domination locked out countries throughout Europe who aligned with the Soviet Union. Countries on the other side of the curtain—those aligned with the West—enjoyed freedom and independence. Until its final fall in 1990, anyone from the East trying to tear through that impenetrable barrier was shot.

On Easter we celebrate the tearing of a curtain far more consequential than the Cold War one described by Winston Churchill.

In the Jewish temple, a sixty-foot four-inch-thick curtain separated the Holy of Holies from the rest of the temple. No one could go behind that veil and enter God's presence but the high priest, and he could enter only once a year to atone for the people's sins. All that changed on the first Good Friday. At the very moment Jesus died on the cross, this massive barrier that blocked common people from entering into the presence of God ripped from top to bottom.

That torn curtain changed everything. Those bound by the oppression and domination of sin could now cross over into a country of freedom. Those restricted from being in God's presence could now run unafraid into his open arms. The torn curtain bought us a heaven-bound ticket.

When Jesus gave up his spirit, his cry became our song of liberty. That includes you. And me. Maybe we should linger at the torn curtain a little while. Soak in the enormity of its power. And let the love it took to dissolve the threads of bondage drench us as we bow before our Savior. Our Liberator. Our Curtain-tearer.

The Curse Is Broken

(Our God, however, turned the curse into a blessing.) —Nehemiah 13:2 (NIV)

It has to be the most *un–parenthesis worthy* statement in the Bible. Maybe that's why other versions use a simple period or dash. But the NIV version puts a parenthetical around the fact that God turned a curse on Israel into a blessing. Seems way too powerful a statement to surround it with punctuation that typically indicates an afterthought!

The passage in Nehemiah refers to the time Balak, king of Moab, hired Balaam to put a curse on Israel (Numbers 22). Every time Balaam made an attempt, the Lord intervened and changed his intended curse into a blessing. Four times, Balaam tried to prophesy a curse, and four times God turned his words into a blessing on his people. God's power to turn curses into blessings and alter the flow of history cannot be overstated.

Nowhere is this more evident than at Calvary. Galatians 3:13 says Jesus became the curse for our sins. We were condemned to hell, but because of Jesus' sacrifice, the curse was broken. Fallen man was given the opportunity to become redeemed man, redeemed woman. No matter how indebted to our sinful lifestyles we've become, Jesus paid the price to secure our freedom. The curse was turned into a blessing, no matter how many Balaams try to convince us otherwise.

Don't be deceived. We who are born of God have received the seed of Christ. He now lives within us and empowers us to become like him. Sin CANNOT enslave us. Not anymore.

Maybe you've been the victim of condemning words. *You will never change. You can't possibly overcome that temptation. You're insignificant, a failure.* The empty tomb says differently! Jesus overcame the greatest curse on mankind to make available eternal blessing. It's a power accessible to all who believe.

Don't underestimate God's power to change our circumstances or our destiny. As you worship the risen Christ, let all those past sins be just an . . . *(afterthought).*

What's Next?

And if I go and prepare a place for you, I will come again and will take you to myself, that where I am, you may be also. —John 14:3

A little boy in our church recently asked his parents if there would be toys in heaven. His dad assured him, "Yes, there will be toys in heaven." I guess the five-year-old needed more clarification because he responded, "Lots of toys?"

We all have questions about this place Jesus is preparing for us, don't we? What's next? Is there a heaven? What's heaven like? Are there any toys there?

I believe it's important to learn as much as we can about heaven. Of the sixty-six books in the Bible, fifty-four mention heaven/eternity. And in the book of Matthew alone, Jesus mentions heaven about seventy times.

Paul warns us in Colossians 3:2 to set our minds on things above, not on the earth. Thinking about heaven not only reassures us about our future, it gives us the context we need to live in the present.

Those who find the greatest contentment on earth realize this life is not all there is. We can appreciate the pleasantries of tasty food, thoughtful conversations, and a good book. Of football games and fireplaces and lifelong friends. But we recognize they come as shadows of what lies ahead. So, we don't hold on too tightly. One person has compared this side of heaven to the *smell* of a pie baking in the oven. The best is yet to come.

Heaven also teaches us how to deal with the not so pleasant moments of suffering. Romans 8:18 says our present sufferings can't compare with the future glory headed our way. In light of eternity, our pain lasts but a short moment. We rise from our suffering with fire-tested courage and up-from-the-ashes beauty when we understand God uses our pain for higher purposes.

So for every follower of Christ the answer to "What's next?" is what makes life worth living.

A Mite Big Investment

And he said, "Truly, I tell you, this poor widow has put in more than all of them. For they all contributed out of their abundance, but she out of her poverty put in all she had to live on."—Luke 21:3–4

You're probably familiar with the story of the "widow's mite." Some people would say she was foolish to put all she had in the offering. Some might say she stewarded her finances poorly. But I think she wanted to make the best use of her money. She wasn't looking at the immediate, but the future. She wanted to invest in something bigger than herself, bigger than the now. So, she gave it all. And you know what? Jesus commended her. And two thousand years later this unknown widow is still inspiring people. I would say she got a pretty good bang for her buck . . . or more like a *monumental* return for her mite.

Scripture warns us to put our hope in God rather than money. In spite of all its promises of the good life, money will never satisfy us in the long run. Proverbs 23:5 says, "Cast but a glance at riches, and they are gone" (NIV). So, if our sense of security and contentment comes from those riches, be warned, they will soon "sprout wings." And if we're driven by our love for money, we risk plunging into all kinds of evil. Then, friend, we lose everything.

God has given us all we have—resources, capabilities, opportunities. In our brief moment of stewardship, we can spend it exclusively on ourselves or use it for eternal investments. Make no mistake, heaven records every act of generosity, of kindness, of sacrifice.

Every season is the right season for charity. I remember how my mother never passed a Salvation Army bucket at Christmas without putting in a few coins. She didn't have a lot, but she had her tithe check ready every Sunday. I believe her willingness to give in small areas actually increased her generous spirit.

So I pray that no matter how much earthly treasure you have, that you give it back to God. Let him lead you into some *mite big investments.* Your return will be out of this world.

Do You Want to Go There?

Do not work for the food that perishes, but for the food that endures to eternal life, which the Son of Man will give to you. —John 6:27

The man was explaining to my husband about an out-of-body experience he had. He described what he saw in heaven with great detail and conformity to Scripture. He clearly expected my husband to react and call him crazy. But instead, my husband listened, then asked, "Do you want to go there someday?" The man responded with silence.

A question bearing tremendous implications.

Author Tim Keller writes in *Hope in Times of Fear*, "what we believe about the future is one of the best predictions for how we act today."[11] Increasing suicide rates, popular books, and movie trends affirm we're living in a culture of hopelessness. Yet, as Keller notes, "we are hope-based creatures." Hope-based creatures who no longer know where to find meaning.

The wisest man who ever lived said meaning can't be found in temporary things. Not in wisdom and knowledge, not in pleasure, not in successful work. Neither power nor money can satisfy our search for meaning. These will all pass. They simply aren't large enough to provide us with hope. With a sense of significance. Only God can do that because what he does endures forever (See Ecclesiastes).

Eternity, for believers, reigns as our ultimate goal. In fact, it encompasses every aspect of earthly life and infuses it with meaning. All the temporary things in life—the joys, the disappointments, the losses, the gains—have value because they are cast into the bigger picture. Our hope for today springs from our hope for the future.

If you are a follower of Christ who struggles to find hope and meaning, perhaps it's a good time to revisit the promise of eternal life. Jesus warns us not to work for food that perishes, but for food that lasts. Maybe you need to be eating more of the good stuff. Soak yourself in the reality of eternity. Don't let silence be your answer to *Do you want to go there?*

Part Three

What Does the Oil Provide?

CHAPTER SIX

The Oil Provides Gratitude and Praise in a Thankless World

"People who are filled with such radical gratitude are unstoppable, irrepressible, overflowing with . . . the supernatural, refreshing love of God that draws others to Him."

Chuck Colson
—Breakpoint 5/17/05

It's impossible to overstate the necessity of developing hearts of gratitude. Nothing shades the light of Christ more than a complaining, grumbling spirit of ingratitude. Thankfulness provides a prism through which we view all of life's circumstances—the good, the bad, and even the ugly. When we choose to praise God, we affirm his sovereign goodness, acknowledge our desperate need, and embark on a road that leads us to final victory. So, let's never underestimate the power of grateful praise.

When King David established the officials of Israel, he appointed not only the leaders of the army, but also hundreds of priests to offer prophetic praise! Both were essential for victory. Gratitude and praise position us for the inevitable battles we face. They fuel the sustaining oil in our lamps when the shadows deepen.

Front-load Your Day

Give thanks to the LORD, for he is good, for his steadfast love endures forever. —Psalm 136:1

There are many things I tried to pass on to my children. But probably one of the most important: front-load your days with gratitude. According to the dictionary, front-loading occurs when you "allocate most of your efforts, costs, etc. at the beginning of a process or enterprise." I wanted my kids to know that every twenty-four hours they have the opportunity to begin the enterprise of living a new day by allocating thankfulness in their "efforts."

Holocaust survivor and psychiatrist Viktor Frankl, in his book, *Man's Search for Meaning*, writes "that everything can be taken from a man but one thing: the last of the human freedoms—to choose one's attitude in any given set of circumstances."[12] Because Frankl chose optimism, he was able to endure the horrors of the Holocaust. We, too, have the freedom, even in the most difficult of circumstances, to look for something that merits thankfulness.

I know a woman who is fighting two types of cancer in her body. Her focus on all the things she's grateful for is transforming a devastating circumstance into a thing of beauty and hope. Another man recently lost his battle with the disease, but as long as he still had breath, he woke up every morning thanking God for another day. He died in peace and with dignity.

Psalm 136 encourages us to thank God because of his goodness, his enduring love, his faithful provision. The psalmist recounts how God worked miracles in creation, delivered Israel from bondage and gave them victory over enemies. Things which should elicit their eternal gratitude. And not by accident. "His steadfast love endures forever" follows each reason for thanksgiving.

Gratitude and love connect at the hip. You simply can't have one without the other. Each virtue reinforces the other.

That's why I believe one of life's greatest lessons includes starting our days with gratitude. We begin with expressing thankfulness for the little graces of everyday living, from a good night's rest to hearing your favorite song come up on the radio. Gratitude leads to love. And nothing surpasses the significance of loving God with all our heart, soul, strength, and mind. Love is the ultimate goal.

And front-loading our days with gratitude will help us get there.

Blah, Blah, Blah

And do not grumble, as some of them did—and were killed by the destroying angel. —1 Corinthians 10:10 (NIV)

What's wrong with a little complaining? *A little grumble here; a little grumble there; here a grumble, there a grumble, everywhere a grumble, grumble.* That describes the problem with complaining. It rarely stops with one grumble.

C. S. Lewis writes, "Hell begins with a grumbling mood, always complaining, always blaming others . . . but you are still distinct from it. You may even criticize it in yourself and wish you could stop it. But there may come a day when you can no longer. Then there will be no you left to criticize the mood or even to enjoy it, but just the grumble itself, going on forever like a machine."[13] In other words, grumblers actually BECOME the grumble!

Grumbling is not harmless. Do you know Scripture says it's one of the four reasons Israel failed to enter the promised land? Right along with idolatry, sexual immorality, and testing the Lord. Paul wants the church to know that if grumbling could cause Israel to stumble, it can cause us to fall short as well (1 Corinthians 10:6–11).

So why do we whine? Why pout instead of praise? Why criticize instead of commend?

I believe the grounds for Israel's demise listed in 1 Corinthians 10 share a common thread. Idolatry, sexual immorality, testing God, and grumbling all reflect dissatisfaction with God's provision. We would rather have our way, and have it now, than wait on His plan.

The other day I was drinking a cup of coffee at my favorite donut shop. Honestly, it tasted awful. I loaded it with as much cream as the cup could hold, but the bitterness persisted. So, it became both distasteful *and* lukewarm. I had a choice in this seemingly insignificant moment. I could dwell on how I got cheated out of my $2.10 or be grateful for the delicious, salted caramel crème pastry sitting before me. Further, I could choose to be thankful for the opportunity to even be there at a public setting in an almost but not yet post-pandemic world.

And you know what? My gratitude caused the grumble to slink away and melt like a slug in the sunlight.

Friend, resist the "blah, blah blah" temptation when things don't go your way. Don't turn into a grumble. Become the praise of God.

Thanks Rules

Give thanks in all circumstances; for this is the will of God in Christ Jesus for you. —1 Thessalonians 5:18

Thank you. Gracias. Merci. Danke. Grazie. Tak, Shurkan. Arigato. Expressing gratitude crosses all cultures and languages. Despite its universality, the climate of the day leans far more toward cynicism than gratefulness. And cynicism kills gratitude.

Followers of Jesus know the importance of thankfulness. They've learned expressing thanks is like turning on a light switch—it dispels the darkness of negativity. They have also discovered the choice to be thankful is an intentional one, especially when circumstances tell them nothing good can come out of it.

When Paul admonished the Thessalonians to give thanks in "all circumstances," he included instructions to always be joyful and pray without ceasing. Rejoicing, praying, and thanking God go together like bread, peanut butter, and jelly. God wants us to view life through the lens of gratefulness. No matter what we face.

A few years ago I received news that one of my students at Lancaster Bible College unexpectedly passed away. He was so young, so vibrant, so devoted to Jesus. I don't understand why God took him, but in my sadness, I began to thank God for the mark Joe left in the world. As I prayed, I thanked the Lord for putting Joe in my class, for letting me know him. My Scripture that morning *just happened* to be from Philippians 1:21, "to live is Christ, and to die is gain." In spite of my sorrow, I rejoiced with the assurance that Joe has found his gain.

I'm disturbed by all the skepticism I see today. I imagine you are too. The negativity of hate and distrust seems to be casting a dark shadow over the world. Let's never forget we have access to the light switch. In the midst of darkness, we can stop negativity dead in its tracks when we exercise thankfulness. It is stronger than the darkness. It's smack dab in the middle of God's will. So, why don't we always give thanks, if not *for,* then *in* all circumstances. Why don't we let thanks rule!

Ready to Praise

Praise the LORD, for the LORD is good; sing to his name, for it is pleasant! —Psalm 135:3

Good. Great. Sovereign. Just. Mighty. The psalmist certainly got it right when he chronicled the reasons we should praise the Lord. Interestingly, in Psalm 135, he begins with the fact God is good. Only through the lens of understanding his goodness can we see reason to praise. It gives us context for why he does what he does, even if we don't understand. God is good. Continuously. Persistently. Permanently. Nothing can alter his goodness.

It's a perspective I want to hold on to. I've discovered when I express my gratitude for his goodness through praise, it actually *cements my sentiments*.

So . . .

I praise him for his goodness to me. When he surprises me with unexpected visits from family who live in faraway places like Tennessee, Rhode Island, and Ohio.

I praise him for his goodness to me. For the ability to enjoy simple pleasures like a good book, a two-mile walk every morning, a dinner date with my husband, a salted caramel cold brew with extra crème.

I praise him for his goodness to me. By letting me "feel his pleasure" when I write and when I teach my college classes.

I praise him for his goodness to me. He comforts me when some prayers lay unanswered and unsettling situations distract me. He enables me to let go of disappointments, big and small.

I realize the more I choose to praise God in my circumstances, the more I am able to see his goodness. In fact, I start looking for it! I could focus on the negative aspects of many situations but praising God through them helps me not get engulfed by the pain. Acknowledging his goodness not only gives honor to whom honor is due, it increases my love for him.

So how about we engulf ourselves up in a mindset of his prevailing goodness. Think about the *specific* ways God has been good to you. Make a list! Then praise him for each instance. Let the awareness of his goodness overshadow everything else. And be ready to give him praise each and every day.

Paralyzed or Thank-you-ized

Afterward Jesus found him in the temple and said to him, "See, you are well! Sin no more, that nothing worse may happen to you." —John 5:14

The man had no faith. He didn't even know who Jesus was. Whether he felt comfortable in his status as a beggar or whether after thirty-eight years living as an invalid, he had simply given up hope, we don't know. But we do know when Jesus told him to pick up his mat and walk, a miracle occurred.

Perhaps even more curious is the man's response. You might think he would fall on his face and worship the One who set him free. Gratitude would wash over him like the healing waters of Bethesda he had been denied. How could someone experience such a complete restoration of his paralyzed body and still have a paralyzed heart? When Jesus saw him later, he even warned him to stop sinning. But this man used his now fully functioning legs to run to the Jews and rat Jesus out.

Unthinkable!

But that's what ingratitude does to us. It locks us into our own perspective and hinders us from recognizing God's grace. It is both the cause and effect of our immobility. The less we give thanks, the more fixed on ourselves we become. Our failure to discern Jesus' work in our lives turns us into cynics; it causes us to view the world with a skeptical eye.

A life of gratitude, however, illuminates our perspective in all of life. As we learn to give thanks in all things, we learn to see Jesus in every situation. We learn to recognize him even in the middle of pain's paralysis, and in those times when it seems like everyone is jumping into the pool ahead of us.

Oh friend, don't miss the thousands of opportunities every day you have to give God thanks. Let gratitude be the first thought in the morning when your (un-paralyzed) feet hit the ground. Let gratitude cap your last prayer at night for the privilege of living another day. Let it infuse each waking moment.

Don't let ingratitude paralyze you. You have places to go and people to meet who need to hear why you're so thankful.

What's A Win?

And let the peace of Christ rule in your hearts, to which indeed you were called in one body. And be thankful. —Colossians 3:15

I was at a conference once when the speaker challenged us to think about what we consider a win. I've never forgotten the illustration he used. He said a "win" for the sound team at their church occurred when no one looked back at the sound board during the service. Their "win" was simply not to draw attention to themselves by messing up!

I think it's important to look for wins in the small areas of life. Someone has said good is the enemy of the best. And it may well be if our standard devolves into a permanent "good enough" mentality. But focusing on the best can negate all the good steps it takes to arrive at the end goal. I've known women who desperately wanted their husbands to change. When their husbands started to take tiny steps, the women still complained because their progress wasn't moving quickly enough. They ended up sabotaging the very thing they hoped for. "Striving to better, oft we mar what's well," penned Shakespeare.

Although I definitely don't fall into the perfectionist category, over the years I've found much freedom in lowering my expectations on people and plans. I remember when a whole evening out for dinner could be spoiled because I didn't like where we were seated. Now I spend more time being grateful that we got to eat out in the first place.

Failing to appreciate the small wins in life stifles gratitude. Once we limit our wins to the end goal, we stop enjoying the journey. Paul admonishes us to let the peace of God rule in our hearts by being thankful. It's amazing how many wins we can pull out of losses if we look hard enough. Focusing on mistakes, defeats, and disappointments robs us of God's peace and only adds to our frustration. Trusting God to use them redemptively makes way for contentment and happiness. I would call that a win!

So the next time something or someone doesn't live up to your expectations, don't focus on the loss. Intentionally shift your attention to those small pockets of victory. Your thankful heart will make you a true winner.

BEEF-y Christians

We give thanks to you, O God   we give thanks, for your name is near. We recount your wondrous deeds. —Psalm 75:1

One of my students gave his demonstration speech on how to make a successful free throw shot in basketball. He should know. He held the high school record for successful free throw shots in the state of Maine. To explain how he does it, he used the acronym BEEF to explain his strategy.

Most people familiar with the game have probably heard of BEEF: B—maintaining balance, E—eyes focused on the target, E—elbows aligned in 90-degree angle, F—follow through. If players hope to swish the ball through the net, they need to master these steps.

I couldn't help but think how the acronym of BEEF might apply in our Christian walk. Maintaining the *balance* of being in the world but not of it. Keeping our *eyes* focused on Jesus. Aligning our *elbows* at a 90-degree angle as we hold the Word of God. Well, that might be a stretch, but the last step is not a stretch—the *follow through.*

Follow through for the Christian consists of praise. Scripture abounds with directives to praise the Lord in response to what we see him do. "I will tell of the kindnesses of the LORD, the deeds for which he is to be praised, according to all the LORD has done for us" (Isaiah 63:7 NIV). "He is the one you praise; he is your God, who performed for you those great and awesome wonders you saw with your own eyes" (Deuteronomy 10:21 NIV). "Sing to him, sing praises to him; tell of all his wondrous works!" (1 Chronicles 16:9). When we see what the Lord has done, we should praise him for it.

If we hope to strengthen our relationship with the Lord, we must not ignore the follow through. Praise brings completion. It helps us remember what a trustworthy God we serve. I suggest we engage in a little "binge praising" from time to time. Be intentional about praising God for everything we think of, and then some, because praise tends to increase our ability to see him and his works.

Do you want to be a BEEF-y Christian? My student didn't become the best free throw shooter in Maine without practice. Let's practice those areas that make us strong as believers. And especially, let's not neglect the follow through.

Another Thanksgiving

Oh give thanks to the LORD, for he is good, for his steadfast love endures forever! —Psalm 107:1

One of the highlights of our Thanksgiving dinner occurs when we go around the table and share something we're thankful for in the past year. Since our meal includes extended family, it's not unusual to hear twenty to thirty people express their gratitude.

Over the years we've given thanks for everything from new babies to Penn State football winning seasons. One year we all ganged up on my brother who was visiting from Ohio with his new girlfriend. Unbeknown to him or her, when it came our turn, we each thanked God with how happy we were that Marty finally had a girlfriend! Everyone had a good laugh, (even more so when he and Lisa got engaged that Christmas). And every year it seems at least one person expresses gratitude that we can all be together another Thanksgiving.

The Bible mentions some form of thankfulness over 144 times. The priests in the Old Testament regularly presented thank offerings for deliverance from sickness or death. Some Levites were selected specifically to give thanks. Nehemiah appointed two large choirs for the sole purpose of giving thanks. Imagine that. Professional thank-ers!

In the New Testament, Paul thanked God every time he thought of the Philippians, and he couldn't stop thanking God for what he had done in Ephesian believers. He thanked God for the Romans, Colossians, and Corinthians. God clearly wants his people to be filled with thanks.

Thankfulness packs a powerful punch. The other day my husband and I were talking, and the conversation started to turn negative. I said, "Let's take turns mentioning what we're thankful for rather than what's disappointing us right now." It wasn't long before our attitudes took a dramatic shift. We found more to be thankful for than we realized. It's amazing what happens when you focus more on what you have than what you don't have.

So I pray you fill every day—not just Thanksgiving Day—with thankfulness. May you always remember, no matter what the season, to "give thanks to the Lord, for he is good."

Zip-a-dee-doo-dah

Offer to God a sacrifice of thanksgiving, and perform your vows to the Most High, and call upon me in the day of trouble; I will deliver you, and you shall glorify me. —Psalm 50:14–15

The other morning, I was sitting in my little room having my devotions when I spotted a bluebird headed from the holly tree to the bird feeder. Then I saw another, and another. Before they all flew away, I counted at least a half dozen bluebirds! Although Mr. Bluebird didn't exactly perch on my shoulder, the lyrics to "Zip-a-dee-doo-dah" quickly came to mind.

The sentiment stood in sharp contrast to the terrible days many people I knew were experiencing. Serious health issues, marital struggles with bleak prospects of a quick resolution, false accusations carrying life-shattering implications, and regular run-of-the-mill disappointments flooded my landscape. How could I sing a cheery tune when so many were hurting?

It's easy to praise God on zip-a-dee-doo-dah days. There's nothing sacrificial in thanking him for the sunshine beaming all around us. Standing in the midst of a huge storm poses a different story. I think that's why the psalmist calls for the "sacrifice" of "thanksgiving." When the harshness of life threatens to turn us upside down, we don't feel very grateful. It's a sacrifice to let go of our demands and choose to remain faithful no matter what. Yet, it's a mindset that honors God and results in our deliverance.

There is nothing God allows to enter our lives that he doesn't want to use for our good. When I got sepsis a few years ago, it was clearly not a zip-a-dee-doo-dah moment. But as I look back on that experience, I see so much positive in the aftermath. It catapulted both my husband and me to a new depth of appreciation of our life together. We still can't stop thanking God for the little nuances of everyday living. We are quicker to recognize pockets of grace hidden in the struggles. We have more hope, more faith, more love.

So I think one of the best things I can do in the face of what seems like rampant difficulties is to praise God. Not for the circumstances. But for him being with us in the midst of them . . . and turning them into something good.

Something quite *satisfactual!*

Topsy Turvy

I will sing of steadfast love and justice; to you, O LORD, I will make music. —Psalm 101:1

One morning during the pandemic, I was reading a book to my grandson by Josh and Dottie McDowell, *The Topsy Turvy Kingdom.* As I read about a fictional world turned on its head, I recognized a real-life *topsy turvy* world was presently interrupting my kingdom of normal. A *topsy turvy* called COVID-19.

Because nothing felt normal. Suddenly people had no jobs. Images of deserted city streets flooded our TV screens. And even those of us who don't understand how the stock market works knew enough to realize those down arrows with four-digit numbers next to them couldn't be good. Students who left for a week of Spring Break were told not to come back to school. Cancellations of everything from highly anticipated sporting events to long-awaited graduations descended on us like deflated balloons. My heart broke over this crisis.

And yet.

Our college chorale was scheduled to go to Ireland during Spring Break and perform throughout the country. To say these kids were pumped would be an understatement. They had worked hard to raise enough money to go, and many saw the trip as the cap on their college career. Four hours before they were to depart for the airport, the college made the decision—in light of the coronavirus—to cancel the trip.

Then the most remarkable thing happened. The students asked their director if they could sing one last song before going their separate ways. These kids took their demolished dreams and turned them into praise for God. They chose the song, "Total Praise," to express their unflinching confidence in him. As I watched their performance on the internet (several times), I couldn't help but join them in praise. It was all the inspiration I needed for the difficult days ahead.

Scripture records similar responses to adversity. On some of the darkest days in David's life, he chose praise. It's what got him through. It's what got the Lancaster Bible College chorale through. And it's what will get us through.

Because that's what praise does. It brings peace into *topsy turvy.*

The "Great" in Gratefulness

Giving thanks always and for everything to God the Father in the name of our Lord Jesus Christ. —Ephesians 5:20

Thank you. Two simple words. Simple but powerful. Words, according to *Harvard Health* that will make you happier when you express them. And *Psychology Today* reports that showing appreciation builds relationships and improves physical, mental, and psychological health. Even war veterans with high levels of gratitude are found to have lower rates of Post-traumatic stress disorder.

Expressing gratitude should be an ongoing characteristic of the Christian life. Ephesians 5 instructs us when to be thankful—*always,* for what to be thankful—*everything*, and to whom to express our thankfulness—*God the Father.*

But that *always* part can be tricky because we don't always feel thankful, do we. How can we be thankful when it feels like all we have to be grateful for has been stripped away? And for *everything*? What about all those mistakes I make? Does *everything* include times of hurt, betrayal, and loss?

I think the *when* and *what* make sense only in the context of *whom*. It's only as we realize God not only authors all the good things in our lives, but uses the bad stuff for a greater, deeper good, that we can move into a lifestyle of gratitude. So we fail, and God teaches us about humility. Someone hurts us, and we grow more forgiving and kind. Thankfulness in the midst of difficulty becomes a crucible for courage.

I believe we cultivate a mindset of gratitude through everyday life.

I remember one weekend in the fall when my husband and I attended a Penn State football game. Who knew it would snow? We certainly didn't, and our lack of appropriate clothing showed it. But we thanked God for an extra blanket and a thin plastic poncho that cut the wind. I spilled mustard all over my white coat, but I thanked God for how good the hot dog tasted anyway. And worst of all, we lost the game, but we thanked God for the opportunity to just be at Beaver Stadium. We could have left the game feeling frustrated over all the things that didn't go as expected, but instead we counted our blessings.

That's what makes gratefulness so great. It clears our vision to see beyond our present circumstances. And it empowers us to replace life-squelching negativity with words of life.

May you never stop shining the light of gratitude, in everything, to God our Father.

CHAPTER SEVEN

The Oil Provides Holiness for Broken Lives

"Our failures don't define us; they inform us"

Bob Goff
—*Dream Big*

Scripture emphasizes the importance of "perfecting holiness out of reverence for God" (2 Corinthians 7:1 NIV). I don't know about you, but the idea of "perfecting holiness" for this fallen human seems insurmountable. It's ugly work. It's hard to recognize and deal with our sinful nature. But deal with it we must. The saints refer to the process of becoming holy as "sanctification." Without it, we can't see God, and we certainly find ourselves inadequate to shine our light. If we want to keep shining, some hindrances have to go.

But holiness doesn't come by obeying a set of legalistic rules. Holiness develops as we allow ourselves to be put under God's microscope. He will expose our hidden wounds and help us deal with areas of self-preservation, anger, and self-pity that block the light. The Holy Spirit will convict us of where we need to use restraint, shore up areas of neglect, and guard our thoughts, words, and speech. We will never be able to clean up our own act. But as we pursue holiness out of reverence for God, we'll find him to be just the cleaner-upper we need.

Be Holy. Who? Me?

But as he who called you is holy, you also be holy in all your conduct, since it is written, "You shall be holy, for I am holy." —1 Peter 1:15–16

Be holy. What a directive! Both Old and New Testaments call us to it. The purpose could not be clearer. God is holy and his children should be too. But what does that mean? What does a holy person look like?

I grew up thinking of holiness in legalistic terms. I bought into the caricature that "holy" people were strict and unhappy for the most part, and all the women wore beehive hairdos. It took a while before I realized holiness has more to do with what's happening on the inside than the outside.

Did you know there's a big difference between being holy and being religious?

Holy people don't look religious at all. They look a lot like Jesus. They exude kindness and love. They make the people around them feel valued, significant, seen. We may experience conviction in their presence, but never condemnation. Just being around them often makes of think of God.

Holiness means "set apart." But for the religious, *set apart* means "set above." Jesus, although clearly set apart, never exalted himself over other people. He lived as the most non-elitist person who ever walked the earth. He delighted in bringing marginalized people—women, children, tax collectors, demoniacs—into the center. Even betrayers.

The religious always expect something in return, whether it be admiration, affirmation, or affection. Jesus loved freely without expecting anything in return. He washed dirty feet, fed multitudes, healed the sick, and preached righteousness. His only reward was pleasing his Father. He didn't even complain about not having a place to lay his head! Holy people don't give to get.

Peter exhorts us to be holy. To keep walking in the truth. To love deeply from the heart. We're to let go of our temporary troubles by anticipating the inheritance that awaits us. That, friend, is what holiness looks like. And you don't even have to put your hair in a beehive to attain it.

Search Me, God!

Search me, O God, and know my heart! —Psalm 139:23

Has the Holy Spirit ever surprised you with revelations about yourself? Exposed some hidden sins you didn't even know existed? Have you finally come to the conclusion the only one who truly understands you is God?

Psalm 139 reveals a man who understood there was Someone who knew him far better than he knew himself. The One who formed him in his mother's womb and breathed life into his nostrils was the One who continued to see every crack and crevice in his heart. Not one single thought remained hidden from his Creator. Not one word. Not one action. God perceived not only what he did but why he did it. And how does David react to such exposure?

"Such knowledge is too wonderful for me; it is high; I cannot attain it" (Psalm 139:6).

David realized self-understanding proved to be an unreliable tool. If he hoped to walk in "the way everlasting" he would need more than Meyers-Briggs to help him see what he was made of. Don't get me wrong. I think personality assessments and gift evaluations can be helpful. I lived in Boulder, Colorado, in the early '70s. It was a time when introspection reigned. Many participated in psychodramas, Gestalt therapies, and encounter groups in hopes of gaining insight about themselves. Although I did learn a lot about my (emerging) self in those days, I would discover that only God could take me to the depths of who I am and bring me out again.

When God shines light on our souls, it can be shocking. Like Peter, we boast, "I'll never deny you," only to have our feeble courage revealed. We think our faith will stand firm and our devotion unshakeable no matter what the enemy hurls our way, only to recognize the true enemy lies hidden in our heart. But God knows it all along. He allows circumstances to surface those buried relics of our human nature not to condemn us, but to make us whole.

Please don't miss this wonderful knowledge David found. Join his cry: "Search me, O God, and know my heart! Try me and know my thoughts! And see if there be any grievous way in me, and lead me in the way everlasting!" (Psalm 139:23–24).

The Virus Within

For everyone who does wicked things hates the light and does not come to the light, lest his works should be exposed. But whoever does what is true comes to the light, so that it may be clearly seen that his works have been carried out in God. —John 3:20–21

Not long after our son graduated from college, he was diagnosed with Type 1 diabetes. The doctors said a virus triggered his once dormant predisposition to the disease. It struck me how he had been living all that time with tendencies toward such a serious condition without knowing it.

I believe the same can be true with issues involving our emotions. We lead fairly normal lives for a number of years, then a crisis of some sort surfaces a wound hidden deep in our souls. The crisis triggers a release of anything from fear and insecurity to depression and anger. The point of pain makes its way to the surface and causes havoc.

It happens to us all in one form or another. Even if we are born-again, Bible-believing, sold-out followers of Jesus. He allows those hidden areas of hurt to surface at just the right time in order to heal us. And be assured, his desire is not to condemn us, but to see us whole. It reminds me of a remark I recently heard:

> *Religion says: I messed up; my dad is gonna' kill me*
>
> *The Gospel says: I messed up; I need to call my dad.*

Jesus came to save. He saves us from eternal condemnation. But he also saves us from everything that hinders us from living like him. From loving like him. From trusting our heavenly Father like he did. If that means we must endure pain to surface festering wounds of rejection or betrayal, he will allow it. If something within us keeps blocking our trust in God or interferes with being able to forgive those who hurt us, he will let the fire of the Holy Spirit come with refining power.

So when the Lord allows a crisis to surface unresolved issues in your life, don't resist the truth. Embrace it. Let the light of the Holy Spirit expose all the hidden darkness and be healed. Let him crush that virus within.

Push Pause

Be still, and know that I am God. —Psalm 46:10

Holiness comes as an inevitable outcome of being in God's presence.

The Lord God Almighty who promises to be with us, even if the earth gives way and the mountains fall into the sea, calls us to be still and know he is God. I'm working on it.

I'm trying to become more conscious of God's presence. Not just in morning devotions, or Sunday services, or when people ask me to pray for them, but in every part of my life. I want to sense his presence when I walk across campus, when I prepare a meal, when I'm drinking a cup of coffee at a café. I want to be like the early Christians Mark Buchannan describes in his book, *Your God Is Too Safe.* He writes about "how unconscious the people were of their consciousness of God."[14] They lived and breathed the awareness of God. And they didn't have to strive to make it happen.

The thought of being so conscious of God that I'm unconscious of it, grabs hold of my heart like a sunset on Cadillac Mountain, Maine. Beautiful. Big. Haunting. How do you learn to *see through* the secular to the sacred? How do you let unceasing prayer capture your thoughts? And can you get to the place where you hear God's voice whispering through music, conversations, and newscasts?

Of course, it begins with the first part of Psalms 46:10, *Be still.* Not an easy task in our noisy world.

I have a friend who's been experiencing the same longing to be more aware of God's presence. The two vertical parallel lines (||) on his TV remote—the pause symbol—came to mind. He felt the Lord directing him throughout the day to raise his arms in a similar fashion (||), pause, and focus on Him. In essence, take a conscious moment to be still and know God is God.

Although it sounds a bit unorthodox, I decided to try it. I was surprised at how that simple physical motion tore right through *my* thoughts and redirected me to *his.* Even if just for a few minutes, arms lifted in pause became arms lifted in praise.

This discipline may not work for you. But I pray the Holy Spirit leads you in some way to grab the remote. Push pause. And in the quiet, consider God.

Chisel Plow Christians

He said to him the third time, "Simon, son of John, do you love me?" Peter was grieved because he said to him the third time, "Do you love me?" and he said to him, "LORD, you know everything; you know that I love you." Jesus said to him, "Feed my sheep."—John 21:17

When Jesus touches our brokenness, we can't help but want to be more like him.

Peter needed healing. His bold declarations of unquenchable loyalty to Jesus had withered with the rooster's third crow. He denied even knowing Jesus, let alone being one of his closest friends for the last three years. When thrust into a life-threatening crisis, self-preservation rather than undying faithfulness surfaced. It exposed him to be a shallower man than he realized.

Before Peter could become the "rock" Jesus declared him to be, he would have to deal with some deeply hidden areas of his human nature. After the resurrection when Jesus asked Peter if he loved him, he gave opportunity for Peter's guilt, shame, and failure to surface. Three times Jesus asked. Three times the penetrating question opened the wound of his denial. But it also exposed him to a dimension of forgiving love he had yet to experience. It healed him. It equipped him to feed God's flock. It prepared him to one day die rather than deny Christ again.

Peter became a chisel plow Christian.

Chisel plows are farm implements used primarily to break up hard, packed dirt. Their iron claws rip through the soil and prepare it for planting. They get rid of stones and weeds that would otherwise hinder seeds from taking root and bring fresh nutrients to the surface. Without chisel plows, fields would be far less productive.

Without the chisel plow of the Holy Spirit, we too would be unproductive. Until we let the Lord dig deep into our hearts and surface our hidden faults, we can't hope to grow. We need him to expose stones of bitterness and rejection. To cut off weeds of shame and guilt so they don't overrun us like crabgrass.

Do you desire to have a deeper walk with Jesus? Then don't be afraid of what might surface in your life. He loves you no matter what. Whether you've betrayed his character or fallen short of loving his sheep, his love will reinstate you, just as it did for Peter.

A great harvest awaits our participation. Let's get ready. Let's become chisel-plow Christians.

Pity Party Invite

I'm so angry I wish I were dead. —Jonah 4:9 (NIV)

Self-Pity. There's nothing attractive about it. Like quicksand, it draws us in and pulls us down, down, down, until we drown in SELF. Self-pity accepts no responsibility for our beleaguered state of mind and soothes our bruised egos with the balm of blame shifting. It never draws us to the high bar of forgiveness, but to the low bar of revenge. It deceives us into thinking we don't deserve the inevitable hardships that accompany fallen life. It keeps our light from shining.

I hate everything about self-pity, but most of all when I find it in myself. Like Jonah, I sulk under the leaf of a plant whose shade I don't deserve and think I'd rather die than not get my way. "Oh poor *me!* This injustice shouldn't happen to *me!* Lord, why don't you care about *me? Me, me, me.* How do we throw off the mantra of *me?*

It's a lot easier to deal with self-pity if we nip it in the bud. When the first inkling of feeling sorry for ourselves starts to shadow our hearts, treat it like the sin it is and repent. Don't try putting lipstick on a pig by calling it a "struggle." Acknowledge it as a selfish response to not getting our way.

Then turn to the Word of God.

Thankfully, Scripture provides us with powerful examples of those who refused to give in to self-pity. If anyone had justification for feeling sorry for himself, it was Joseph. But he refused, and when reunited with his brothers, his response pointed to God, not himself. "You meant evil against me, but God meant it for good" (Genesis 50:20).

Paul suffered much because of Christ. But his epistles burst with gratitude to God, not grievances. "I count everything as loss because of the surpassing worth of knowing Christ Jesus my Lord. For his sake I have suffered the loss of all things and count them as rubbish" (Philippians 3:8).

And of course, Jesus. His life exemplifies the very opposite mindset of self-pity. "Father, forgive them, for they know not what they do" (Luke 23:34).

So, the next time you're invited to a pity party, refuse that invitation. Wad it up, stomp on it, and throw it in the trash. You have better things to do with your time!

Misplaced Anger

Be angry and do not sin; do not let the sun go down on your anger. — Ephesians 4:26

Anger eclipses the light of love. Yet it's showing up everywhere. In all kinds of situations, all kinds of people. To say we've become an easily offended society understates the issue. We are living in an atmosphere of misplaced anger, where we would rather focus on the speck in someone else's eye than deal with our own planks. Christians should know better.

Even when anger is justified, we are warned not to let the sun go down on our wrath. It's important to deal with anger when the first hint of resentment makes its way to our consciousness.

Recently someone reneged on a major commitment to me. At first, I was stunned. Then as the reality began to sink in, I found myself replaying the consequences in my mind. The offense started to take hold. I knew if I didn't deal with it right then, the negativity would grow into full- blown anger.

I had a choice: continue to stew about it or replace the resentment with something better. I shifted my focus to the Lord, recalled Scripture, sang praises, and asked the Holy Spirit to help me forgive. I believed the Lord would work out the situation for my good, but I wanted to trust him *before* it resolved. So, I fanned the flames of worship instead of anger.

The circumstance turned out better than I could have imagined. But the greater victory probably occurred in my soul. As I resisted the pull toward resentment and anger, the Lord was able to unearth areas in my own life that needed washing. He answered my prayers and threw in some sanctification along the way.

God wills for each of us to be sanctified, to be made pure, holy. It's not a once-and-done process. Every day we face life in a fallen world. When injustices erupt, we are called, as God's children, to deal with them in a righteous manner. Meeting sin with sin—anger with anger—rejection with rejection—never works.

Although we will never be able to stop all sin and anger, we must be willing to allow God's sanctifying fire to burn out the misplaced anger in ourselves. Let's not contribute to our "angri-culture." Let's ask the Holy Spirit to take our resentments and turn them into something far better than anger.

Unfiltered

Finally, brothers, whatever is true, whatever is honorable, whatever is just, whatever is pure, whatever is lovely, whatever is commendable, if there is any excellence, if there is anything worthy of praise, think about these things. —Philippians 4:8

What does it mean for something to be *unfiltered*? I'm sure you've seen the term on photographs and certain items like olive oil, honey, and apple juice. Sometimes people's actions earn them the title of being *unfiltered* when they lack self-restraint or when they display a reckless, self-absorbed attitude.

Filters protect our computers and television screens from harmful content. Filtered water promises to make what we drink healthier. My coffee would be full of grounds without a coffee filter. But what about our minds? How often do we allow our minds to wander—*unfiltered*? At times, I have to remind myself about the importance of filtering what I think about. Especially when my thoughts whirl around like an endless swirl of negativity.

We actually can determine what feeds our thought life. Paul exhorted the Philippians to choose what things they thought about. He told them to dwell on the true, noble, right, pure, and lovely, filtering out thoughts that were deceptive, ignoble, impure, or ugly. Paul knew that to a large extent people *are what they think.* The more they directed their thoughts to the admirable, the more admirable they would become.

But for the process to be complete we need to be aware of what not to filter.

When my heart is hardening toward someone who has hurt me, I don't want to filter out God's love. When I face what appears to be an impossible obstacle, I don't want my logic to filter out God's supernatural power. I don't want pride to filter out truth that might make me look bad and consequently keep me from repenting. I don't want self-centeredness to filter out an awareness of those with whom I share this planet.

So, maybe like me, it's time to consider your filters. Are you filtering out those thoughts   that have no other purpose than to drag you down? Are you free to let the Holy Spirit lead you into an unfiltered life of holiness?

I hope so, because that, friend, is my *unfiltered* desire for you.

Creepy Little Friend

And these are the ones along the path, where the word is sown: when they hear, Satan immediately comes and takes away the word that is sown in them. —Mark 4:15

Do you know distractions can interfere with our pursuit of holiness?

A beautiful house with a wraparound porch set on a mid-size lawn surrounded by woods. I was beyond excited for the opportunity to spend a week alone in this setting as a place to write, study, and pray. Bring it on! "Speak, Lord, your servant is listening!"

As I look out over the lawn, I notice something moving. Not a squirrel, chipmunk, deer, or fox, as I might expect. This something looks unnatural. It IS unnatural! This moving unnatural something turns out to be a robotic lawnmower. Since this is a second home for the owner, he bought the robot to keep his lawn in shape while away. It runs 24/7, returning to the battery station to get recharged when it starts to run out of juice.

It's actually kind of weird to be sitting at my worktable, only to look out the window and see the robot nonchalantly moving across the grass. In the front, in the back, in the morning, in the afternoon. I started calling the distraction my creepy little friend.

Distractions come in all shapes and sizes. Most prove to be harmless in and of themselves. It's how much we allow them to detour us from our goal that determines their impact. One of the most harmful effects takes place when used by Satan to impede our walk with the Lord.

In *The Screwtape Letters* written by C.S. Lewis, a senior devil instructs a junior demon on the best way to keep his "client" from pursuing God. Right at the moment the man starts to think about spirituality and seems to be moving toward God, plant a thought in his mind like, "How about lunch." As he goes to lunch, he quickly forgets about godly issues.[15]

Has something like that ever happened to you? Rather than tempting us with blatant wickedness, Satan uses distractions to move us to a different train of thought. Like those people Jesus described who hear the word but lose it because Satan quickly snatches it away. Let's not be in that crowd.

Let's not give in to creepy little friends of distraction, lest they turn out to be creepy little fiends.

Are You Infected . . .With Neglect?

How shall we escape if we neglect such a great salvation? It was declared at first by the Lord, and it was attested to us by those who heard, while God also bore witness by signs and wonders and various miracles and by gifts of the Holy Spirit distributed according to his will. —Hebrews 2:3-4

Our brokenness sometimes emerges due to neglect.

I woke up one morning with this passage from Hebrews 2 on my mind. How do we find any hope in life if we neglect God's great salvation? Scripture indicates we have no excuse. The Lord declared it; eyewitnesses affirmed it; signs, wonders, and miracles confirmed it. The Holy Spirit continues to provide us with spiritual gifts pointing to it. So much evidence exists that we have to ignore its truth *with intentionality* in order to avoid it.

But I'm afraid that's exactly what many of us try to do. We numb ourselves to the reality of our condition. We're like people infected with the coronavirus who have no idea of their vulnerability. Only when temperatures spike and breathing becomes labored do we realize the danger. Danger not only to ourselves, but also to others. We need to heed the warning signs.

Some of us try to deceive ourselves by God-words as a cover for our neglect. We talk about how much we "love Jesus." But then we do things we know he disapproves of. We skip right over the part where Jesus says if we love him, we'll do what he commands (John 14:15).

I think neglect for most of us probably begins with small, seemingly insignificant, decisions. Busyness cuts into reading Scripture as a priority. Prayers become flavored more with our interests than God's. But most of all, we stop acknowledging God as the source of all the good we experience. The *New Living Translation* puts it starkly: "Don't you see how wonderfully kind, tolerant, and patient God is with you? Does this mean nothing to you? Can't you see that his kindness is intended to turn you from your sin?" (Romans 2:4). Gratitude works like a vaccine against apostasy.

Friend, let's avoid getting infected with the bacteria of neglect. The consequences run too high. Our God has designed us for life. Abundant life.

How's Your Infrastructure?

Unless the Lord builds the house,
  those who build it labor in vain.
Unless the Lord watches over the city,
  the watchman stays awake in vain. —Psalm 127:1 (NIV)

There's a lot of talk these days about "infrastructure" in our country. It refers basically to the physical systems needed for a government to run smoothly. Safe bridges and roads, adequate power grids and sewer systems, and up-to-date communication networks provide the foundation that enables everything else to function.

But what about you? How's your *spiritual* infrastructure? Maybe you're experiencing some potholes in your faith. Or the power of the Holy Spirit needs a bit more amperage. Perhaps you've let some unforgiveness or disappointment clog up pipelines purposed to carry life-giving waters.

Infrastructures—whether physical or spiritual—share a common problem. They often grab our attention after a crisis occurs.

When we accepted Christ, we entered into the most radical transaction known to man. God himself came to dwell in us. He wants to turn our humble bungalows into something akin to Westminster Cathedral. But it can be painful at times to stay within the confines of his blueprint. We let down our guard and open the window to seemingly harmless compromises. We stop maintaining the "systems" for a variety of reasons until devotion to God gets squeezed out. And that's when the infrastructure starts taking a hit.

Solomon said unless the Lord builds the house, we labor in vain. Maybe the first step in repairing our infrastructure comes in remembering God is both the builder and sustainer, not us. When we start to take pride in our moral goodness and works, we lose sight that the foundation of the whole house rests on grace. In fact, our house would not even be in existence were it not for grace! And it certainly can't withstand the turbulence of spiritual warfare without it.

So if you find your "infrastructure" in need of repair, don't wait for the house to collapse. If you realize you've *grown* out of grace and are *groaning* under the weight of self-sufficiency, ask God to patch up those cracks. Don't let yourself become worn down by the winds of compromise and by neglecting spiritual disciplines. Return to the blueprints. You will rediscover all the resources you need to fulfill God's plan and become a habitation for his glory.

CHAPTER EIGHT

The Oil Provides Truth Over Deception

"You can resolve to live your life with integrity. Let your credo be this: Let the lie come into the world, let it even triumph. But not through me."

Aleksandr Solzhenitsyn
— *The Gulag Archipelago*

Deception slips into our conversations, newscasts, and advertisements. Even our hearts. I don't think I have ever lived in a time where so many people are wondering where to look for truth. Where can men and women of integrity be found? People who speak truth even when it makes them look bad? Folks who don't fudge the truth to get the end result they want? As believers, we follow the One who called himself the Truth. As we purpose to adhere to his standard of truth, no matter what, we will shine a desperately needed light into the fog of deception.

Nothing But the Truth

And Jesus began to say to them, "See that no one leads you astray."
—Mark 13:5

One of my students recently gave a speech on the importance of telling the truth. She cited a study stating a whopping 60 percent of people lie at least once during a ten-minute conversation. The most common culprit behind the lies was a need to feel "likable or competent." She described how even small, seemingly harmless deceptions can weave a dangerous web.

As believers, we should stand as beacons of truth, beginning with our personal lives. If we get comfortable rationalizing our small detours from honesty, it won't be long until we create a pattern where full-blown deception feels quite welcome to kick off his shoes and lean back in the easy chair. We'll become so accustomed to his company that we'll actually forget he's there (2 Thessalonians 2:10).

It's vitally important to love the truth. Love the truth. Love the truth. Even when it hurts. Even when it makes you look bad. Don't coddle misperceptions that nurse grudges and give you an excuse not to forgive. Don't be afraid to speak the truth when it goes against the cultural grain. Walk with so much integrity that you cement a foundation that cannot be breached by lies, no matter how convincingly they're packaged. Make truth-telling a habit.

Because it's not going to get any better.

Deception reigns as a hallmark of the last days. When the disciples asked Jesus about signs of the end times, he warned them about deception (Mark 13). "See that no one leads you astray" (v. 5). "Be on your guard" (v. 9). Keep awake!" (v. 33). He told them there would be a rise in false prophets and false messiahs who would dazzle people with wonders and miracles designed to deceive. But the more they immersed themselves in the truth, the quicker they would detect deceit.

So how is your truth-detector? Are you among the 60 percent who give in to telling those little white lies? Don't let deception move in and carve out a groove in your mind. Love the truth. The whole truth. Nothing but the truth.

Too Much Freedom

For you were called to freedom, brothers. Only do not use your freedom as an opportunity for the flesh, but through love serve one another. — Galatians 5:13

When my daughter, Bethany, was around eight years old, she wanted to go along with my mother-in-law and me to a women's meeting where I was the main speaker. We met in the banquet room of a local restaurant. Bethany wore her new white dress and came prepared with her little notebook and pen to take notes. I could not have been prouder.

They served a buffet-style dinner before the meeting with a smorgasbord of delicious desserts. The combination of being a bit preoccupied with my upcoming message and wanting it to be a special night for her, caused me to be more relaxed than usual with *what* she was eating and *how much*. I'm guessing it was somewhere around a fifth helping of chocolate mousse that she told me her stomach hurt. She seemed miserable, so I led her from the banquet room to the bathroom. Right as we reached the door, disaster struck. All those helpings of chocolate mousse came flying across the bathroom floor and on her once white dress. (Thankfully, my mother-in-law came to the rescue and helped me clean her up.)

I realized had I been more watchful and given her some limits, the whole mess would have been averted. She was too young to handle unlimited chocolate mousse. She suffered the consequences of too much freedom.

Paul warned the Galatians not to use their freedom as an excuse to indulge. Of course, he was speaking to more than the folks in Galatia. Our human tendency always seeks to push the limits, to bend the restrictions. But rules, as much as we might resist them, keep us from turning into slaves of our own passions.

God gives us freedom but sets fences around that freedom to protect us from ourselves as well as each other. If I would have limited the chocolate mousse to no more than two helpings, it would have resulted in a much more pleasant night for all of us.

So don't buy the lie that freedom means an absence of rules. We will remain free only as long as we walk in the truth. And truth sets boundaries.

Truth-Shaming

For whoever is ashamed of me and of my words, of him will the Son of Man be ashamed when he comes in his glory and the glory of the Father and of the holy angels. —Luke 9:26

Fat-shaming. You've no doubt heard of it. It's when people are mocked or ridiculed because of being overweight. The purpose is to humiliate them for carrying extra pounds. Although it has become more prevalent in our weight-conscious society, there's another kind of shaming that is also on the rise. I call it truth-shaming.

Truth-shaming occurs when people belittle those who speak the truth . . . especially those who profess there is only one truth. Truth-shamers declare no one has the right to claim the existence of only one truth. They see truth as fluid. *I have my truth. You have your truth.* They classify those who believe in one truth as naïve at best, dangerous to society at worst. They cast an ominous shadow over our culture.

Don't let truth-shaming pull you down. No one endured more truth-shaming than he who is the *Truth*. Jesus was accused of blasphemy, of casting out demons by the power of Satan, of being a sinful rebel-rouser. He was spit on, mocked, and subjected to the degradation of the cross. But do you know how he dealt with all the shame being hurled his way?

He scorned it! (Hebrews 12:2).

We can too. The author of Hebrews says we are to consider how Jesus handled the shame, lest we lose heart. It's not easy to be the butt of late-night comedians' jokes or the targets of social pressure. It's hard to be labeled as haters when we love, as insensitive when we respect the dignity of all people, as fools when we possess the wisdom of the ages. But as followers of truth, we must have the courage to stand firm, keeping our hope on what lies ahead, just like Jesus did "for the joy that was set before him" (Hebrews 12:2). Jesus warned if we are ashamed of him in this life, he will be ashamed of us in the next. That's a warning I want to heed, and I imagine you do too. Let's keep fixing our eyes on the author of our faith rather than the contempt of the truth-shamers. There's a whole cloud of witnesses counting on us not to fold.

So is Jesus.

Lightsaber-ers

And he departed with no one's regret. They buried him in the city of David, but not in the tombs of the kings. —2 Chronicles 21:20

What a eulogy! King Jehoram died "with no one's regret." In his eight short years as king of Judah, he managed to murder all his brothers, lead the country into idol worship, and fight constant wars—wars that resulted in defeat and plunder by surrounding nations. A painful bowel disease took his life. And everyone was relieved at his passing.

Jehoram was Jehoshaphat's oldest son, and Jehoshaphat, although imperfect, was one of the good guys in the annals of Judah's kings. So, what happened? Scripture indicates Jehoram was influenced by his wife, who happened to be a daughter of the infamous Ahab. She was evil to the core; she almost succeeded in wiping out the whole Davidic line of kings in Judah.

Evil only needs a small piece of our heart to take over. Although we may have experienced the light of the gospel, we need to be diligent in not succumbing to the dimming fog of compromise. I like how one missionary puts it, "Just as the light penetrates the darkness, so the darkness catches up with the light." And the "darkness that follows the light is the worst kind." Jehoram had basked in the light under the reign of his father Jehoshaphat. But he allowed the darkness to snuff it out, and the whole nation plunged into apostasy.

According to "Wookiepedia," lightsabers are the laser swords used primarily by Star Wars Jedi. The power radiating from them can be offensive or defensive. They can cut through just about anything, even deflecting back shots lodged toward them by their enemies.

The thought of lightsabers intrigues me. I can't help but think we followers of Christ are like those lightsabers. God has given us the responsibility to fend off the darkness—the darkness within ourselves as well as the encroaching darkness that threatens to overtake the world. It's an assignment that extends to every believer everywhere.

So, my fellow lightsaber-er, don't let any part of your light be compromised. Don't let the darkness take even an inch. Let your light shine brightly and boldly. You'll have no regrets.

One-Eyed Christians?

But Nahash the Ammonite said to them, "On this condition I will make a treaty with you, that I gouge out all your right eyes, and thus bring disgrace on all Israel." —1 Samuel 11:2

Are you a one-eyed Christian?

The Ammonites were pressing hard against the little Israelite city of Jabesh. Vastly outnumbered, the men of Jabesh asked their enemies if they would make a treaty with them. The Ammonites agreed, but on one condition. They would gouge out the right eye of every inhabitant in the city.

That the men of Jabesh entertained the idea of making a treaty with the Ammonites in the first place reveals how far they had fallen from the Lord. Their covenant with God stipulated they were not to compromise with the surrounding Gentile nations. Yet when faced with taking a stand against the imposing threat or negotiating a way out, they abandoned God and sought to negotiate. Only when the brutal terms of their

surrender became known, did they seek help from their fellow Israelites.

In spite of Jabesh's spineless lack of valor, the tribes of Israel responded to their cry for help. They completely routed the Ammonites
and rescued their countrymen from defeat and degradation. All right
eyes were left intact!

I think compromising with the enemies of God is like having our
right eyes gouged. I'm afraid some of us are running around with im-
paired vision. And we probably don't even realize it.

We now live in a culture attempting to steamroll over every Christian principle in sight. It's challenging to stand firm on the rock of truth
when society's influencers present a new definition of truth every day.
The more we allow the world's perspective to cloud our vision, the
more we look like one-eyed Christians.

But there are other, subtler enemies tucked securely in our hearts.
These are the truly powerful ones, capable of gouging out both eyes.
When we fail to fight the forces of self-centeredness, judgmentalism,
and pride we in essence are making a treaty with the enemy of our souls.
We give him access to our vision, and in the end, we bring disgrace
upon the body of Christ because we distort what he looks like.

But we don't have to compromise! We can cry out to God and fellow
believers for help. Help to keep us from becoming one-eyed Christians.

I Love Me

*For people will be lovers of self, lovers of money, proud, arrogant, abu-
sive, disobedient to their parents, ungrateful, unholy.* —2 Timothy 3:2

An article in *The New York Times* written by a law professor at San
Francisco University described divorce as an expression of "radical
self-love." Far from being the shameful event we've known it to be, she
says divorce liberates us from being tied to responsibilities keeping us
from reaching self-fulfillment. She readily admitted she still loved her
husband, but she just loved herself more.[16]

A sign of the times.

Today's culture seems bent on self-love. If someone hurts you, deal with it by indulging on a quart of death by chocolate ice cream and binging on episodes of *The Office*. Feel like you're giving more than receiving from a friendship, from your church, from your job? Ditch them and move on to places where you get more bang for your buck. And don't forget virtue-signaling to let everyone know how you're a tiny bit better than the rest of us.

Self-love covers all generations. It transfixes Baby Boomers into perpetual *baby* mindsets of wanting what we want and wanting it now. It tells Gen Xers to X out anything that crosses their own agenda. And it transforms millennials into *me-llennials.*

In this haze of self-love, truth becomes whatever we say it is. So, you have *your truth* and I have mine. No *inconvenient truths* that might threaten our well-being in the landscape! But truth that is not true will never last.

Paul warns us to mark such days as the precursor to "terrible times" (2 Timothy 2:1, NIV). How could they not be? Because self-lovers relish in what gives them pleasure, what gets them ahead. In their conceit, they lack humility, forgiveness, and gratitude—all the virtues necessary for fallen people to live together.

So how do we respond to such a dire forecast?

No matter how crazy the times, stand firm in the truth. Cultivate forgiveness, kindness, and thankfulness. Jesus said if we love our life, in the end we will lose it. He created us for a far higher purpose than loving ourselves. If we love him with all our heart, and seek our neighbor's good, we'll guard ourselves against this prevailing cultural madness. That, friend, is *true love*. Far better than *me love*.

Pacifying Evil: No Such Thing

But Saul was ravaging the church, and entering house after house, he dragged off men and women and committed them to prison. —Acts 8:3

Evil cannot be pacified. It will keep spreading until it is stopped dead in its tracks.

Stephen was wise, courageous, and full of the Holy Spirit. He also holds the distinct honor of becoming the first martyr because of his faith in Jesus Christ. After confronting the Sanhedrin with the truth about what they did to Jesus, they were so incensed that they ran him out of town and stoned him (Acts 7:57–58). Even though Stephen stood innocent of any wrongdoing, they got away with it. Like blood in the water attracting sharks, his death fed their maniacal pursuit. A great persecution of the church broke out after his martyrdom.

The enemy of our souls never finds contentment with one victory. Success only feeds his ravenous spirit. There are times to compromise in life, but when it comes to evil, we dare not give an inch. As Oswald Chambers says, "There's no heaven with a little corner of hell in it."[17] Hell will eventually take over if we give it a place to land.

Wholesale evil is on display in far too many regions. Take Russia. Afghanistan. North Korea. Across the Middle East, believers are being maimed and martyred by extremists. Young Christian girls continue to be abducted and forced to convert to Islam. Early successes have made the terrorists hungry for more. Christian leaders in those lands describe the onslaught as "pure genocide," but the evil continues. Although we might not be in a position to alleviate the suffering of our brothers and sisters in other parts of the world, we can pray for them.

And one other thing we can—and should—actively pursue is having a zero tolerance for evil in our own lives.

Don't let even a smidge of unforgiveness or deception lie hidden in your heart. If you try to justify any semblance of evil in your thoughts or actions, be assured you will come out on the losing end. Ask the Lord to keep washing you clean in his love. Leave no room for evil.

Don't Be Deceived by Power Brokers

Whoever finds his life will lose it, and whoever loses his life for my sake will find it. —Matthew 10:39

"One Ring to rule them all, One Ring to find them, One Ring to bring them all, and in the darkness bind them.[18]

J. R. R. Tolkien presents possibly the strongest case in literature about the danger of power. In *The Lord of the Rings* trilogy, he shows how its lure can entice even common folks (like hobbits). The "ring of power" turns reason into insanity, normal longing into deadly obsession, and noble intentions into dishonorable betrayal. Beware!

Power's clutches reach far beyond the confines of the Shire. The lust for power lurks in marriages where husbands and wives forget their call to *complete* one another, not *compete* for control. Bullies, whether on the playground or in the boardroom, think power over others will quiet their noisy insecurities. And don't get me started on the drive for power in politics. How many politicians sacrifice their integrity to satisfy its addicting snare? Power is insatiable . . . the more you get, the more you want.

So, Jesus told us not to pursue this treacherous commodity. He showed us true power—the kingdom of heaven kind—exists for giving, not for acquiring. It's the kind that heals the sick, raises the dead, cleanses lepers, and casts out demons. It's in the business of freeing people, rather than coercing them to bend to its will.

The kingdom of heaven kind of power can get us into trouble because it refuses to play along with what the world values. But Jesus tells us not to worry. No one has power over our souls, and that proves to be far more important than what anyone can do to us. When we choose to lose our pursuit of power and instead take up the cross of Jesus, we find more than we ever imagined.

I think it's time we stop listening to the deceptive voices of the world's power brokers. Don't let their rings of power deceive us. Jesus offers us the opportunity to escape from all the power grabs. Let's give it all to him. We'll discover the One who breaks the power of sin and death is the greatest power broker of all.

Un-listening Rebels

But you, son of man, hear what I say to you. Be not rebellious like that rebellious house; open your mouth and eat what I give you. —Ezekiel 2:8

I remember the first time I took my then three-year-old grandson to a playground to release some of his unspent energy. At one point I asked him to slow down and be careful. His response was priceless: "I don't think I can hear you." What a shock to learn this adorable bundle of joy shares undeniable traits of fallen humanity! His perception of what was good at the moment had more pull than instructions from his (very wise) grandma.

As much as we say we want to hear God, each of us must deal with our rebel hearts. The nation of Israel was no exception. In the book of Ezekiel, the prophet is told to speak to the people *even though* they would not listen. In the space of six verses in Chapter 2, Israel is referred to as "rebellious" six times (vv. 3–8). Not listening to God is the first sign of a rebel heart.

One of the direst consequences of not listening comes in the form of deception. People who refuse to listen to the truth need to justify their behavior, so they make up their own truth and in time actually believe it (2 Thessalonians 2:10). I know people, and you probably do too, who literally rebuild reality in order to rationalize everything from their refusal to forgive to why it's okay to cheat. I even heard a woman once say she had to leave her husband in order to serve Jesus. But what it all boils down to is our human proclivity to rebel against the God who created us.

It isn't always easy to hear God. It could be "I don't think I can hear you" reflects an honest appraisal of our situation. In those cases, all we need to do is take a little wax out of our ears. That's very different than saying *I can't hear* because I don't want you to interfere with what I'm doing. It's a dangerous mindset. In fact, it's right-down foolish. Refusing to listen to God turns once soft hearts into rebellious habitats of deception.

Keep walking in truth, friend. Nothing offers your heart greater protection.

Going Green

But be doers of the word, and not hearers only, deceiving yourselves.
—James 1:22

One of the most subtle forms of deception occurs when we believe we possess a certain quality simply because we've heard about it. It can not only stifle our growth, but over time will desensitize us to truth.

In 1974, Chip and I transformed our van into something that resembled an RV. With a makeshift bed and cooler-turned-refrigerator we left Florida for a month-long trip across the country. One of our destinations included attending the World's Fair in Spokane, WA. The theme of the Expo was the environment. We took in exhibit after exhibit extolling the virtue of caring for the earth's resources. This was the early '70s when not many people had jumped on the environmental bandwagon. We left feeling quite enlightened, maybe even a bit "ecologically smug." We patted ourselves on the back because we determined to do our part in taking care of the planet.

So, you can imagine our horror when we got back to our apartment and realized we had forgotten to turn off the oven! That's right. I had been warming up some coffee cake to take for our first breakfast on the road, and I left the oven on for a whole month! Thankfully, nothing caught fire. But Chip spent hours repainting the now yellowed walls surrounding the oven. Our ecological smugness faded as quickly as plastic straws in San Francisco.

Clearly, hearing about the importance of caring for the environment did not make us environmentalists. Hearing about the necessity of getting rid of anger doesn't make us gentle. Hearing about the call to generosity doesn't make us charitable. And hearing about someone else's heroism doesn't make us courageous. If *hearing* doesn't lead to *doing*, we can kiss *becoming* goodbye.

According to James, it's easy to deceive ourselves into thinking we're something we're not when we don't follow up on what we hear. If we want to cultivate a particular virtue, we have to go beyond mere listening. We have to move on it in order to incorporate it as a part of our lifestyle. Otherwise, we're like people who look at their faces in a mirror and promptly forget what they see (James 1:23–24).

Friend, don't let yourself be deceived. Put into practice the things God calls you to do. The world doesn't need more folks who fail to practice what they preach. When the light signal turns green, don't sit there just thinking it's a nice color. Go!

Not Just a Slogan

Let us acknowledge the LORD; let us press on to acknowledge him. — Hosea 6:3 (NIV)

A few years ago, we had the opportunity to tour the fabulous United States Naval Academy in Annapolis, MD. I couldn't help but notice the pin our tour guide was wearing: BEAT ARMY. When asked about it, she said, "*Beat Army* isn't just a slogan here; it's a way of life!" The academy even sports a case in the athletic building displaying all the winning footballs gained against their archrival. Did I say the footballs were painted gold? I have a feeling any plebes coming with a half-hearted mindset toward Army will, after four years, have mastered said "way of life."

So, what about the phrases we commonly use in our Christian walk? Have they deteriorated into mere slogans, or do they reinforce how we live? Expressions like *Praise the Lord, I'm praying for you,* or *God bless you* disclose something that should be a part of every believer's "way of life." But do our words truly reflect our mindset? Does our acknowledgement of God synchronize with our words, or have our words become empty syllables of self-deception?

The book of Hosea records one of the most severe charges against Israel: they had stopped *acknowledging God.* Even though they gave him lip service, the people went about their days as if he didn't exist. They deceived themselves into thinking as long as they were offering sacrifices, they'd be okay. But failure to truly acknowledge him resulted in love as enduring as the morning dew (Hosea 6:4). They would be healed of their evaporating faithfulness to the Lord only after they began acknowledging him again.

Friend, the days ahead are not ones where empty slogans are going to cut it. If you have been walking down a path of compromise and simply been going through the motions, STOP. TURN AROUND. Stop lying to yourself and repent! Make acknowledging him a way of life. The world is searching for authenticity. For people whose words match their actions. Be one of those people.

As you do, you'll be ready to defeat *your* arch enemy. You will BEAT SATAN!

CHAPTER NINE

The Oil Provides Faith in Lieu of Unbelief

"Everything begins with faith."

Max Lucado
—*Glory Days*

Persistent faith in God illuminates a skeptic-driven world like the Ocracoke Lighthouse in a dark and turbulent North Carolina sea. It shows us how to navigate through the crushing waves of disappointment and directs us to an anchor of hope when hope is lost. Faith calls us to believe for things unbelievable. To keep believing because God's Word tells us to believe. To focus on what God can do when believing in ourselves runs aground. Faith shores us up against Satan's temptations to doubt. And it enables us to shine a legacy of courage for those adrift in the waters of unbelief.

Too Important to Forget

They did not remember his power—the day he redeemed them from the oppressor. —Psalm 78:42 (NIV)

The miraculous signs making possible their exodus from Egypt. The parting of the Red Sea. Water gushing from rocks and manna falling from the sky. The defeat of enemy after enemy. How could Israel ever forget the power of God? But the psalmist says they did.

I don't think their forgetfulness was an *Israel-problem*. I think it was a *human-problem*. Scripture is replete with admonishments to remember what God has done. To recall what he has done in the world as well as in our own lives. If we forget his power, our prayers become little more than lip service, "having the form of godliness but denying its power" (2 Timothy 3:5 NIV).

Remembering the power of God replenishes our faith. Faith—even mustard-size faith—ignites the engine that gives us access to his power. It makes miracles happen, for "with God all things are possible" (Matthew 19:26). Mark Batterson writes in *The Circle Maker*, "The greatest moments in life are the miraculous moments when human impotence and divine omnipotence intersect."[19] There is nothing too hard for God. He wants us to know that. To *really* know that. To know it so thoroughly that we don't forget.

Friends, we are engaged in a great spiritual battle. Our Father has given us the privilege of fighting that battle with him. Our prayers make a difference in the outcome because he designed it that way.

I was recently praying for someone whose situation seemed pretty desperate. But as I began to reflect on the power of God and pray accordingly, I experienced a great release of faith. When I *remembered* the power of God, I no longer felt hopeless. I started praying boldly for a miracle with a confidence I didn't have before.

I'm not suggesting every time we remember the power of God, we will experience a miracle. But I am saying if we do not remember, we will miss opportunities to honor him and to impact the world for his glory.

Let's not be like Israel. Let's remember the power of God. Recall it. Rehearse it. Tell others about it. And walk in faith. It's too important to forget.

Where Do Those Ifs Come From?

*The devil said to him, "If you are the Son of God, command this stone to become bread." —*Luke 4:3

If . . . if . . . if . . . I think Satan has a packet of doubt seeds beginning with the word *if.* He tries to sow them in our hearts whenever he spots a vulnerable moment.

You're familiar with his tactic against Jesus. After forty days of fasting in the desert, Satan appears to him, beginning every temptation with that insidious word. *"If* you are the Son of God, command this stone to become bread" (Luke 4:3). *"If* you, then, will worship me, it will all be yours" (v. 7). And again, *"If* you are the Son of God, throw yourself down from here" (v. 9 emphasis added). He wanted to make Jesus doubt his identity as well as God's plan and purpose.

We can be sure if Satan had the audacity to try and sow seeds of doubt in the Son of God, he'll attempt blocking our faith with the same strategy. *"If* you are really following God, why are these bad things happening?" *"If* you were a good parent, why is your child rebelling?" And one of my favorites, *"If* you had faith, why aren't you seeing miracles?"

Believe me, *ifs* can completely uproot our faith. They rob us of the confidence we need to carry out God's will. And they make us forget our call comes from God—the God who promises he himself will bring our work to completion (Philippians 1:6). The longer we linger over all the *ifs,* the deeper they get entrenched in our soul.

So what do we do with the *ifs?* We do what Jesus did and let the Word of God cut them down. Even when the enemy's accusations hit the bullseye, we call upon the One who promises to redeem our past, "Therefore, if anyone is in Christ, he is a new creation. The old has passed away; behold, the new has come" (2 Corinthians 5:17).

Friend, we have been given an outlandish opportunity to shed the light of truth in a dark world. How important it is to counter Satan's seeds of doubt with seeds stemming from the Word of God. Faith comes from hearing his word. It's a faith that stands strong enough to over-come all those weedy *ifs*.

Believe What You Heard

Does he who supplies the Spirit to you and works miracles among you do so by works of the law, or by hearing with faith? —Galatians 3:5

We are saved because we *believed what we heard.*

The Holy Spirit lives in us because we believe what we heard.

We witness miracles because we believe what we heard.

We run into trouble when we stop believing what we heard and be-lieve more in what we do. That's what happened to the Galatians, and I'm afraid it didn't stop with them. We continue to face the challenge of whether to rely on God or on our own efforts to obtain the results we desire. Paul doesn't mince words in describing our return to self-reli-ance. It's foolish! (Galatians 3:1.)

I can't help but ask if the reason we don't see many miracles is be-cause we stop believing what we hear. Or maybe we don't stop to listen in the first place. There are circumstances in my life right now that war-rant supernatural intervention. But even though I pray for miracles, all too often I find myself wondering what I can do to make things happen. I worry, I fret, and I fail to develop the kind of trust God wants me to have. I should know better.

The foundation of Christianity rests on faith. From the call of Abra-ham, who *believed what he heard*, to Mary, the mother of Jesus, who *believed what she heard,* God calls us to believe in something greater than ourselves. If our faith goes no further than our efforts, the fruit we produce will have a short shelf life.

Yes, miracles happen. They're not due to some formula we work out or because we deserve to have God answer our prayers. We find mira-cles occurring when we see people *believing what they heard.* Has God told you to have faith for the salvation of an unbelieving family mem-ber? Don't stop *believing what you heard.* Has he told you to pursue your dreams? Don't stop *believing what you heard*. Has he spoken to you about a specific situation? Don't stop *believing what you heard.*

Faith comes by hearing the Word of God (Romans 10:17). If we want to have earth-shattering, mind-blowing, miracle-working faith, then resist becoming like those foolish Galatians. Believe and keep believing what you have heard.

Withered Fig Trees

As they passed by in the morning, they saw the fig tree withered away to its roots. And Peter remembered and said to him, "Rabbi, look! The fig tree that you cursed has withered." —Mark 11:20–21

My first response after reading the eleventh chapter of Mark was *Lord, don't let us become withered fig trees!*

Jesus and his disciples were on their way to the temple when he spotted a fig tree in leaf. Even though it wasn't the season for figs, its leaves indicated the presence of fruit. But when Jesus approached the tree, he discovered none of the tasty figs, only leaves giving the false impression of fruitfulness. He cursed the tree, but not because he was *hangry*. He used the tree to illustrate something far more important than satisfying his hunger.

When he arrived at the temple courts, he saw a whole orchard of human fig trees. The Pharisees and teachers of the Law waved their leaves as if they bore the fruit of God. But they were as barren as the tree Jesus cursed. They *should* have been bearing life-giving fruit to seekers of God, but their spiritual lives had long ago dried up.

What caused these human fig trees to wither?

They lacked faith. No one can walk in God without faith, let alone have food to feed the spiritually hungry. The Pharisees refused to believe in Jesus, and so cut themselves off from the source of hope and power.

I find it necessary to do a *Pharisee-check* in my life from time to time. Are there factors cutting into my faith? Am I doing more judging than loving? Does my diet consist of an ample supply of old manna but runs short on new wine? Have I begun limiting God's power to the confines of my understanding? Is my desire for comfort trumping sacrifice?

Let's not let the fruit God wants us to produce dry up by allowing the harshness of the world to steal our faith. Let's keep believing in the God of miracles. And do whatever he tells us to do.

One summer some dear friends brought us a basket of figs from their trees. I still remember how delicious that fruit tasted. As believers, we have some pretty soul-satisfying fruit to offer the world. But only if we don't become withered fig trees.

Even Now

Martha said to Jesus, "LORD, if you had been here, my brother would not have died. But even now I know that whatever you ask from God, God will give you." —John 11:21–22

"Yet Lord, I know even now you can deliver her." I was surprised to find myself writing those words while praying for someone who was doing irreparable harm to her body. I'd prayed for her before. If anything, her situation had become worse. Deception was running rampant in her thoughts, lassoing every last trace of truth. But as I presented her before the Lord, something felt different. Although I had little to base my hope on, the words—*even now*—ignited a spark of faith that went beyond wishful thinking.

Even now. Where had I heard that before?

John, chapter 11, recounts the story of Lazarus' death. When he fell ill, his sisters, Martha and Mary, sent for Jesus to come and heal him. But by the time Jesus arrived at their home, Lazarus was not only dead, but lay three days in the tomb. If ever a situation appeared irreversible, this qualified. Yet Martha, who apparently didn't recognize the power of her words says, "But even now I know that whatever you ask from God, God will give you."

Martha may not have had the faith at that moment to believe what she said, but Jesus did. He asked God for the impossible, and God delivered the impossible (vv. 41–44). Lazarus rose from death.

As believers in Christ we ought never limit God's workings to our natural thinking. We have precedent in Scripture to trust him to come through in situations that seem hopeless. And even if what we pray for turns out differently than we expect, *even then* we can continue to put our hope in a God of limitless power, love, and grace. Nothing exists in his universe that he will not turn into good for those who love him.

Today, are you struggling over some "irreversible" situations? Are you carrying burdens for people that require from you a lot more than wishful thinking? God remains in the miracle-working business. He hears you. He desires for you to have faith in him . . . *even now*, my friend, *even now*.

A Legacy of Courage

"We can't attack those people; they are stronger than we are." And they spread among the Israelites a bad report about the land they had explored. —Numbers 13:31–32 (NIV)

Do you recognize these names: Shammua, Shaphat, Igal, Palti, Gaddiel, Gaddi, Ammiel, Sethur, Nahbi, and Geuel? Probably not. These are the ten out of twelve men Moses sent to spy out the land God promised to give Israel after their exodus from Egypt. Although the spies acknowledged Canaan "flowed with milk and honey," they filled the people with fear when they described the giants who lived there. No way could Israel's ragtag army take the land from them!

But it was never about *them* taking the land. It was about God taking the land *through* them. A fact not lost on the other two spies, Joshua and Caleb—names I'm sure you're familiar with. These two men had the faith to believe God would help them. Their faith infused them with courage not only to take on Canaan's giants, but to stand up to their faithless brothers. They weren't afraid to be mocked and ridiculed. To speak the truth when about a million people stood against them. We know today which ones landed on the right side of history.

The ten had experienced God's miracles when leaving Egypt. They walked under the protection and guidance of the cloud by day and the fire by night. Excuseless, they knew what God had done for them, but they refused to believe he would help them overcome the obstacles they now faced. They became spineless cowards.

Joshua and Caleb stand in stark contrast. They believed God would give them the land, and their unshakeable faith resulted in a legacy of courage. The kind we still name our kids after. I've known a number of Joshuas and Calebs over my life, but I've never met one Shammua or Igal.

Who wouldn't want to leave a legacy of courage?

It begins with believing God. Then standing strong against all the arguments that deny his power. No small task in today's culture of doubt, fear, and skepticism. But God encourages us to stand like those two faithful spies. Let's not let our legacy die in the desert for lack of faith.

Let's keep believing. Let's leave a legacy of courage.

Who Has Believed?

Who has believed our message? —Isaiah 53:1 (NIV)

Are you having trouble believing for things *unbelievable*?

The prophecy describing the coming of the Messiah in Isaiah 53 shocks us to the core. The Creator God of all majesty and power was coming to the earth as a suffering servant. Rather than being hailed as the Mighty King, he would be "despised and rejected." He would be identified as the slaughtered lamb. Not the conquering lion. Deceit would crush the One who knew no deceit. Hatred would inflict incomprehensible anguish on the author of love.

Anyone looking on might conclude God was punishing this suffering servant. The religious leaders of the day certainly did. They accused him of blasphemy as an excuse to cut his life short. They nailed his body to a mocking cross and threw him into a grave marked, *It's over!*

But it wasn't over. Isaiah's message proclaims news even more incredulous. So unthinkable that it stretches our imagination beyond every natural instinct. His suffering atoned for our sin. My sin. Your sin. Every single sin in the whole world. Such intercession on our behalf would give each of us a shot at eternity.

No wonder Isaiah asked, "Who has believed our message?"

Yet this unthinkable message remains as vibrant as when it was first proclaimed. And God, by his grace, has given us many more prophecies to verify his plan. Not one has failed to come to pass. From how and where Jesus would be born to how he would die, every prediction proves true. God gives us such evidence to help us believe this incredible message.

Ronald Reagan's famous line, "Trust but verify," works well when dealing with fallen man. But God is infallible. His words stand true. What he says will happen, will happen, no matter how outlandish or improbable. He has already verified his trustworthiness.

So, about those *unbelievable* things in your life. Believing Isaiah's message lays the foundation for trusting God in things we don't yet see. As long as we live, he will give us opportunities to deepen our faith. Don't be discouraged when faced with challenges that require more faith than you think you have. Let him stretch you. And when he asks, "Who has believed our message?" heartily respond with, "I do!"

Don't Stop Believing

It had been revealed to him by the Holy Spirit that he would not die before he had seen the Lord's Messiah. —Luke 2:26 (NIV)

A few years ago, my husband pruned our holly tree. Boy, did he! I wondered if any of those beautiful red berries would ever appear again. And since that time, I've had to work at getting enough boughs to decorate the house at Christmas. But not this year! I have never seen so many holly berries on any holly tree ever! It's absolutely stunning. Who would have believed it? Certainly not me. After a couple years of not seeing any results, I had given up.

Failing to believe what I can't see rears its head in other areas of my life more consequential than Christmas décor. How often do I prematurely jump to the wrong conclusion when I don't see what I hoped to see? I'm still learning that God's timing doesn't always line up with mine.

You know the story of Simeon. A devout Jew, he had waited his whole life to see the coming of the Messiah. And when Mary and Joseph brought the baby Jesus into the temple, he immediately recognized the Son of God. All those years of waiting honed his spiritual acuity. He never stopped believing.

And neither should we.

Many people linger in the waiting room. Some hopes and dreams have been pruned and the new growth has yet to appear. Maybe you're one of them. It seems like what you expected is on back-order, interrupted by a supply chain fiasco. So, you're still waiting for that check to arrive, for the doctor to pronounce you cancer free, for a son or daughter's return to the faith.

Don't lose heart! Instead of worrying about the future (which changes absolutely nothing), choose to trust God. Nothing in the universe rivals his faithfulness. Let him use the waiting time to trigger new growth. Simeon waited his whole life to receive God's promise. As he, at last, held the very Son of God in his arms, I doubt he regretted the pruning of one moment of unmet expectations.

Friend, I pray no matter what season you're in today, that you trust God. Don't stop believing.

·

So What Are We Gonna Do?

He said this to test him, for he himself knew what he would do. —John 6:6

"So what are we going to do with all these people?" Jesus asked Philip. A crowd of five thousand was flooding the countryside. But the disciples didn't have enough money to buy even a scrap of bread for each one. And if they did, no Paneras graced the landscape. The best they could come up with was a small boy toting five barley loaves and two small fish. *For over five thousand people?*

Scripture says Jesus already knew what he was going to do. He asked Philip to test his faith. Could Philip look beyond the natural and believe Jesus was able to miraculously meet the need? Only as the disciples faced impossible situations would their faith have opportunity to grow.

And so it is for us. I think Jesus still puts his disciples in impossible situations to increase our faith.

I was recently struggling over a situation that seems as formidable as feeding thousands of people in the desert. Interestingly, I was reading the sixth chapter of John at the time, and it seemed like the Lord was saying, "What are we gonna do about it? Will you recognize the five loaves and two fish I'm providing? Will you believe I can work a miracle from that small amount?"

Our faith grows when we choose to believe in Jesus, even when we don't understand how he will come through. We realize he already has the answer, and we trust him, even if the only answer we see comes in the form of a mustard seed (or five loaves and two fish).

The Bible uses the word *believe* (or its derivative) 257 times. So, believing in Christ, no matter at what level, can hardly be over emphasized. In fact, John says the whole Bible was written that we would believe Jesus is the Son of God, and by believing have life in his name (John 20:31).

So, the next time you're facing a way-over-your-head problem, consider the Lord has put you in that situation to test your faith. Not to see you fail, but to empower you to pass with flying colors.

Lord, we believe!

Friend of God

And the scripture was fulfilled that says, "Abraham believed God, and it was credited to him as righteousness," and he was called God's friend. —James 2:23 (NIV)

Believing God opens the door to many things. But one of the most important—it offers us the opportunity for friendship with him. It's almost too outrageous to believe, but nevertheless, it's true. God wants us to be called his friend.

I hadn't really considered friendship with God as a specific life goal. I think of aspirations more in terms of letting my light shine and of doing my best to walk in truth, integrity, faith, and love. To use my gifts to advance his kingdom and one day hear him say, "Well done." Yet deeper reflection on being God's friend opens up a whole new universe of how to do life.

God offers those who seek him the intimacy of friendship. It's a friendship strong enough to rescue us from the horrors of hell, yet tender enough to comfort us when our circumstances don't work out like we hoped. It's a friendship that inspires us to be our best but remains faithful when we're at our worst. It meets us in our lonely hours and surrounds us with sweet companionship. How profound, how incredible, how amazing to be called God's friend!

Far from lessening our worship of God, our friendship with him deepens it. He remains our Lord and Savior even as he broadens the relationship. Like many relationships in life, they can be multifaceted. My mom became my friend at some point, yet she remained my mom to the end. We ought not think it sacrilegious to consider God in terms of friendship.

Scripture tells us Abraham was God's friend. He believed God and obeyed what he told him to do, even packing up all his belongings and heading toward an unknown destination. Such trust endeared him to God, resulting in a bond you and I are given the opportunity to emulate.

It makes me wonder about my life's aspiration. I don't think, in the end, my accomplishments in life (or lack thereof) will matter a whit. I think the greatest epitaph I could hope for might be: *She was God's friend.*

How about you? Does this realization pull at your heart? Do you *know* at this very moment, you may become the friend of God? I pray you have faith to believe it.

Don't Act Like a CHINO

If you are not firm in faith, you will not be firm at all. —Isaiah 7:9

I imagine you're familiar with the acronym, RINO—*Republicans In Name Only.* It's used as a derisive term to describe people affiliated with the Republican Party who are perceived not to adhere to conservative principles. The Democratic Party has their DINOs as well—*Democrats In Name Only*—those who fail to pass muster with the liberal wing of their party. I don't consider myself a RINO or a DINO, but more important than either, I don't ever want to be a CHINO—*Christian In Name Only.*

CHINOs profess faith in Jesus, but you would never know it by the way they act in time of crisis. Or how they regularly rely on themselves rather than God. They may use all the right words, but somehow those words don't connect with their hearts.

When Ahaz was king of Judah, Syria and Ephraim joined together to conquer his country. Overwhelmed at the thought of such a powerful alliance, Ahaz shook like trees in the wind (Isaiah 7:2). But the Lord sent Isaiah to encourage him not to be afraid. He told him the rulers coming against him would not succeed. He was to stand firm in his faith in God. In fact, Isaiah instructed him to ask the Lord for a sign to help him believe! But he didn't.

God wanted Ahaz to believe he was with them. Judah would never be able to stand against the trouble heading their way if they did not stand firm in their faith.

Neither will we.

I don't know what lies ahead for followers of Jesus, but I do know the Lord continually gives us opportunities to strengthen our faith. To get rid of anything that sabotages our reliance on him. Anything that makes us CHINOs.

I act like a CHINO when I forget my faith. When I obsess over difficult situations rather than entrust them to God. Or when I doubt whether God will bring good out of heartbreak and devastation. Whenever I lean on my own understanding rather than believe the God of all power and love will make a way, I'm acting like a Christian in name only.

How about you? Do you ever find yourself sliding into unbelief, letting your circumstances turn you into a CHINO? You don't have to. Heed Isaiah's words and stand firm in your faith, friend. Don't be shaken like a tree in the wind.

Part Four

How Do We Replenish the Oil?

CHAPTER TEN

With Humility in a Culture of Selfie-Sticks

"This way is first humility, second humility, third humility, and however often you should ask me I would say the same."

St. Augustine
—*Letters*

It's hard to imagine a culture more self-absorbed than the one in which we live. A *#mefirst* mindset infiltrates everything from choosing the food we eat to the careers we pursue. Yet the more we seek self-satisfaction, the more discontent we become. Maybe it's because we were never created to view life from the other end of a selfie-stick. God created us to find our life by losing it. He gently brings circumstances our way to shake us out of our self-centered worlds and teach us humility. Well, sometimes, not so gently. But whether in major or minor ways, cultivating humble hearts replenishes the oil needed for us to keep shining toward the higher way.

Position Wanted

For God knows that when you eat from it your eyes will be opened, and you will be like God, knowing good and evil. —Genesis 3:5

It's a position everyone with a beating heart wants, no matter the age, gender, or nationality. People have been applying for it since the Garden of Eden. Satan even tried to get Jesus to apply! This job allows us to be the captain of our own ship, to do things "our way." Its authority ranges from our personal sphere to worldwide dominion. So, what is this most sought-after spot?

Being God.

Anyone around children knows this drive manifests itself in a baby's first cry. Oh, we don't call it that in the beginning. But as those little ones mature in their fallen nature, so does the sophistication of their demands. When I was young   my grandpa spliced together a series of home movie clips and called it *Becky Creech, This Is Your Life.* I thought I was the queen bee. It would take a few years before I learned, as Francis Chan puts it, my life consists of two-fifths-of-a-second-long-scene in a movie that's not even about me. Life is not about being God but serving him.

Although dedicating our lives to serving God might sound like a noble mindset, I think more than noble, it's just plain smart. The God we're trying to be is the God who knows us better than we know ourselves. He created us with a plan and purpose before the foundation of the world. We'd be far better off relying on his assessment of what we're to do than on our limited perspective.

Satan played on Eve's desire to be like God. He tricked her into thinking her Creator was a celestial killjoy who didn't have her best interests at heart. It's a tactic he continues to use against Eve's offspring. Let's not fall for his schemes against us, no matter what temptation we face. Let's quiet our rebellious hearts against God's plan and spit out the forbidden fruit.

I can't help but think we could eliminate much of the pain and suffering in the world if folks would just acknowledge all we need to know about the position of being God.

It's already been filled.

I Pledge Allegiance to Myself

Never let loyalty and kindness leave you! Tie them around your neck as a reminder. Write them deep within your heart. —Proverbs 3:3–4 (NLT)

"Loyal, loyal to our West High; raise those banners high; we will fight for you forever; fight, fight, fight's our cry." You know you're getting old when you can't remember the rest of the words to your high school fight song. And I was a cheerleader! Fortunately, one inquiring post on social media and the missing lines were supplied.

But it got me thinking about loyalty. I haven't lived in my hometown since I left for college, but I guess there's a part of me that will always be a "west sider." Although I still have great affection for my roots, the lofty pledge of fighting for West High forever has been replaced with other bonds. Different seasons call for different allegiances. But the quality of loyalty ought never be discarded.

Scripture tells us to never let go of loyalty and kindness. It pleases God (as well as people) when our lives display loyalty. Devotion to something outside of ourselves helps us move away from the predominant *it's all about me* mentality. Loyalty pushes us beyond our momentary expectations. We love our team, even when they lose. We stay committed to our spouses even when they disappoint us. We don't abandon our country even when we disagree with policy. We remain devoted to God even when we don't understand what he's doing.

It seems like the biggest threat to loyalty lies disguised in self-worship. We remain loyal only if it benefits *me*. This, of course, isn't a bad thing when it comes to consumable items. But brand loyalty doesn't fit in how we see people. Or God. Especially God.

No one displays more loyalty to you and to me than God. He has given *everything* in order to set us free from sin and condemnation. He promises not to let anything separate us from his love—ever. He will always fight for us and with us so we can walk in victory (Romans 8:31–39). Given his unmatched faithfulness, isn't he worthy of receiving our utmost loyalty in return?

Friend, don't be deceived in pledging allegiance to yourself. Humble yourself and pledge devotion to the One who deserves it.

It Is Not About You

I have been crucified with Christ. It is no longer I who live, but Christ who lives in me. And the life I now live in the flesh, I live by faith in the Son of God, who loved me and gave himself for me. —Galatians 2:20

I had been invited to do a TV interview about my book, *Between the Lamp Posts.* Full of excitement for the opportunity, I arrived at the station bright and early. After a brief tour of the studio, we settled in the green room until it was time for my makeup. Up until now, things had gone pretty smoothly. But as soon as the makeup artist started applying my makeup, my comfort zone evaporated. I don't wear much makeup anyway, and to have a total stranger literally inches from my face, trying to cover up every single facial flaw proved to be a bit unnerving.

So, when she asked why I wrote my book, all coherent thinking escaped my mind. I tried to answer, but as I talked, all I could think about was mascara and lip gloss. *I'm going to be on TV in a few minutes, and I can't even remember what prompted me to write the book!* When she finished, I asked the producer if he had a copy of my book laying around. I wanted to reread the introduction to jog my memory!

My anxiety now on high alert, my husband reminded me of what I always say to my Public Speaking students before they give a speech: "It's not about you. It's about your audience." So, I took my own advice, and by the time the interviewers asked me the first question, I wasn't thinking about myself anymore. My desire to communicate with them about the book superseded my self-consciousness.

Paul said the life he lived was no longer about himself; it was about the One who lived within him. He must have encountered many circumstances that pushed him out of his comfort zone, but I doubt he ever defaulted on his set focus. It's only when we make life about ourselves that self-consciousness has the opportunity to derail us.

God has a purpose for you and for me much greater than a TV interview. But it will only come about if we remember this: Life is not about you. It's not about me. It's about Jesus.

I AM or I am?

God said to Moses, "I AM who I am." And he said, "Say this to the people of Israel, 'I AM has sent me to you.'" —Exodus 3:14

Who's in charge of your life? "I AM" or "I am"? The contrast between following God's agenda or our own could not be more drastic.

When God gave Moses the unenviable task of leading his one million people out of Egyptian slavery, Moses reacted with an "I am" mindset. "Who am I that I should go to Pharaoh and bring the Israelites out of Egypt?" (Exodus 3:11). He had tried forty years earlier to help his Hebrew brothers and failed miserably. What made this time any different?

This time I AM was sending him. God knew Moses was now ready to make the shift from self-dependency to God-dependency. God assured Moses the call was not about him or his capabilities. It was about God working through him. He would be able to accomplish the task because I AM would be with him.

This human fallen tendency to be our own god (I am) is what Oswald Chambers calls the "disposition of sin." It's clinging to our right to be in charge.

Every decision we make stems from a mindset of either "I AM" or "I am." When we say, *"I am* too afraid to use my gifts," or *"I am* more comfortable when *I am* in control," or "*I am* unwilling to change," we actually block God's power. But when we embrace I AM, we let him take the reins of our lives. We surrender our so-called rights to him.

I can pinpoint the time when I made the shift from "I am" to "I AM." Everything turned upside down. Oh, I had believed in Jesus, but somehow my plans always seemed to slip in ahead of his. It's only when I truly wanted God's will more than my own, that I discovered the powerful intersection of the two. But I had to first let go of my "I am." I had to first seek his kingdom. When I did, he gave me more than I could have ever imagined.

Friend, don't base your life on the limitations of "I am." Bow before your King and go for abundance. Go for freedom. Go for the great I AM.

The Ring Story

Do nothing from selfish ambition or conceit, but in humility count others more significant than yourselves. Let each of you look not only to his own interests, but also to the interests of others. —Philippians 2:3–4

I call this The Ring Story.

Some years ago, a dear friend asked me to be the maid of honor in her wedding. The ceremony took place in the downstairs of an old rustic inn. The upstairs held quaint little rooms where we dressed and prepared. The bride had just helped me get my dress on when disaster struck. As her only attendant, it was my responsibility to take care of the groom's ring. As she started to give me the band, it slipped from her hand. Noting all the cracks and crevices in the floorboard, I panicked. I felt like Gollum as he watched the *ring of power* descend into the fire on Mount Doom!

In a desperate attempt to grab the ring before it landed, I dove to the floor. Unfortunately, the dress didn't follow my lead. As I reached for the ring, my zipper tore, leaving my back gloriously exposed.

Thankfully, we managed to find a needle and thread and do a makeshift sew job. It at least lasted through the receiving line, that is, until I extended myself to hug one too many people. I ended up wearing a sweater the rest of the evening to cover the gap!

I'm so glad God designed us with a sense of humor. The ring story still makes me chuckle. My ripped zipper didn't ruin the wedding, and at least my friend realized how seriously I took my duty! But I admit, it was humbling.

Humility makes it possible to laugh and not take ourselves too seriously. To realize we don't have to be the "most-together" person in the room. We don't have to dissect our social *faux pas* and obsess over what others think of us. Paul describes humility as valuing others above ourselves. It runs counter to our natural inclination toward selfishness and conceit. So it's hard, but not unattainable, or Scripture wouldn't urge us to have the same humble mindset as Christ (Philippians 2:5).

It costs something to put others above ourselves. Time, energy, maybe even a torn dress. For Jesus, it cost the splendor of heaven. Now that's a story!

Whatever Happened to R-E-S-P-E-C-T?

Show proper respect to everyone, love the family of believers, fear God, honor the emperor. —1 Peter 2:17 (NIV)

One of the ominous shadows hanging over our culture lies in a growing lack of respect for our fellow humans.

Everyone longs to be respected, no matter who they are. Aretha Franklin spelled it out in her iconic song, *"R-E-S-P-E-C-T."* Although we live in a world of voices demanding respect, it seems fewer and fewer are trying to find out *what it means* to the person in front of them.

Whatever happened to respect?

The apostle Peter tells us to respect everyone who shares the unique commonality of being human. But in today's market, showing respect to people who differ from us has become a liability. Even in the church. And honoring authority? Forget it.

When people stop having a holy fear of God, they dismiss both his authority and standards. They no longer look on his creation as something to cherish. The deluge of crudity, vulgarity, and irreverence we're now experiencing in our culture desensitizes us to what is real and true and beautiful. When skepticism replaces respect as the *modus operandi*, the world becomes very ugly very fast.

If we hope to reclaim R-E-S-P-E-C-T, we have to begin with another word: H-U-M-I-L-I-T-Y. Humility teaches us how to view life. But humility isn't about focusing on how small we are; it's about realizing how great God is. Groveling over our sin doesn't humble us. Basking in the light of undeserved grace does.

Jesus Christ's domain extends over all existence. Incredibly, he calls us to steward that domain. To do it well means we show respect for all who bear his image. People just like us, who make poor choices, who resist his love, maybe even spit in his face. But people he died for. We may not like what some do. In fact, we may fervently disagree with them. But we are fellow guests in the same house. We don't make the rules. The owner of the house does. So, we obey.

I doubt a song titled "H-U-M-I-L-I-T-Y" will ever make it to the Billboard charts. But if we're not humming its tune, we can sing "R-E-S-P-E-C-T" all day long and never find out what it means.

Don't Bet On It

For by the grace given to me I say to everyone among you not to think of himself more highly than he ought to think, but to think with sober judgment, each according to the measure of faith that God has assigned. —Romans 12:3

My senior year of college some of my girlfriends and I thought it would be a great idea to take a road trip from Delaware, Ohio, to the Kentucky Derby. None of us had been there before, but it seemed like a *cool* item to add to our résumé of adventures, and in those days, nothing sounded more appealing than being thought of as *cool*.

The first thing I noticed when we arrived was the long, long lines. I had never seen bathroom lines that extensive! I began to panic, thinking of what a predicament I would be in if I had to go.

As you may have figured out, those long lines were not people waiting to go to the bathroom. They consisted of people waiting to bet. On horses. Who knew? Obviously, we thought we knew what we were getting ourselves into, but we didn't have a clue. We assumed people went to *watch* the horses race, not *bet* on which one would win! Our coolness factor took a pretty big hit that day. Naivety and coolness just don't go together.

I guess we all experience those times when our estimation of ourselves exceeds our knowledge and capabilities. Scripture warns us not to think more highly of ourselves than we should.

I recently heard a sermon on the importance of having a teachable spirit. It requires cultivating a humble heart, one not threatened by correction or guidance. Ecclesiastes 4:13 says, "Better was a poor and wise youth than an old and foolish king who no longer knew how to take advice." I don't ever want to get to the place where I think I know it all. Where I replace sober judgment and honest self-assessment with pride. You probably don't either.

Well, I'm not as naïve as I was in college, and I'm still not very cool. But that's okay. I've found something better to pursue. I'm going after a humble heart, one filled with grace. Will I ever let conceit and vanity get in the way? Perhaps, but as long as the Holy Spirit helps me, I wouldn't bet on it!

The Danger of Doubling Down

Before destruction a man's heart is haughty, but humility comes before honor. —Proverbs 18:12

It's one of the hardest things we humans have to do. Our words get stuck trying to express it. We're afraid our reputation will experience too big a hit if we yield to it. And most politicians run from it like the plague. But so do wives and husbands, employees and employers, and children who want to avoid unfavorable consequences. Yet we find freedom and relief every time we experience it.

I guess most of us have trouble admitting we were wrong. Instead, we double down.

Doubling down occurs when, rather than acknowledging our mistakes, we wax stronger in our defense. Even when we realize we're incorrect, we intensify our efforts to save face by grabbing justification for our actions wherever we can find it.

Scripture clearly teaches us about the consequences of doubling down in pride. David doubled down in unlawfully taking a census of Israel, and 70,000 people died (1 Chronicles 21:14). Herod doubled down in receiving praise to himself as God. He was eaten by worms (Acts 12:23). The Pharisees doubled down in their opposition to Jesus, and the whole world went after him (John 12:19). Refusing to admit we are wrong leads to the very opposite of what we sought.

Isn't it refreshing to hear someone in a prominent position admit he or she made a mistake? Oh, wait. Have you *ever* heard a person in a prominent position confess a failure? How about a politician? A celebrity?

Turning from mistakes requires humility.

Humility acknowledges we don't know everything but emanates a quiet power. Humility makes us look like Jesus (Philippians 2:3–8). It can heal a nation (2 Chronicles 7:14). It protects us from humiliation (Luke 14:11). And it opens the door to grace, wisdom, and honor (James 4:6). So, if you double down on anything, double down on having a humble heart, one fixed on truth, love, and righteousness.

Whether you are dealing with big issues or small, refuse to let pride push you into doubling down in the wrong direction. Turn around and admit when you're wrong. Better to have a little egg on your face than put yourself and even others in danger.

Don't Eat the Cheerios!

But he said to me, "My grace is sufficient for you, for my power is made perfect in weakness." Therefore, I will boast all the more gladly of my weaknesses, so that the power of Christ may rest upon me. —2 Corinthians 12:9

The day finally came. Six weeks earlier my husband had been scheduled to be operated on for a shoulder replacement. But the day before the surgery we got a call saying the insurance company would not pay for the operation until Chip underwent six weeks of physical therapy. A month and a half later, his MRI revealed he still needed the surgery. He was more than ready . . . or so he thought.

We arrived early at the hospital. They sent us to the pre-op room where he discarded his clothes and donned the lovely blue gown. One of the nurses proceeded to take his vitals while another asked him a series of questions, like "When was your last meal?"

"Dinner last night," he responded.

"No, remember, you ate breakfast this morning," I inserted.

"Oh, yeah, I forgot I had a bowl of Cheerios."

The nurse's face fell flat. "You have to wait eight hours before you can undergo anesthesia. I better get the surgeon." The surgeon entered the room and affirmed the nurse's assessment. Surgery would have to be rescheduled. Again.

My husband was mortified. He had forgotten that bit of information from the prior instructions. He apologized profusely to the surgeon, the nurse, the staff, to me. Hating the inconvenience he'd caused everyone, he knew he had only himself to blame.

I felt bad for him, but as we drove back home, the irony struck my funny bone. Chip definitely does not fall into the foodie camp. Some days he doesn't even remember to eat breakfast. He's the last person I would expect to miss surgery because of food. I couldn't stop laughing, and eventually he, too, found the humor in it.

As long as we exist in this human frame, we're going to run smack dab into the middle of our human weaknesses. Paul said his "thorn in the flesh" kept him humble. It reminded him of his ongoing need for Christ. He realized he would never reach a point where he didn't need God's grace. Neither will we.

So, the next time your circumstances humble you, embrace God's grace. And if you're my husband, "Don't eat the Cheerios."

Because of Someone Else

And when the LORD your God brings you into the land . . . and houses full of all good things that you did not fill, and cisterns that you did not dig, and vineyards and olive trees that you did not plant—and when you eat and are full, then take care lest you forget the LORD. —Deuteronomy 6:10–12

His words humbled me.

I found my eyes getting misty as I listened to the former Lancaster Bible College president. Dr. Teague's prayer prompted the college faculty and staff to remember we were there that day because of others who came before us. We shared in the privilege of working at a place where someone had previously dug wells and filled the house with good things. His words reminded me I was part of something far greater than the present moment. I'm a piece of the ongoing legacy of the school. I would not be teaching there had it not been for the "wells" others dug. But more than that.

I live in a beautiful farmhouse because of the seeds planted by someone else. Within its walls we raised a family, discipled fellow Christ-seekers, and entertained angels. Celebrations from marriages to birthday parties as well as passages from life to death have echoed in this place I call home. But none of it would have happened had my husband's parents not previously planted "vineyards and olive trees" on these grounds.

And what about our country? It's often noted we experience the kind of freedom we do in the United States because of the sacrifices others have made. We hear phrases like "We will never forget," but I'm afraid we too often do forget. And we fail to appreciate the long line of fellow countrymen and women who gave themselves to secure the liberty we've come to expect.

Before Israel entered the promised land, Moses cautioned the people to remember the source of their abundance. God was giving them land, a beautiful land filled with good things. They had done nothing to earn any of it. Someone else had done the work, and the Lord was allowing them to benefit from it. That awareness should have protected them from pride.

It's humbling to realize we're a part of the enduring saga of humanity on the earth. Every day affords us the opportunity to remember we belong to this great story because of Someone Else. May it cause us, always, to fall on our knees in humble gratitude.

CHAPTER ELEVEN

With Dependence on God's Strength in Our Needs

"God doesn't expect us to *handle* this. He wants us to *hand* this over to Him." [emphasis mine]

Lysa Terkeurst
—It's Not Supposed to Be This Way

We will never outgrow our need for God. Sometimes we think we've been around the block a few times and can take it from here. When this happens, we start to experience what I call "independence creep." Our old nature of relying on anything but God starts to creep back in. We rely instead on our wisdom, our strength, or our wealth. We carve them out of our experiences. Then we overlay them with a heavy coat of deception and mistakenly think these gods of self-reliance will protect us from uncertainty. They will somehow provide the security we long for. And it may work for a while. But Jeremiah cautions us about the danger of boasting in any other thing than knowing God (Jeremiah 9:23–24). Nothing has the power to lead us successfully through life more than depending upon the God we have learned to know, love, and worship. And nothing will make our light shine brighter.

I Have Nothing

Blessed are the poor in spirit, for theirs is the kingdom of heaven. —
Matthew 5:3

I need God. And the more I sense my spiritual poverty, the richer I become.

I teach Public Speaking at a local college, and one semester I experienced a first. One of my students had an epileptic seizure in the middle of class. Although I realized what was happening, I had no idea what to do. With the help of some of the other students, we were able to lay her on the floor. Someone said, "Roll her on her side." Another student called 911, and another gently put his jacket under her head. We felt helpless as we watched her limbs stiffen and her eyes glaze with fear.

Lord, how can I help her? I have nothing.

I knelt beside her and did the only thing I knew to do. I prayed for the Lord to touch her, to calm her twisting body, and to quiet her spirit. The seizure lasted about ten minutes, but it seemed more like thirty before she "came to." The medics arrived, checked out her vitals, and gave her the okay to go back to her dorm, accompanied by her Resident Director.

The next day I spotted her on campus. She came running up to me. "Can I give you a hug? Thank you so much for staying with me the whole time." She told me she had never felt so much peace during a seizure. For in the midst of the epileptic fog, she kept hearing someone say, "Jesus."

Here's where my spiritual poverty comes in. I had nothing to offer my student. But when I cried out to the Lord, he filled me with compassion and calmness. He showed me how to intercede, and *he* provided exactly what she needed.

Jesus told his disciples the kingdom belongs to the poor in spirit. I experienced it that evening. I do every time I lay down my paltry provision and cry out for him. I have nothing, but I'm connected to the One who has everything.

So, friend, if you've been feeling poor in spirit these days, don't fret about it. Jesus says if you know your spiritual poverty, you are blessed.

The Right Man on our Side

If it had not been the Lord who was on our side when people rose up against us, then they would have swallowed us up alive —Psalm 124:2–3

Do you know the right man is on your side? Sometimes I think all of life is purposed to teach us that one unassailable truth.

Maybe you're encountering new territory. Until now, you've gotten away with relying on yourself. But something is forcing you out of your comfort zone. What succeeded before no longer works. The devil's chomping at your heels and seems about to overpower you. You see no alternative but defeat. You would be a goner were it not for this:

The right man is on your side.

Or maybe your heart is aching for a loved one who is making all the wrong decisions. You've tried talking. Warning. Threatening. Even begging. But your attempts to shed light prove as effective as convincing a four-year-old who hates vegetables to eat his broccoli. Your predicament would be utterly hopeless if not for this:

The right man is on your side.

Take it from someone who knew. David was no stranger to danger and despair. Time and time again, the leader of Israel's army found himself outnumbered and out equipped. He cried to God on every occasion, and God never failed to deliver. Not. One. Time. In Psalm 124 David recounts those victories and gives praise to the Maker of heaven and earth who created a way of escape when escape looked impossible. To the One who provided safe haven when treacherous floods threatened to sweep Israel away. He acknowledged deliverance occurred because of this:

The right man was on their side.

Martin Luther wanted believers to know we never have to face life's battles alone. We have a mighty fortress, a never-failing defense, a helper who causes the Prince of Darkness to shrink in fear. Words some of us may need to hear today.

Did we in our own strength confide,
Our striving would be losing;
Were not the right Man on our side,
The Man of God's own choosing:
Dost ask who that may be?
Christ Jesus, it is He;
Lord Sabaoth His name,
From age to age the same,
And He must win the battle[20]

So friend, no matter what you may be facing, never forget this powerful truth . . . The right man is on your side.

Why Rely?

Indeed, we felt that we had received the sentence of death. But that was to make us rely not on ourselves but on God who raises the dead. —2 Corinthians 1:9

After what seemed like a marathon of work—writing, editing, rewriting, re-editing—the manuscript for my 365-day devotional book was finally ready for the printer. I was going through one last look (for the umpteenth time) when panic struck. The entry for September 4th was nowhere to be found! I could hardly believe my eyes, but the gap between September 3rd and September 5th glared at me with astonishing certainty. Changing the subtitle to *364 Devotions for God-Seekers* did not seem like a good option.

Right then, my publisher called with what she referred to as "good news" and "bad news." The good news: the printer had given the go-ahead to print. The bad news: my credit card had a glitch that needed to be fixed before beginning the process. After relaying to her my "very bad news," she also panicked. She searched for the missing September 4th in her files, but to no avail. However, she said because of the delay caused by the credit card problem, if I sent her the original entry, she would have time to correct the mistake and still make our deadline.

Not only did we corral the runaway September 4th, I believe it happened for a reason. The Lord was sending me a gentle reminder that no matter how hard I try to cross every *"t"* and dot every *"i"* reliance on my own efforts is never enough. The God who let me discover the mistake and who kept the credit card from processing—he's the one I need to rely on.

Paul knew all the circumstances he faced, even death, happened to remind him that the God he served was far more sufficient than he was. Relying on God had become his *modus operandi.*

So what about you . . . when you experience a difficult breakup? Maybe this happened so you might rely on God. When your car runs out of gas? Maybe this happened so you might rely on God. When your "thorn in the flesh" refuses to go away? Maybe this happened so you might rely on God.

Why rely? The real question is why not.

Okay Google

That they should seek God, and perhaps feel their way toward him and find him. Yet he is actually not far from each one of us. —Acts 17:27

I love the voice activation on my phone. All I have to do is say, *Okay Google,* and access to whatever information I'm looking for opens up. The other day Chip and I were traveling in the car, and he happened to say the two magic words in conversation. Suddenly, we heard a little voice from my purse asking how to assist! Kinda' creepy. But that's our world today.

I wish our culture relied on the Holy Spirit as much as we rely on Google to give us direction. But looking to sources other than God has been with us for a very long time.

Take first century Athens.

The people living there depended on gods—and lots of them—for guidance. When Paul arrived and saw all their idols, he explained how they could discover the one true God. The God over all other "gods" was in fact reachable! If they turned from their idols and sought him, they would find him. They didn't have to be seeped in human knowledge or perform great exploits. The source of truth was closer than they could imagine.

I think we're not all that different from the Athenians. Oh, we don't worship idols of stone, but it seems we're apt to rely on anything other than a God who holds us accountable for our actions. We can control our self-constructed substitutes for God. They're safe and comfortable, not too demanding. But they're also false.

The true God "is not far from each one of us." He's even more accessible than our phones and smart speakers. And he wants us to seek him. He desires for us to rely on his wisdom rather than man's. To come to him in our decision-making. To rely on his supernatural power and love. And to help other people reach out to this reachable God.

So I'm taking a tip from my phone activation app. I'm going to be more intentional in seeking God in all I do, whether it's teaching a class or taking my neighbor an apple pie. I want to follow his leading. Ready?

Okay, Holy Spirit!

I Just Need You

Blessed be the Lord,
 who daily bears us up;
God is our salvation. —Psalm 68:19

I pulled into the church parking lot listening to Toby Mac's "I Just Need U" on the radio. I waited until it was over before entering the building. The worship team was practicing for the morning service, singing "I

Need You Now." A different song, but the same message, one which I evidently *needed* to hear.

I probably need God most in those times when I don't realize I need him. Things are moving fairly smoothly. No big crisis at hand. My concerns aren't driving me to my knees. I fall into a "good enough" mentality. But as Oswald Chamber writes, "The greatest enemy of the life of faith in God is not sin, but good choices which are not quite good enough. The good is always the enemy of the best."[21]

The good can blind us from our need. It can keep us satisfied with praying nominal prayers and expecting nominal results. It can short-change us from experiencing the fullness of life God intends. But more importantly, it can keep us from a deeper intimacy with the Lord. When we're aware we need him to infuse everything we do, our love for him grows exponentially.

David declares in Psalm 68, "Blessed be the Lord, who daily bears us up." *Daily.* God wants us to know he is our *daily burden-bearer.* His plan for us doesn't include spinning our wheels in the stagnancy of "good enough." David learned to depend upon God in everything from caring for his sheep, to facing down Goliath, to leading Israel into battle.

Sometimes David's needs were obvious. Sometimes they were not. When they were not, he let his guard down and made one of the worst mistakes of his life. He needed God to deliver him from his lustful desire for Bathsheba. If he would have asked God, God would have answered. But he didn't ask. He let his wants overshadow his need.

How about you? Do you sometimes forget how much you need God? Ah, friend, don't let that happen. Every time you acknowledge your need for him, the door to spiritual growth opens. And if Toby Mac can acknowledge his need, I guess we can too.

I Like to Walk, Just Not Uphill

Listen to me...who have been borne by me from before your birth, car-
ried from the womb even to your old age I am he, and to gray hairs I
will carry you. I have made, and I will bear; I will carry and will save.
—Isaiah 46:3–4

I was talking with my friend the other day. She said, "I like to walk, just not uphill." How I resonated with that! My guess—many of us prefer walking on level ground.

But I know a lot of people these days whose situations are forcing them to walk uphill. Circumstances they didn't expect threaten to shove them right off the path. Health related issues, false accusations, divorce papers, betrayal, and oppression burden them to exhaustion. They are weary as they search for that elusive plateau.

Christian author Lysa Terkeurst writes in *It's Not Supposed to Be This Way* how an avalanche of unexpected events flipped her world upside down. Try as she might, she couldn't rally enough strength to cope with her circumstances. She finally realized God wasn't asking her to. He wanted her to come to him with her heavy load and lay it down.[22] When life overwhelms us, God doesn't intend for us to keep walking up that hill on our own. He wants us to lean on him.

Even in our rebellion, God calls us to cry out to him. Israel's years of idolatry threatened to destroy their identity as a nation. They were headed to exile in a foreign land with foreign gods, stripped of everything that distinguished them as God's people. They would be "walking uphill" for seventy years.

Yet into this bleak future, Isaiah assures them of God's promise to sustain them, to carry them as he had since their birth. In spite of their hard hearts, he planned to rescue them. And they would come out of this a stronger, more faithful people. Walking uphill tends to do that.

So how are you doing? Are you relying on God totally? Or do you find yourself striving to climb that hill on your own? Never forget God's mercy. He promises to be your strength. Trust him no matter what the terrain.

Follow the Cloud

And the LORD went before them by day in a pillar of cloud to lead them along the way, and by night in a pillar of fire to give them light, that they might travel by day and by night. —Exodus 13:21

Self-sufficiency and the Christian faith do not run parallel tracks. God created us with needs. We need to be seen, to be touched, to be loved. These needs (and many others) help us depend on him. Without them, we might think of God as irrelevant. We need God. We need each other. Sometimes it takes a crisis—maybe even a pandemic—to reveal how insufficient we really are.

The stay-at-home order during COVID-19 certainly revealed our need in the church. How do we continue to meet the spiritual needs of the people? Do we gather? What precautions should we take? "We do not know what to do, but our eyes are on you" (2 Chronicles 20:12). The structure we typically depended on was no longer an option. Like Israel, we needed to "follow the cloud."

When Israel exited Egypt, they knew the Promised Land was their destination, but they had no idea how to get there. God, however, provided them with their own GPS. During the day, he led them by a pillar of cloud, and by night with a pillar of fire. They needed to know which way to go. But even more, they needed to learn how to depend on God.

In our small part of the body of Christ, we found relying on God for direction through the pandemic to be invigorating. Whether directing us to temporarily hold drive-in services on Sunday mornings or showing us ways to support local businesses, the Lord led us. So much so, that "follow the cloud" has become a common refrain among us.

My husband has all the data from his computer stored in the Internet cloud. He's dependent on accessing that information when he needs it. But pastoring the church during a pandemic taught him, and all of us, there's a far more consequential cloud we need to depend on.

So how are you doing in following the cloud?

Perfect Strength

But David strengthened himself in the LORD his God. —1 Samuel 30:6

Sometimes we forget the road that leads to strength often takes us through the valley of humble dependence.

The other day I was reading a devotional on *"Joy."* To be honest, I wasn't feelin' it. My bucketload of concerns had left me depleted, unable to see the world in anything but gray, ashen hues. My mood positioned me as an open target for Satan's arrows. "You can't win this battle." *Zing!* "You're done." *Zing!* "Admit you're a loser." *Zing!*

I wonder if that's how David felt in the situation described in 1 Samuel 30. He had led his 600 men into battle, only to return home and find their city burned to the ground, their wives and children taken captive by the Amalekites. In the face of such devastation, they "wept until they had no more strength to weep" (v. 4). The bitterness toward David for getting them into the mess ran so strong, the men talked about stoning him. So, what did David do?

He found strength in the Lord. He refused to give up or give in to the circumstances. Instead, he instinctively sought the Lord's guidance. Consequently, he and his men pursued the Amalekites, routed them, and recovered their wives, children, and all the plunder. "Nothing was missing" (v. 19). Quite the turn of events.

Events turned because of where David turned. As overwhelming as the situation was, David didn't linger in its shadow any longer than he did in Goliath's. He humbled himself, never forgetting the source of his strength.

Neither must we.

We're living in enemy-occupied territory. And God has called us here at this place, in this time, to sabotage Satan's plans. A call that I'm sure doesn't include allowing ourselves to be target practice for the devil's lethal lies. His strength may be hideous, treacherous, and overpowering. But it is no match for the strength we find in the Lord.

Don't be deceived, friend. And don't delay. Put up your shield of faith and renew your dependence upon the Holy Spirit to help you deflect all those fiery darts. After all, it's our weaknesses that lead us to strength. His strength. His perfect strength (2 Corinthians 12:9).

Zing! Zing! Zing!

In Good Hands

Now to him who is able to keep you from stumbling and to present you blameless before the presence of his glory with great joy. —Jude 1:24

In my Public Speaking classes I like to show an insurance commercial, *The Recession That Made Us Great*, to demonstrate the power of the pause. The narrator, Dennis Haysbert, voices over pictures showing how the past recession taught us "things are not as important as the future we're building with those we love." Each poignant pause gives the viewer time to reflect on the value of relationships, the importance of "making do" with what we have, and, of course, the trustworthiness of their insurance company to be there, no matter what the crisis. By the time we get to the ending tagline, "You're in good hands," I'm ready to sell the farm and beg an agent to let me sign up!

Do you know as a child of God there is never a moment we are not in good hands? Hands, the Scripture says, that are able to keep us from stumbling, hands that can turn our spiritual recessions into wells of life, hands that lead us on a path of purity and joy. It's knowing we are not only in the hands of a sovereign God, but in the hands of a *good* sovereign God that gives us the confidence we need to move through whatever life hurls our way.

Jude displayed this confidence when he wrote to the early church. He warned them of how there would be people who would ridicule them for their moral stances. They would try to bring division in the body by enticing them to rely more on themselves than the Holy Spirit. Filled with self-interest, greed, and discontentment, they hoped to drag as many people as they could into their wake of rebellion. Sound familiar?

Such people have been around since before Sodom and Gomorrah, and they will continue to exist until the last battle recorded in Revelation 20.

But have no fear. We will not fall into their hands of destruction if we remain firmly fixed in the good hands of "the only God, our Savior" to whom belongs all "glory, majesty, dominion, and authority" (v. 25). After all, He's got the whole world in His hands. That includes you and me, sister; you and me brother.

Yes, we're in good hands.

Soli Deo Gloria

So, whether you eat or drink, or whatever you do, do all for the glory of God. —1 Corinthians 10:31

I had been working most of the day writing a devotional. When it finally came together and I read over it one last time, I instinctively lifted my arm and pointed to heaven. You know, like some athletes do after scoring a touchdown or an actor when he bows at curtain call. I wanted God to know he deserved the glory for what I'd just accomplished. My work could hardly compare with a shout-out to God in front of a massive audience, but the small gesture reinforced a belief I hold dear: I can do nothing without God. And I want to let him know every chance I get.

I've read Johann Sebastian Bach penned the initials *SDG* (standing for *Soli Deo Gloria)* at the bottom of each of his manuscripts to communicate God and God alone should be glorified in his work. Not only was giving glory to God for his immense talent right and good, but it probably protected him from turning his work into an idol.

The problem of idolatry loomed over the early church. Paul warned the Corinthians to flee from it (1 Corinthians 10:14). When a dispute arose as to whether eating food offered to idols would pose a stumbling block for others, Paul insisted the answer could be found in determining whether or not their actions gave glory to God. If they abstained from eating for God's glory, they had nothing to worry about. But no less if they ate for the glory of God. What motivated their behavior? Was it God's glory?

It's a good question to ask of ourselves.

Giving God the glory in all we do protects us from worshiping whatever we create. It rightly acknowledges him to be the source of all that is good, creative, and beautiful in our lives. If I offer meaningful counsel to a friend . . . *Soli Deo Gloria*. If I prepare a creative meal for my family . . . *Soli Deo Gloria*. If I write words that help someone . . . *Soli Deo Gloria*.

All we have comes from God. Every day he gives us the opportunity to do what we do for his glory—whether in small areas or big. May you and I intentionally make the most of each opportunity.

Soli Deo Gloria.

So Much More Than First

But seek first the kingdom of God and his righteousness, and all these things will be added to you. —Matthew 6:33

"Don't view God as your first priority!" What?

The speaker explained that all too often many believers spend devotional time with God in the morning, then proceed to their next priority of the day. God becomes a box we check off, the first assignment to be completed in a day of many. He said rather than seeing God as a priority, look at him as the motor that runs the whole system, the brain that enables all the parts of the computer to work. Instead of leaving him at the table with our empty morning coffee cup, we invite him into every aspect of the day.

I think that's what C. S. Lewis meant when he wrote, "I believe in Christianity as I believe that the sun has risen: not only because I see it, but because by it I see everything else."[23] We view our relationships through the lens of Christ. We view our work through the lens of Christ. Our pleasures, our pain, our interactions—all seen through the lens of Christ. This doesn't mean when I go to a Penn State football game that

I yell John 3:16 while everyone else is screaming "Let's go State!" It means I become God-aware everywhere. Christ *in* me goes *with* me wherever I am. I realize he's right there in the bleachers enjoying my enjoyment.

When my husband and I got married, I inscribed Matthew 6:33 on his wedding ring. Our relationship reflected the first time I had wanted God's will more than my own. Chip was one of those "things" Jesus added to my life when I sought his kingdom first. Through it, the Lord taught me I could trust him to provide for all my needs, from the food I eat to the clothes I wear. To the man I would spend the rest of my life with.

When we see Jesus as the very core of our life, he infuses "all these things" with himself. And I've found there is nothing that makes our light shine brighter. Or more beautifully.

So I agree with the speaker. Let's not relegate God to a priority, even if it's the first one. Let's rely on him in every part of our lives. Let him be so much more than first.

What Kind of "Holic" Are You?

Let me sing for my beloved my love song concerning his vineyard. — Isaiah 5:1

Addictions of all kind flood the world. What started as a simple pleasure or temporary escape has become, for a countless number of people, a prison of insatiable dependence.

It shouldn't surprise us. We humans are designed to live passionate lives. Lives filled with fruitfulness, joy and whole-hearted devotion. The fall of man twisted that plan, redirecting us from finding that fulfillment in our Creator to seeking it in other places.

The house of Israel paints a clear picture of this. Although God had provided everything his "vineyard" needed to thrive, they were producing wild, useless grapes. Isaiah 5 describes the reasons why. They had allowed other passions to take the place of God. Drunk on the love of money and pleasure, lies, pride and injustice, they became greed-ahol-ics, deceit-aholics, conceit-aholics, and cheat-aholics. The song he sang over his vineyard was a sad one.

I want to hear God sing over me a love song of joy. To be part of a vineyard that yields the wine of gladness. You probably do, too. It will no doubt make us God-aholics. We will get addicted to his ways of goodness and mercy. We will become totally dependent on his love to help us forgive. And on his light to show us the truth. He will be the first thing we think of in the morning and the last thought before we drift to sleep.

I like to tell my students to segue their speeches toward the one thing about a particular topic that interests them. Similarly, God-aholics find themselves segueing all their circumstances back to the One who takes center stage in their interests. They are quick to express gratitude to him for every positive, pleasant happening in their lives. And when situations turn south, they *know* God is able to turn even the worst into something good. So they trust him to work his deeper plan, and depend on his "deeper magic."

So what kind of "holic" are you? Do you realize you are created to be a God-aholic? He will never take advantage of your dependence on him. He will use it to help you flourish.

Flourish as part of his beloved vineyard.

CHAPTER TWELVE

With Mercy in a World of Offenses

"When Christ calls a man, he bids him come and die."
Dietrich Bonhoeffer
—The Cost of Discipleship

Perhaps two of the hardest words to say in the English language are "I'm sorry." And sometimes they're the hardest to hear. We too easily forget the mercy we receive is purposed to pass on to those whose sins affect us. The mercy of God calls us to let go of offenses, grudges, and unforgiveness. To do the unexpected and season justice with mercy. It may feel like *Mission Impossible* at times, but as we know, there is nothing God demands that he won't help us accomplish. If we hope to replenish our oil, it won't happen without, as Shakespeare penned, the "twice blessed quality of mercy."

Beware of the "O" Word

A brother offended is more unyielding than a strong city, and quarreling is like the bars of a castle. —Proverbs 18:19

We have become an *offended* people, haven't we? Jesus warned it's impossible to live in a fallen world without encountering offenses. We fail to meet others' expectations; they don't meet ours. We get hurt; we hurt others. It doesn't take much to rouse our suspicions and divisions, especially if past wounds lay dormant.

It's been over fifty years since a friend of mine served in Vietnam. He still occasionally reacts when he unexpectedly comes upon something that looks "unusual" in a field or the woods. His reaction stems from seeing the consequences of hidden land mines taking their toll on unsuspecting soldiers. Our emotional landscape works much the same way. A relationship explodes in front of us, and we find it difficult to trust again. We parse our words and withhold our feelings for fear of stepping on another hidden explosive device, an IED of offense, if you will.

John Bevere, in his bestselling book, *The Bait of Satan,* describes offenses as being a way Satan traps us into becoming unforgiving, grudge-bearing people who show little resemblance to Jesus. He writes throughout the book how those who consume offenses eventually produce the fruit of "anger, jealousy, resentment, strife, bitterness and hatred."[24] Nothing beautiful or valuable results from the enemy's scheme against us.

So how do we deal with the "O" word? How do we protect ourselves from ingesting its deadly venom?

Spit out the bait! Choose not to dwell on the offense, whether that offense is directed toward you or toward someone you love. Lay your hurts and judgments at the feet of Jesus. No greater offense exists than the offense of the cross. Yet Jesus overcame and he promises to help us overcome as well.

Scripture compares an offended brother to an impenetrable city. He stays locked behind his perceptions and refuses any input that differs with his reasons for perpetuating his offended status. Don't be that person. Ask God to help you listen to the other side, even if it seems to bear little resemblance to reality. It takes humility. Vulnerability.

Courage. But the consequences of letting the "O" word destroy us could not be more deadly.

Let's trade the "O" word for the "M" word and show . . . *mercy.*

Forgiveness Completes

I am angry with you and your two friends, because you have not spoken the truth about me, as my servant Job has. So now . . . go to my servant Job and sacrifice a burnt offering for yourselves. My servant Job will pray for you, and I will accept his prayer and not deal with you according to your folly. —Job 42:7–8 (NIV)

Studying the book of Job inspires me to be ready to forgive in all circumstances.

The completion of Job's trial came in a way no one could have imagined. God told him to pray for the people who had falsely accused him. You know, the ones who concluded Job's sufferings were due to his wickedness. The ones who said his "evil was abundant" and there was "no end to his iniquities." The ones who charged him of withholding justice, food, and clothing for the needy, and who accused him of sending away widows and crushing orphans. The ones who said he was getting exactly what he deserved.

In order to pray for his accusers, Job had to first forgive them. It completed him and it will complete us as well.

If I could put it into perspective, it's like someone falsely accusing you of bigotry because you disagree with an immoral behavior. Or someone accusing you of stupidity because truth is more important to you than trends. Or someone you've made a gazillion sacrifices for accusing you of not caring. Who wants to pray for those people?

It sounds a lot like what Jesus told us to do in Matthew 5:44, "Love your enemies and pray for those who persecute you." Job, after receiving his own dose of grace from God, was able to see his accusers in the same light of God's mercy.

I don't know about you, but all the hatred bubbling up in the world today troubles me. I'm especially disturbed when the brunt of blame lands on followers of Jesus who have done nothing wrong. I want to voice my indignation and hurl my own insults at the accusers. But Jesus says there's a better way. A way that breaks our own chains of bitterness and has the power to release others from its grip. It's the way of mercy, the way of love. Love prays, it forgives, it completes.

Let's not miss this important lesson from the book of Job.

He's Got All the Numbers

Indeed, the very hairs of your head are all numbered. Don't be afraid; you are worth more than many sparrows. —Luke 12:7

"People are receiving their third stimulus checks and we haven't even gotten our second one!" We wondered if the check was lost in the mail or stolen. Eventually, my husband contacted the IRS. The massive form we had to fill out proved to be both confusing and unsuitable for our situation. Who knew dealing with the IRS would be complicated?

A few weeks later Chip was collecting the leaves around the pachysandra on our patio. As the leaf blower sucked in the foliage, he noticed some white paper making its way into the shredder. He stopped the machine to investigate. And there, along with fragments of fallen maple leaves, he found the tattered remains of our second stimulus check that I must have dropped when bringing in the mail. Yep, $1,200 lay scattered in the debris.

Like children putting together the pieces of a jigsaw, we scoured our yard looking for every fragment of the check we could find. We managed to reassemble about two thirds of it. But when Chip took the pieces to the bank to see if they would cash it, they said no.

Then a friend told him he could make an e-deposit if he had the router number from the bank issuing the check. Since our friend's stimulus check was sent from the same bank, he supplied us with the numbers. When my husband took the check back to Wells Fargo and supplied the missing information, the teller called out to the manager, "He's got all the numbers." And we received the belated $1,200.

It made me think of a shattered relationship we had recently experienced.

When broken trust litters a once thriving friendship, what remains is as worthless as our torn stimulus check. No matter how hard we try, we can't piece it back together. We need someone with "all the numbers" to accomplish such a task.

Jesus has all the numbers. He knows everything from the number of hairs on our head to the number of times wounds from others cause us to feel worthless. He alone is able to cancel the debts of unforgiveness and fix the brokenness. We have no reason to fear when we lay all the crumpled pieces of offense at his feet.

So, no matter what kind of "shattered check" you might be experiencing, let the One who values you way more than $1,200 bring you restoration.

Divided We Fall

Finally, all of you, be like-minded, be sympathetic, love one another, be compassionate and humble. Do not repay evil with evil or insult with insult. On the contrary, repay evil with blessing, because to this you were called so that you may inherit a blessing. —1 Peter 3:8–9

We haven't seen this amount of divisiveness in our country since the Civil War (or at least the '60s). A hungry media, high on clickbait but low on substance, has stoked our differences. We can no longer just disagree with people who think differently. We have to hate them in order to somehow justify our positions. It's not surprising to see such behavior in the world.

But in the Church?

Scripture doesn't deny differences among believers. In fact, Paul says divisions are necessary in order to discover the truth (1 Corinthians 11:19). But the kind of vitriol fellow believers have been expressing toward one another these days should make us all hang our heads in shame. *You can't be a Christian if you vote for . . .* or *If you support . . . !* Really? How does it bring God glory when we mimic the world's lack of compassion and humility? When we repay insult with insult? When, in our quest to be right, or relevant, or cool, we trample all over someone's dignity?

I'm afraid the divisive spirit in the world has infiltrated the Church. We have to stand against it. And the only way to do that is get back to our first love.

Jesus. Raise Jesus above politics. Jesus above careers. Jesus above family. And Jesus above culture. If we hope to be "like-minded" with other believers, as the Scripture exhorts us to be, we have to remember why we're here. Jesus does not call us to show the world how to do life a little bit better, but how to display a radically different way of doing life altogether. Like how to be merciful toward people who disagree with us.

Sister, brother, let's not miss this opportunity to show the world the true cure for divisiveness. And trust me, it's not going to happen by singing endless renditions of "Kumbaya. "

Grudge-Free Zone

Do not seek revenge or bear a grudge against anyone among your people, but love your neighbor as yourself. I am the LORD. —Leviticus 19:18

We're all familiar with *drug-free zones*—designated areas, usually close to schools, where the distribution or possession of controlled substances warrants a greater fine than in other places. They serve to protect vulnerable children.

I've recently been thinking about another kind of "substance" we need to guard against: grudges. Holding grudges can prove to be as destructive as crack cocaine.

If you are part of the human race, you—or someone you love—has been the brunt of another's insensitivity, irresponsibility, or downright meanness. We can't go through life in a fallen world without our share of bruises, especially in a culture saturated with offenses. We're offended by words people speak; we're offended by symbols people use; we're offended by the past, the present, and the future. We're offended when someone picks on our kids, when someone misinterprets our intentions, when someone opposes our causes. We live in an atmosphere ripe for nurturing grudges.

Don't be deceived into thinking you can follow the Lord with integrity while carrying the insatiable drive for revenge. If you don't deal with the pangs of resentment, those grudges will keep festering until you find yourself locked into a world of isolation.

Jesus shows us a better way.

In calling us to love our enemies, he reinforces the command given in Leviticus. "Do not seek revenge or bear a grudge against anyone among your people but love your neighbor as yourself." Rather than feeding grudges that eventually turn into hate, we're to choose love. Even if we can't see the "justice" in forgiving, we do it because the Lord requires it. That should be enough motivation to help us get over ourselves. But sometimes it isn't.

Because that's what grudges do. They keep us absorbed on ourselves rather than on the God who refuses to hold a grudge toward us. When we focus on the bigger picture of God's love and purpose, his Spirit lifts us out of the sludge of self-importance.

Grudges destroy friendships, families, and churches. Perhaps even nations. Let's choose to let go of offenses and trust God to deal with the injustices we encounter. How about committing to make our hearts *grudge-free zones*?

No Time to Quarrel

And the Lord's servant must not be quarrelsome but must be kind to everyone, able to teach, not resentful. —2 Timothy 2:24 (NIV)

Some of the greatest areas of offense lie in our words. Especially when we fall into quarrels.

It masquerades as communication but leads us to polarization. It elevates our need to convince others above our need for truth. We are warned it ruins all who participate in it. Yet in our culture, especially through social media, it has risen to new heights. Quarrels.

Quarreling differs from discussion. Respectful discussion stems from a desire to discern the truth. Quarrels originate from a desire to get what we want (James 4:1–2). We use words to prove we're right—that we're the smart ones, the ones who should be listened to. Once we start quarreling, our positions harden. We push others into corners while backing into our own. Love and respect disintegrate in the process, whether in our families, in politics, or in the church.

The late Chuck Colson suggested in his book, *My Final Word,* the reason the Church falls into traps of quarreling is because we've adapted a "peacetime mentality."[25] We fail to recognize we are at war. War with Satan and with a world who hates everything we stand for. Our quarrels with one another keep us from fighting against the real enemy of our souls. Colson says if we really understood this, we would be taking bullets for each other, not quibbling over things that in the end don't matter. We simply don't have time to quarrel!

Paul warns us not to quarrel. He says we are to extend kindness and gentleness toward those who disagree with us. He knew "foolish and stupid arguments" that lead to quarreling would never win someone to the cause of Christ. When the world sees Christ-followers fighting each other, we lose the war. How are we reflecting the Lord when our Facebook feeds and Twitter accounts degrade and disrespect those who think differently but who fall within the arc of God's mercy?

The Church may be imperfect, divided, and battered. But the Apostles' Creed declares we believe in the church. Just as we believe in God the Father, Jesus Christ, and the Holy Spirit. Let's not separate ourselves by indulging in senseless quarrels. Instead, let's do all we can to foster unity and love. We may be running out of time.

You Can Have My Room

Who is a God like you,
who pardons sin and forgives the transgression
of the remnant of his inheritance?
You do not stay angry forever
but delight to show mercy. —Micah 7:18 (NIV)

The season for mercy never expires.

Have you heard the story about the little boy who played the innkeeper in his church's Christmas pageant? He was a big kid for a nine-year-old. Mentally slow and awkward, he was often the butt of jokes from the other kids. He wanted more than anything to be a part of the upcoming Christmas play. And somehow, he ended up landing the role of the innkeeper. It was an easy part. All he had to do was brusquely turn Mary and Joseph away when they knocked on the door of his inn.

And that's exactly what he did. "No room!" he thundered. In perfect fashion. But then, as he watched the poor couple walk away dejected and disheartened, his eyes began to fill with tears. With an emotional flush of the impromptu, he cried out, "Come back! I changed my mind. You can have my room!"

You can have my room. It's what Jesus says to all of us, you know. He left his *inn* of splendor to make room for you. For me.

In spite of all the times I've messed up, times I've hurt other people, pushed my kids too hard, insisted on my own way, God's mercy has never turned me out in the cold. Every time I've been insensitive, judgmental, or self-centered, he's offered me another knock at the door. No way do I deserve it. But that's what makes mercy so powerful. It undoes us, then changes us from the inside out. It offers second chances and third chances and even seven times seventy chances if needed.

No wonder the prophet Micah, when seeing how the undeserving Judah was being given another chance, cried out, "Who is a God like you?" The leaders had abused their power and brought untold misery on the people. Yet the God who delights to show mercy had compassion on them and forgave their sins (Micah 7:18–19).

God's mercy never runs out. And it's a good thing because we will never outgrow our need for it. Friend, do you hear Jesus saying, *You can have my room?*

A World Without Repentance

My dear children, I am writing these things to you so that you may not sin. But if anybody does sin, we have an advocate with the Father, Jesus Christ the righteous. —1 John 2:1

Shining mercy into offenses requires an encounter with repentance.

Imagine a world without repentance. It would be run by hypocrites, since repentance is what keeps us honest. Words like *forgiveness, mercy,* and *pardon* would be foreign to our lexicon. The ugliness of pride would replace the beauty of grace. Our knees would not become calloused from too much prayer, but innumerable cases of stiff neck would surface.

If you think bitterness is strong now, ramp it up one hundred-fold where people never say, "I'm sorry." We would have no hope for our land to be healed because we'd be stuck in our wickedness. There would be no means for drawing close to God, no access to his heart. Even heaven's joy would be diminished due to the lack of repentant sinners. And worst of all, the horrors of hell would be chomping at the bit for our arrival.

I don't think that's a world any of us welcome. But it seems more and more we speak less and less about repentance. It's tough stuff. Who likes having their dark places exposed to the light? It's much easier to blame someone else or rationalize our behavior as *not all that bad.* Funny how often *not all that bad* can mushroom into *stone cold bad.*

Eventually we become blind and deaf to the only good news that could set us free. Repentance keeps that from happening.

We are among the "dear children" John writes to in his first letter to the church. He assures us our sins have been forgiven. But he warns us about our susceptibility to the world, how it will tempt us with things like pride. He tells us not to sin, but if we do, there's a way back.

Repent!

Run to our Advocate! Run to Jesus! "If we confess our sins, he is faithful and just to forgive us our sins and to cleanse us from all un-righteousness" (1 John 1:9). That's not religious jargon. It's what keeps us on the road. It's what picks us up when we fall.

Don't live in a world without repentance. Turn around. You'll find it's not as hard as you think.

Dwelling on Justice and Mercy

Let me fall into the hand of the LORD, for his mercy is very great, but do not let me fall into the hand of man. —1 Chronicles 21:13

I've always been intrigued by trials and courtrooms. I'm one of the few people I know who has never been called for jury duty but wishes they were.

When Chip and I were first married, we moved to Ft. Pierce, Florida, where he and his brother began a business. He worked long hours. Since at that point I had neither friends nor a job, I found myself looking for ways to occupy my time. There wasn't a lot happening in a town whose population consisted primarily of construction workers and retirees. However, a murder trial was taking place at the city courthouse. A for-mer sheriff's deputy was accused of killing two teenage girls. I decided to observe the daily proceedings along with many of the over-65 resi-dents. Perry Mason move over!

Don't we all long to live in a world where justice prevails? Or maybe we don't. When David sinned against God by taking a census of Israel's fighting men, he was given three options as a consequence: 1) three years of devastating famine, 2) three months of debilitating war, or 3) three days of ravaging plague. David chose the latter, acknowledging the possibility God's mercy might intervene. He was right. As the plague reached its height, God relented and stopped the destruction.

So, I must admit, as much as I love justice, I'm grateful I don't get what I deserve any more than David did for his foolish actions. God sent Jesus to balance the scales of justice for my sin. Although I might have to suffer natural consequences for my behavior, his mercy prevails, washing me with forgiveness. And not only me. His mercy extends for all who ask, no matter how badly we mess up.

Of course, we believers know this. But I wonder if the interaction between God's mercy and justice isn't one of those areas we don't allow our minds to dwell on enough.

The Florida man was convicted and sentenced to prison. I don't know if he ever called out to God, but the truth is that if he did, even he would have found mercy and forgiveness. Something to dwell on.

Goodwill Toward Men

Fools mock at making amends for sin, but goodwill is found among the upright —Proverbs 14:9 (NIV)

Goodwill. Although expressions of "peace on earth" and "goodwill toward men" flourish in the Christmas season, peace remains fragile and elusive. And if goodwill describes willing good for others, I'm afraid we're falling short. No surprise in a fallen world, but when the tentacles of division and bitterness slip into the church, the consequences could not be more serious. The often-quoted assessment by George McDonald that division has done more to hide Christ from the view of people than all the infidelity rings truer than ever.

I recently read an article about the huge divide in evangelical churches that's taking place over cultural issues. I believe there's an underlying reason. A recent Barna poll indicates 62 percent of American Christians don't believe that the Holy Spirit is a real person. And

61 percent say all religious faiths are of equal value.[26] When the Church doesn't offer sound biblical teaching, people look to the culture for truth. No wonder we're mimicking the world's lack of mercy and forgiveness!

Even if we hate the unrighteousness some people display, we are not allowed, as followers of Christ, to denigrate them for their opinions. It is so tempting for me to think of snarky remarks when someone says something I disagree with. But what does the Lord think of my smart remarks? Do I actually think he doesn't care when I spread *bad will* toward my fellow image bearers?

This doesn't mean we never call people out. Jesus called out the hypocrites as sharply as anyone. So, spreading goodwill doesn't mean we never oppose anyone. But we don't oppose people by dehumanizing them, as has become commonplace. Instead, we cultivate kindness, humility, gratitude, and respect for others even as we address uncomfortable truths.

In business, *goodwill* refers to the intangible asset that increases a company's value. Variables like the company's brand, or its customer relationships, come into play when one business acquires another. The stronger the *goodwill* developed by the corporation, the greater its worth.

I think we can learn a lesson from this. If we consider ourselves as part of the company of the "upright," let's make sure goodwill toward others can be found among us. Let's view goodwill as the powerful commodity it is. It yields an inestimable return.

CHAPTER THIRTEEN

With Grace When It's Undeserved

"Grace is sufficient even though we huff and puff with all our might to try and find something or someone that it cannot cover. Grace is enough."

Brennan Manning
—*All Is Grace*

I think it's nearly impossible to shine the light of God's favor on those we deem undeserving until we first come to grips with our own undeservedness. Only when we see all of life as a gift, a gift none of us deserve, do we have a well to draw from. His gift of grace enables us to forgive when people (just like us) don't meet our expectations. It protects us from nasty things like self-righteousness and increases our gratitude for all the unmerited blessings he sends our way. Birthed from a holy fear of God, it helps us keep in step with the truth and avoid false messages of everything from *tolerance* to *works*. Let yourself be surprised by this priceless virtue, then shine it brightly.

Don't Miss It!

As God's co-workers we urge you not to receive God's grace in vain.
—2 Corinthians 6:1 (NIV)

How could we forget to access something so powerful? Why do we struggle far longer than we need to? Where did we get the idea that our need for grace stopped at the cross?

Grace.

In the NIV version of the Bible, Paul *urges* believers not to receive God's grace in vain. Other translations say beg, appeal, beseech, entreat, plead. It makes me think missing the grace of God looms as a real possibility for even mature Christians.

God gives us grace because he wants us to use it. A friend compared it to giving his son a new bicycle. He said, "I hope he wears it out to the point I have to get him another one." The last thing this dad desired was for his boy to keep his bike safely locked up in the garage, used only for special occasions. It pleased him to see his gift being put to use. I think it pleases God in the same way when we call on his grace to help us in our time of need.

I was recently confronted with a situation where I'd let my expectations move past reality. Disappointment landed with a giant thud. I experienced frustration, guilt, and plain down sadness. The more I mulled over it, the worse it became. I had overlooked what Paul urged me not to forget.

Grace.

Because of grace, I didn't have to stay stuck in the quicksand. Access to God's grace provided a way of escape. I could forgive. I could repent. I could look beyond the disappointment. God's grace takes us further than we could ever take ourselves. If we let it.

It is far too easy for us to move from divine dependence on God to our own self-efforts. When trouble comes, we default to how we can resolve it. We don't remember there's a Grand Canyon of help awaiting us. There is no dilemma we face his grace can't reach.

So, friend, I hope you're better at accessing the grace of God than I sometimes am. I urge, beg, beseech, and entreat you not to miss it. Let's get on those bicycles and ride, ride, ride.

A Quarantine Cry

When the righteous cry for help, the LORD hears and delivers them out of all their troubles. —Psalm 34:17

In the winter of 2020, sometime BC (Before Covid-19), my husband and I made plans to go back to one of our favorite places for summer vacation. We secured a campsite at Blackwoods Campground in Acadia National Park for the third week in June. Then came the pandemic. And we joined the long list of people across the world facing unexpected cancellations. The campground was closed for the whole season.

As summer continued, and the virus seemed to lessen, we thought about reserving a cottage where we had once stayed outside of the park. We called the owners who said they were open, but we would need to have negative Covid-19 test results within 72 hours of entering Maine. So, we arranged for the test with the assurance we would have our results in seven to ten days. Well, ten days came and went with no results. We were told there was a sudden backlog. But we continued to prepare and left home fueled on the fumes of faith. It was day twelve.

We entered Maine with our test results still pending. When we got to the cottage, our host said we could stay, but we had to agree to being quarantined until we received notification we were healthy. We were wondering if we had traveled all that way only to turn around the next morning and head home. Everyone likes road trips, right? But just as we opened the door to our cottage, I got the text we were waiting for. We were negative!

My husband often responds, "Better than I deserve" when someone asks how he is. It's his way of thanking God for his grace. The door opening for Acadia felt like a bomb of grace landing on our laps. We knew we didn't deserve it, yet the Lord heard our prayers.

The psalmist says the Lord hears the cries of the righteous and delivers them from their troubles. We can align ourselves with the righteous not because of anything we have done, but because of what the Lord has done in making us—and all who receive him—righteous.

As children of God, we have no right to demand he give us anything. But he seems to like delivering us from our troubles. So, don't be afraid to cry out to the God who hears—even in quarantines.

Holy Fear

But the God in whose hand is your breath, and whose are all your ways, you have not honored. —Daniel 5:23

If I saw a hand out of nowhere writing something on the wall, I guess my face would pale and my knees would knock too. That was the reaction Babylonian King Belshazzar had during a night of revelry with his friends when he called for the gold and silver goblets taken from Jerusalem's temple to be used. As they drank from those sacred vessels, they praised the gods of gold and silver in defiance of the true God.

Belshazzar should have known better. He saw how God stripped his father, Nebuchadnezzar, of his high position due to his pride and arrogance. Nebuchadnezzar had been at the top of his game, the most feared man in the whole world, but in one minute it all came crashing down. He lost his kingdom as well as his sanity and lived with the wild animals in the field until he was willing to acknowledge the Most High God (Daniel 4).

Pride has a way of deceiving us into thinking we can beat the odds.

Belshazzar intentionally used the vessels set apart to worship the Sovereign God for his own pleasure. He blatantly set himself up against the One who held his life in his hands. His blasphemy cost him his life that very night.

Belshazzar lacked a holy fear of God. I think we do, too, at times. We focus on how much God loves us and forgives us. Rightly so. But if not careful, we can view him as a doting grandfather who winks at our blasphemies of self-adulation. We are not as self-made as we think. We have nothing and are nothing without him. That alone should elicit never-ending reverence.

God takes much pleasure in giving both saints and sinners unmerited blessings. But let's not take his grace for granted. Our society has come a long way from the fire and brimstone preachers of the 1700s. But maybe the pendulum has swung too far. Let's not take lightly the One who holds our breath and all our ways in his hand.

We sing, "You are worthy of it all." Indeed, He is. So, let's live like it. Let's remember his grace and worship him in holy fear.

Grace-Substitutes

And the Word became flesh and dwelt among us, and we have seen his glory, glory as of the only Son from the Father, full of grace and truth.
—John 1:14

Sugar substitutes have become familiar commodities in our diet. Some claim to be more healthier alternatives than others, but all share the commonality of providing an alternative to that sweet substance we all love.

Substitutes take the place of what some consider the "real" thing, from sugar to milk to second-string quarterbacks. But there's another common substitute. Grace substitutes fill the aisles of our culture, our schools, and our churches.

The most predominate grace-substitute in our culture resides under the label of tolerance. Supposedly, the more tolerant we appear, the greater our grace. The truly tolerant accept all behavior (except, of course behavior that doesn't tolerate bad behavior).

But embracing the low standards of the world should never be confused with grace. Genuine grace doesn't make people feel comfortable in their sin. Genuine grace thrives within the parameters of truth. Tolerance might make us popular but also irrelevant.

Another common substitute for grace, of course, is works. Rather than humbly accepting what Jesus did on the cross to save us, we seek God's favor through our own efforts. This inevitably leads to legalism and pride in our accomplishments.

The danger of grace-substitutes surfaces when we encounter situations where we really need the grace of God to get through. The false pillars of cultural definitions of "truth" and other forms of self-righteousness crumble like a house of cards. Fake grace just doesn't cut it.

Jesus had nothing to do with grace-substitutes. His life displayed the real thing . . . real grace, real truth. He never compromised to make the call of repentance more palatable. At the same time, he refused to embrace the legalistic ways of the Pharisees. He showed the world what his Father looks like, and he challenges us to do the same.

So let's be on guard. Let's not fall for those slickly marketed substitutes called grace. The more we delve into the riches of God's unmerited mercy toward us, the less tempted we'll be to accept powerless imitations.

It's *stevia* for my morning yogurt. But no substitute for grace in my life.

Pricey Misperceptions

But the princes of the Ammonites said to Hanun, "Do you think, because David has sent comforters to you, that he is honoring your father? Have not his servants come to you to search and to overthrow and to spy out the land?" —1 Chronicles 19:3

Have you ever found yourself seeing what you thought you would see rather than perceiving what really is? Misperceptions can be costly. For the Ammonites it was deadly.

When Nahash, king of the Ammonites, died, King David sent a delegation from Israel to express his condolences to Hanun, his son. But rather than receiving this act of kindness, the Ammonites accused them of being spies, sent to prepare Israel's army for war against them. They retaliated by humiliating the delegation—shaving their beards, cutting their garments, and throwing them out of their country in disgrace. Their ignorance so incensed David, that he mustered his army and went to battle. The Ammonites were completely destroyed. Forty-seven thousand men lost their lives due to a simple misperception.

It makes me wonder how much misperceptions play in the conflicts and separations we face. If I expect someone not to like me, my defenses go up. Without saying a word, I send a message that says, "Stay away." My behavior changes in anticipation of what I think—based on my perception. The gap between us widens. Like the Ammonites, any hope of connection is destroyed.

But what if we looked at people with a different perspective? What if we treated them with grace? Jesus says to love our enemies. That command stands regardless of whether our perceptions are right or wrong. We are called to love people, even the difficult ones. Maybe separations that seemed inevitable wouldn't turn out to be so inevitable if we were just willing to shake off any perception that hasn't first taken a bath in God's grace.

So, let's hold our perceptions lightly. Rather than jumping to conclusions about someone and creating a divide, let's do the opposite. Be willing to look beyond what you think you see. Don't let your perceptions cloud reality, but check them out with God before allowing them to settle in.

It costs the body of Christ too much not to.

Goodbye Guilt, So Long Shame

In Christ God was reconciling the world to himself, not counting their trespasses against them, and entrusting to us the message of reconciliation. —2 Corinthians 5:19

"How do I know God isn't punishing my friend now for sin he committed 20 years ago?" she asked me.

"Did he repent of that sin?" I questioned.

"Yes, not long after it happened."

"So what you're wondering is whether God held on to that sin—that *repented* sin—until an opportune time to punish him?"

"I guess I am."

"It seems to me the God you're picturing bears little resemblance to the God of the Bible. Scripture tells us God does not count our sins against us. When we repent, we're forgiven. No strings. No delayed punishment hanging over our heads. Jesus paid the price for every sin, from our ugly thoughts to our dastardly deeds. The God of the Bible is all about reconciling us to himself."

I think a lot of us get trapped in shame from our past as evidenced in this conversation I had with a friend. It's hard to imagine a God of grace who accepts our repentance. A God so generous as to grant us opportunities to walk daily with a clean slate. A God who offers us new-every-morning mercies. What kind of God is it who refuses to use our guilt to manipulate us into better behavior? God says I want your good works to be done in gratitude for forgiveness, not as a means to obtain it.

We're much more accustomed to our human tendencies. We hold grudges and secretly hope our enemies *receive their just due.* Sadly, our judgments tend to boomerang. The grace we deny to others, we deny to ourselves. We end up working our fingers to the bone, thinking if we try really hard God will overlook all our bad behavior. It's a standard no one can meet. God designed something far better.

Friend, don't let your past keep you from enjoying the freedom of today. Don't waste your time trying to trust in a god who looks more like you than the God of the Bible. He calls you to be a messenger to others about this great gift of reconciliation, but you can't unless you first say goodbye to that guilt and so long to that shame.

Speak Well

Let no corrupting talk come out of your mouths, but only such as is good for building up, as fits the occasion, that it may give grace to those who hear. —Ephesians 4:29

Our words are a pretty good indicator as to whether we are shining God's grace toward others.

The text I use for my Public Speaking classes is *On Speaking Well* by Peggy Noonan. I thought of that title when thinking how the Bible encourages us in another kind of *speaking well* that is far more consequential. It's how we are to use our words to bring life.

So, what does *Spiritual Speaking Well* look like?

First, we *speak well* when we speak the truth. Paul exhorts us to speak the truth in love (Ephesians 4:15). We might *be right* about an issue, but we don't *have the right* to speak it in ways that undermine the message. Judgmental words don't get past the hammer, anvil, and stirrup of the middle ear. People are more desperate to hear the truth than we think, but they are also desperate to have an excuse not to listen. Speaking the truth in anything but love gives them justification for turning us off.

When we *speak well,* we deliver grace. "Let your speech always be gracious, seasoned with salt, so that you may know how you ought to answer each person" (Colossians 4:6). Grace builds up other people. It gives them space to change. When my Public Speaking students critique one another's *uh's* and *like's,* they often precede their comments with, "I do the same thing." Their expression of grace unlocks the door to receptivity.

The art of *speaking well* from a spiritual perspective is becoming increasingly rare. We're bombarded with crass speech on social media and in entertainment. Negative comments that deride people we disagree with seem to flow as quickly from Christ-followers as they do from nonbelievers. Do we really think graceless comments and harsh criticism advance the kingdom of God?

I'm not saying we shouldn't address wrongs. But if we hope to win anyone over to our side, it won't happen through reckless words and sarcastic put downs. I know it's hard sometimes. Taming the tongue takes more than a halfhearted effort. But every time we choose to speak light into darkness by the grace of God, we speak life. We *speak well.*

Surprised by Grace

But grace was given to each one of us according to the measure of Christ's gift. —Ephesians 4:7

Christianity. It's a faith full of surprises. For example, C.S. Lewis wrote of being surprised by joy. N. T. Wright's book, *Surprised by Hope*, digs into a Christian's view of eternity. But one of the most surprising aspects of my walk with Christ lies in the unsuspecting, mysterious expressions of grace. You could say I've been surprised by grace.

I've known about grace all my life. "God's Riches at Christ's Expense," right? Anyone who has even a slight brush with Christianity has probably sung "Amazing Grace." But we become so familiar with the concept of grace we almost miss its power.

Grace offered me salvation when I didn't even realize I needed saving. It still does. When the Holy Spirit reveals hidden pockets of darkness in my soul, it's grace that enables me to repent rather than fall prey to self-justification. And grace helps me hold on when my feelings shout "give up!"

Grace keeps me aware that all the undeserved pleasures I experience in life are gifts from a good Father. Who am I that I should be able to appreciate so many pleasantries in life? I can enjoy a good book. Be in a stadium with over 100,000 fans cheering on my football team. Roast chestnuts and relish a quiet evening with my husband. The fact I can even see these things as gifts from the God who loves me is grace saying, "Surprise!"

Grace shows up in unexpected places when we let its spirit saturate us. I'm angry at the behavior of a fellow believer, but when I go to confront her, loving concern instead of righteous indignation over-comes me. That's grace. Disappointments that used to hang on me like the odor of rotting potatoes no longer linger. That's grace. Someone lobs a hurtful remark my way, but I let it go. That's grace.

Paul says God has apportioned a measure of grace to each one of us. He expects us to apply it in our own lives and then extend it to others. Because that's the nature of grace: the unmerited riches are meant to be passed on. And as we pour out our "measure," our storehouse of grace actually increases! Yet another surprising quality of this precious virtue.

Friend, don't be suspicious of this lavish gift from God. Get soaked in its surprises!

The X Factor

And because the gracious hand of my God was on me, the king granted my requests. —Nehemiah 2:8 (NIV)

You have undoubtedly heard of the *X factor*. It refers to a variable in a situation with the potential to significantly impact the outcome. A whole music franchise was developed by Simon Cowell to determine which contestant possesses that undefinable quality of star power known as the *X Factor*. In sports, it refers to the player who carries the team to victory. I'm told online dating services use the *X factor* to des-ignate "a very special personal quality."

But I believe there's an *X factor* far more potent than any we could dream of. It has the power to turn impossible situations into something beyond imagination. It shines light into the darkest of days. And it stirs us to take courage when desperation whispers, "Quit."

So, what is that underestimated variable?

God's grace. No matter how discouraged, disappointed, or defeated we feel, never leave the *X factor* of God's grace out of the equation. Nehemiah certainly didn't.

If anyone had reason to despair, it was Nehemiah. For seventy years, Jerusalem lay in the ruins of burnt gates and crumbled walls. Thousands of its inhabitants—-including Nehemiah—had been exiled to Babylon. The once proud city was reduced to a state of utter defenselessness and disgrace.

But Nehemiah didn't give in to desperation. As cupbearer to the Persian king, he used his position to ask the king's permission to return to Judah and rebuild the city. What must have seemed like an impossibility became a reality, not because of the king's goodwill or Nehemiah's persuasive powers. Nehemiah had cried out to God in prayer. When the king released him to go, Nehemiah knew it was due to one factor. One *X factor*: "the gracious hand of God."

The book of Nehemiah records all the obstacles and opposition the returning exiles experienced in the rebuilding process. But again and again, Nehemiah gives credit to God's grace for giving them success. They certainly didn't deserve it. But when has man's undeserving plight ever stopped God?

Friend, never discount the *X factor* of God's grace working in your life. Remember the God who loves you fiercely doesn't want you to live under the shadow of destroyed walls and charred gates. Trust his grace to make a most significant impact in your circumstance.

Even If It's Just a Paragraph

John answered, "A person cannot receive even one thing unless it is given him from heaven." —John 3:27

When I pick up a book, it's always interesting to me to see various affirmations on the first pages from people recommending it as a good read. Some authors include pages of statements acknowledging the value of the work, others one or two assertions. It seems like a metaphor on life. Some people's lives brim with glowing accolades. If they were a book, those front pages would comprise a novel in and of itself. But for most of us, we feel fortunate to contain a paragraph.

The other day I experienced one of those "I'm just a paragraph" moments. It happened because I started comparing myself to someone else.

Before I knew it, my thoughts had fast-tracked into all the areas where I feel I don't measure up.

Thankfully, God doesn't view me—or you—that way. He portions to each of us the amount of grace we need to live our stories. And to live them with great success.

When John the Baptist was baptizing people in the Judean country-side, his disciples approached him with alarming news. Jesus' disciples had started baptizing people and everyone was going to him. The new kids on the block were taking over! John's response indicates what made him the greatest born of woman (Luke 7:28). "A person cannot receive even one thing unless it is given him from heaven." He was doing exactly what God called him to do. He decreased so Jesus could increase.

A few years ago I had a student in my class with an unusually high-pitched, squeaky voice. At the beginning of the semester, I wondered how he would make it with such an annoying vocal quality. But as the term progressed, he proved to be one of the most effective speakers in the class. He had the ability to think out of the box, and he used it to develop some of the most creative speeches I had ever heard. What he did well overshadowed a limitation he could do nothing about.

The apostle Paul said, "By the grace of God I am what I am" (1 Corinthians 15:10). So are you. So am I. Let's use that grace to make the most of what we've been given. Even if it's just a paragraph.

CHAPTER FOURTEEN

With Persistence in Prayer, Problems, and Tight Places

"'Go back?' he thought. 'No good at all! Go sideways? Impossible! Go forward? Only thing to do! On we go!' So up he got, and trotted along with his little sword held in front of him and one hand feeling the wall, and his heart all of a patter and a pitter."

J.R.R. Tolkien
—*The Hobbit*

Persistence births some of life's richest treasures. It's what enables us to keep pressing on, long after feelings of inspiration have dimmed. The flame of persistence keeps our hearts burning with determination when everything within us wants to give up. Perhaps no aspect of our lives requires persistence more than our prayer life. Some situations require worn-out carpets and empty tissue boxes from incessant intercession. The importance of persistence in prayer, but also in our work, in realizing our dreams and in fighting spiritual battles, can't be overstated. Don't give in to the weariness of waiting. You will have no regrets if you keep pressing on.

The Power of Passionate Persistence

And he told them a parable to the effect that they ought always to pray and not lose heart. —Luke 18:1

Passionate persistence consists of faith, desperation, and sometimes tears.

Tears like those shed by Monica, the mother of early church father, Augustine. Alarmed at her son's wanton abandonment of his faith, in desperation she went to her priest, Ambrose, and implored him to speak to Augustine. She wanted him to convince Augustine about the errors of his ways. He refused, sensing Augustine was not ready for correction. But Monica was undeterred. Flooded with tears, she pleaded with Ambrose again and again to speak to her wayward son. Exasperated, Ambrose finally told her to go away because it was impossible that the son of such tears would perish.

Ambrose recognized the great faith behind Monica's passionate intercession. He knew such faith would not go unanswered. He was right. Years later, when Augustine returned to God, he attributed his salvation to his mother's tears. Her tears, faith, and desperation changed the history of Western civilization.

Never underestimate the power of passionate persistence. Commenting on Monica, Peter Kreeft writes "Trying to do good in this world without prayer is like trying to win a war without any air force . . . but it waits for our signals. Those signals are faith, hope, and above all, passionate charity."[27] God hears our faith-filled, hope-inspired, gut-wrenching please.

Remember the parable Jesus told about the widow who kept coming to the judge to obtain justice? Her persistence finally wore the unjust judge down. He granted her request just to get her off his back. Jesus said we should display the same persistence when we approach God in prayer. Don't give up!

If you're like me, there are some circumstances you've been praying about for a long time. Maybe a very long time. You haven't seen any change, but you continue to cry out to the only One who can make a difference. Don't give up, friend! Release those signals of faith, hope, and passionate charity. You never know when the air force might land and dry up those tears.

Pray It Off

The LORD is my rock and my fortress and my deliverer,
my God, my rock, in whom I take refuge,
my shield, and the horn of my salvation, my stronghold.
I call upon the LORD, who is worthy to be praised,
and I am saved from my enemies. —Psalm 18:2–3

Do you see God as your deliverer, the one who saves you from your enemies? Or does that concept seem distant and Old Testament-ish? I believe it's as relevant for us today as it was for David when he penned Psalm 18. Especially when someone falsely accuses us.

I received an email the other day from a person I hadn't seen in years. In it, he launched a venomous attack against me. Even though I knew his accusations were false, it still landed on me like a gut punch. His spitballs of judgment made me feel dirty, like I'd done something wrong, even though I knew what he said wasn't true.

My first reaction was to become my own Perry Mason or John Grisham. I found myself in full defense attorney mode. But no amount of internal arguing could lift the burden this man had laid on my shoulders. I could not "think it off."

I had to "pray it off."

My prayer went something like this. *Lord, deliver me from letting this man's indictments crush me. I know you love me enough to not give me a free pass when I sin, but this does not feel like conviction from the Holy Spirit. You are not the accuser. You are my shield and defender. Save me from this instrument of the enemy.*

God answered my cry. And he taught me how important it is to immediately lay situations like this at his feet. Some issues cannot be talked through, thought through, or smoothed through. They have to be prayed through. God calls himself our refuge and stronghold for a reason. He did not build us to fight our enemies on our own.

Let's learn from Psalm 18. David cried out to God with unshakable confidence even though the "cords of death encompassed" him and "the torrents of destruction assailed" him (v. 4). He didn't fall prey to false guilt, but he stood firm in declaring God shows his mercy to the merciful (v. 25). He exalts the God who is worthy of praise (v. 46).

So when the ugly voice of false accusation comes against you . . . Pray if off!

No Mud Pies for Me

You do not have, because you do not ask. You ask and do not receive, because you ask wrongly, to spend it on your passions. —James 4:2–3

During the presidency of George W. Bush, he challenged educators to avoid the soft bigotry of low expectations. He wanted schools to stop subtle discrimination by expecting poor minority students to fail and so teach from that perspective. The theory: Expecting students to succeed will give them a better shot.

Sometimes I think we experience the "soft bigotry of low expectations" when it comes to God. Oh, we won't come right out and say we don't believe he will answer our prayers. But if we look honestly at our faith, we find we really don't expect him to come through. Especially if we need something in the realm of miracle status. *He's hopeless. She will never change! That's impossible!* Such thoughts say a lot about our view of God.

If we believe we serve a big God, why wouldn't we ask him for big things? C.S. Lewis writes, "It would seem our Lord finds our desires not too strong, but too weak . . . like an ignorant child who wants to go on making mud pies in a slum because he cannot imagine what is meant by the offer of a holiday at the sea. We are far too easily pleased."[28]

According to James, we don't have because we don't ask. Maybe one of the reasons we don't ask is because we fail to see either the vastness of God's sovereignty or the depth of his love. We think he either lacks the power or compassion to intervene in our circumstance. Our puny perspective keeps him at our level.

But as long as our motives stem from wanting his will more than our own, we don't have to be afraid of asking. God will cover our requests. In the biggest ask of his life, even Jesus said, "not my will but yours." He trusted his Father to adjust his prayer. So can we.

If we want to move beyond the bigotry of low expectations on God, there's no better time to start. Let's trust him with our biggest dreams and grandest hopes. Be assured he will bring our best to pass. Let's refuse to be content *making mud pies.*

Who Is in Control?

Also I make a decree that if anyone alters this edict, a beam shall be pulled out of his house, and he shall be impaled on it, and his house shall be made a dunghill. —Ezra 6:11

Sometimes I need a who's in control reality check.

After seventy years in Babylonian exile, the Jewish people were given permission to return to their homeland. Over 40,000 people arrived in Jerusalem and began resettlement. They faced immediate opposition when they started restoring the foundation of the temple. Their enemies sent a letter to the Persian king, accusing the Jews of rebellion, warning him he better shut them down, although they had done nothing wrong. (As many of you know, the "rightness" of our cause does not ensure smooth sailing.) The Jews were forced to stop working.

Thankfully, that's not the end of the story. Fourteen years later, the prophets urged the people to resume the building. When their enemies threatened them again and complained to the king, history records a colossal backfire. Not only did King Darius reinstate permission for the Jews to rebuild, he threatened to impale anyone who tried to stop them!

God has a way of turning the bleakest of situations into shimmering lights of victory. Nothing lies beyond his power. He works through his godly servants but even through ungodly rulers. The God who created the universe and everything in it remains in charge. Let's not let it slip our minds that the "unseen" outpowers, outlasts and outdoes the "seen."

As the Lord calls us to greater persistence in prayer, many seemingly hopeless situations will turn around. The only explanation for the change: the inexplicable power of prayer to "the blessed and only Ruler, the King of kings and Lord of lords" (1 Timothy 6:15).

I pray the next time life starts getting you down, you go for a *who's in control reality check.* Don't give up! The same power that gave the Jewish people favor with a pagan Persian king is the same power that raised Christ from the dead and is the same power that lives in you and in me. Nothing is too hard for him. Absolutely nothing.

Persevering People

Blessed is the man who remains steadfast under trial, for when he has stood the test he will receive the crown of life, which God has promised to those who love him. —James 1:12

My husband and I got married on top of a mountain outside of Boulder, Colorado, with my grandpa officiating. When the wedding party consists of only three people, it's pretty noticeable when one might not show up. Grandpa had been suffering from severe back spasms making him question whether he could make the long flight from Columbus, Ohio, to Denver. Had it not been for my dear Aunt Noreen pressing him to persevere through the pain, he may not have made it. "You will always regret it if you don't go," was her sage advice.

So Grandpa arrived the day before the wedding. That evening, I tucked Grandpa in for the night, hoping he would rest well. But a couple hours later, I heard him cry out in excruciating pain. I rushed him to the ER, where the doctor gave him a shot to relax his muscles. It made him a bit loopy but took care of the pain. And the next morning the three of us hiked up Boulder Canyon where Chip and I made our vows. When we put Grandpa on a flight home that evening, he left with no regrets. His perseverance paid off.

Perseverance always does. I remember the summer I landed a job that proved to be a lot more demanding than I thought. It was my aunt who (again) encouraged perseverance. She helped me see I could put up with anything for a few weeks. Once I decided to stick it out, it's amazing how much lighter the workload became. Plus, I learned an invaluable lesson about not giving up.

I'm glad folks like Job, Joseph, Abraham, Moses, Peter, Paul, and the entire early church kept going when things got tough. I'm thankful Jesus endured the cross and didn't throw in the towel.

Scripture places a high premium on perseverance.

It assures us we will reap if we don't give up (Galatians 6:9). It promises those who persevere will develop a strong character (Romans 5:3–4). Jesus commended the persistent widow who persevered until she secured justice (Luke 18:1–5). And James assures us a crown of life awaits the steadfast.

So, no matter what difficulty you're facing, I pray you don't quit. Be one of those persevering people.

All In

For I am already being poured out as a drink offering, and the time of my departure has come. —2 Timothy 4:6

Every January since the passage of Roe v. Wade in 1973, pro-lifers have traveled to Washington, DC, to march against the legalization of abortion. They come from across the country—young, old, Catholics, Protestants, black, brown, white—all crying out for the rights of unborn babies. They peacefully do what they can do to make the smallest and weakest voices of humankind be heard. You can't help but stand amazed at their unequivocal dedication, year after year after year until at last, their persistence has paid off. I don't think I've ever witnessed a more persevering group of people. Those pro-lifers are all in.

At the college where I teach, a quote from nineteenth century missionary William Borden graces the chapel wall: "No reserves, no retreat, no regrets." Borden grew up in a wealthy family, graduating from both Yale and Princeton. He wrote the words, "no reserves" in the back of his Bible after announcing he would give up his inheritance and go to China as a missionary. When others scoffed him for turning down lucrative positions, he added the words, "no retreat." He set sail for China when he was twenty-five years old, stopping in Egypt to study Arabic. While there he contracted spinal meningitis and died. Many viewed his untimely death as a waste, but as he lay dying, Borden penned these last two words in his Bible: no regrets. William Borden was all in.

When the apostle Paul wrote to Timothy from his prison cell, he believed his death was imminent. In his last letter, he encouraged Timothy to keep fighting the good fight, endure hardship, and preach the gospel. Paul's life was being poured out in a dank, lonely jail, but he voiced no doubts about having given himself to Jesus with total abandon. He urged Timothy to do the same. Paul was all in.

I'm not sure there is any other way to be "in" for Jesus than "all." Authentic Christianity is "all in Christianity." It's radical. No Plan B exists for Christians who are all in. They have their sights set on something far greater than man's temporary approval and applause. They know the One who gave *His all* for them is worth it. Worth whatever it takes to persevere with no regrets.

The Other Side of Righteousness

If the foundations are destroyed, what can the righteous do? —Psalm 11:3

You don't have to be a news junkie to take David's question in Psalm 11 as more than rhetorical. It's hard to watch what's happening across the world without experiencing pangs of despair.

We don't know where to look for truthful assessments anymore. The spirit of divisiveness penetrates every aspect of life, from how we perceive social justice to whether we should wear masks. Violence rather than law threatens to be the new arbiter of justice. Doxing people who hold different views, thus putting their families in harm's way, is becoming common. Judging others' past according to present day standards reminds me of looking in one of those carnival mirrors that distorts reality.

So how are we to live in what seems like the other side of righteousness?

David could have just checked out. "Flee like a bird to your mountain" (Psalm 11:1). Leave the battle to others. Avoid those poisonous arrows aiming for your upright heart. But David would have none of it. Rather than focusing on the crumbling foundations of the world, he turned to the indestructible foundation, the one built by the God who loves justice. And so should we.

When the foundations are being destroyed, the righteous choose to trust a just God. We let the struggles strengthen us. We don't hide in our mountain of Netflix. And we hold on to truth tenaciously, resisting the pull of hatred. We pray. And we learn to pray more. Mark Buchannan writes that we look at the passage in Isaiah 40:31 and think mounting on eagles' wings as the optimum place to be in tumultuous times. He points out, however, that the Hebrews move from the lesser to the greater, making "walking without fainting" the highest goal.[29]

So don't be discouraged if you're not somehow flying above the chaos in the world. God may be calling you to walk. And to keep walking with eyes fixed on him. We each have different assignments to fulfill, no matter what might be happening around us. We might be living in a world on the other side of righteousness but let's not faint. Let's persevere through it with courage, diligence, faith, and love.

How Long?

How long, O LORD? Will you forget me forever?
How long will you hide your face from me? —Psalm 13:1

Who knew perseverance was such a virtue? Certainly, the difficulties of 2020 caused us to step up our capacity for enduring. But how do we keep pressing on when the cruelty and ugliness of the world seems to hide God? When dissension and distrust cast an ominous shadow over much of our thoughts?

It makes me think of a scene from the second movie in *The Lord of the Rings* trilogy, *The Two Towers*. One of the most poignant moments occurs when Sam recalls how all the stories that matter—the ones that inspire us—portray folks who had opportunity to turn back, but chose to keep going, holding on to the end. Frodo, overcome with discouragement, asks, "What are we holding on to, Sam?" Sam's simple response moves me to tears. "That there's some good in the world, Mr. Frodo, and it's worth fighting for."[30]

Do you know the battles you're facing are worth fighting for? Do you know God has a bigger picture to bring beauty from your pain? I lose sight of that in my weak moments.

So did David. Psalm 13 reflects his despair when he can't see God. Charles Spurgeon comments there are so many "how longs" in this six-verse psalm that it could be called the "*howling* psalm." David cries, "*How long* . . . will you forget me? *How long* will you hide your face? *How long* must I wrestle with my thoughts? *How long* will my enemy triumph over me?" (Psalm 13:1–2 NIV, emphasis added).

But as David asks God to hear him, he pivots from his pain to praise. He chooses to trust in a love that has never failed him. And sing to the One whose goodness continues to brace his life. David saw the bigger picture. Like Frodo, he rose above the darkness and set his eyes on the end worth fighting for.

I pray you are doing the same. May you lift your eyes above all the sorrowful, confusing thoughts trying to whittle away your faith. God desires to do more in your trial than just help you get through. Let him transform your *how longs* into undaunting confidence. Don't turn back. Persevere and complete your story.

Battle Savvy

Be strong, and let your heart take courage, all you who wait for the LORD! —Psalm 31:24

A lady called our church office the other day asking if she could meet with me. We set up a time, and as she related all the difficulties she was going through, my heat broke. It seemed adversity was striking every area of her life—physical, financial, marital, as well as emotional and spiritual.

But her story didn't surprise me. I can't remember experiencing a time when so many believers are feeling the brunt of the world and the onslaught of the enemy. They are experiencing one punch after another, as abnormal amounts of life-irritants like kids getting lice, plumbers *causing* damage to water pipes, and unfair treatment at work, compound the serious issues.

Although these situations feel overwhelming, I'm praying the challenges will help us become battle-savvy instead of battle-weary. For every time we go through a difficulty and choose to trust God rather than give in to discouragement, we build up muscles of faith. Satan wants to drive us to despair. He uses every tool in his arsenal to keep us looking down rather than up. He tries to detach us from God's love and make us think God doesn't care. When we stop believing God cares, our faith plummets and all the demons in hell put on their party hats.

That's why I love Psalm 31.

The psalmist urges us to keep hoping in God. No matter what. He knew what it was like to be consumed with anguish (v. 10). How it felt like to be the utter contempt of his neighbors and object of dread to his closest friends (v. 11). To be the brunt of unjust conspiracies (v. 13). Yet he remains faithful to the God who rescues all those who stay true (v. 23). And he encourages us to be strong and take heart.

It reminds me of going to the dentist. When I went for my appointment the other day, the dental assistant asked if I was comfortable. I wanted to say, *Are you kidding? How does comfortable and dentist even belong in the same sentence?* Life in this fallen imperfect world will never feel comfortable. And sometimes it will seem downright overwhelming. But God gives us the opportunity to grow through every uncomfortable, unfair, and unexpected circumstance we face.

Circumstances that will—if we let them—make us battle-savvy.

Unfair!

Forgetting what lies behind and straining forward to what lies ahead, I press on toward the goal. —Philippians 3:13–14

The atmosphere pulsed with electricity. A sea of white shirts and waving pompoms invited football fans to join the frenzied echo of WE ARE . . . PENN STATE! The *white-out* game at Beaver Stadium between Penn State and Auburn—Big Ten vs. SEC (Southeastern Conference)—proved to be a match made in "football heaven."

Although the game remained close, somewhere along the way the officials (SEC officials, I might add), began making questionable calls. In fact, one of the radio announcers remarked he had never seen anything like it. Broadcasters from across the country described the officiating as everything from "awful" to "abysmal." Unintentional grounding discrepancies, disputed ball placements, and an erroneous skipping of a down for Penn State raised eyebrows all over football land. The SEC even had to release a statement the next day admitting they did, in fact, make a mistake in taking away a down from Penn State!

After every "bad call," the announcer would say, "They have to put it behind them and focus on the next play." And that's exactly what the PSU team did. Rather than focusing on the unfair bias, they kept their eye on the goal and pressed forward. It worked. They won the game 28–20.

We have all been the brunt of unfairness at some point in life. Some of us have experienced bigger infractions than others. But whether a small incident of injustice or a life-altering one, when we can't do anything about it, we have to deal with it and move on.

Paul certainly experienced his share of unfairness, as did about everyone in the early church. His encouragement to the Philippians: Forget what lies behind and press on toward the goal. It's a message that everyone who comes face-to-face with unfairness needs to embrace.

Sometimes we can do something to fight unfairness in the world. And if it lies within our capabilities, we should. But other times, our protests fall on ears as deaf as those of the SEC officials when PSU's coach James Franklin objected.

Those are the times to remember the ultimate goal. Put the injustice behind us and focus on the next play. Keep pressing on. We'll find rewards far greater than what the Penn State fans celebrated that night.

Part Five

Where Do We Shine the Light?

CHAPTER FIFTEEN

We Shine Clarity into a Chaotic Culture

"We're in a sad place as a society when somebody's firing and/or cancellation is celebrated more than their life's work. And yet, here we are."

Kelly Sadler
—*The Washington Times*

At one of our Christmas Eve services not long ago, a mother and her nine-month-old child presented a sweet rendition of "This Little Light of Mine." Baby Hazel proved to be a bit stage-wary, but we all gave kudos to her mom for reminding us it's never too early to learn not to "hide our light under a bushel."

God has always called his people to counter the culture. To refuse to let the darkness swallow up the light. But it takes effort to not "let Satan blow out" our life-sustaining, truth-affirming, iridescent light. We have the purpose and privilege of using that light to bring clarity into a chaotic world.

Cancelled or Redeemed?

As far as the east is from the west,
  so far does he remove our transgressions from us. —Psalm 103:12

Everyone from former presidents to guys who make chicken sandwiches is falling to it. Victims of the cancel culture are multiplying faster than homeschool moms lining up for free books at the library. People from every walk of life fear saying the wrong thing lest their careers go into freefall.

Worldviews matter. And in case you haven't noticed, the contrast between Christianity's worldview and the views of the world in which we live keeps growing starker.

Perspectives on the future are the most obvious. Christians believe in a real afterlife where everything we experience on earth serves as preparation for eternity with God. Secularists take John Lennon's lyrics seriously: "Imagine there's no heaven . . ."

How we live day-by-day reflects a combination of influences, but basically Christians try to live by standards set forth in the Bible. Even when we fall short, we acknowledge the principles remain whether we follow them or not. The secular view does not view Scripture as inerrant, relevant, or inspired by God. Certainly not a guide on how to live.

The sudden rise of cancel culture also points to drastically different ways we view the past. Followers of Jesus believe in redemption. We believe he took every mistake we've made and every sin we've committed, to the cross. He has removed our transgressions "as far as the east is from the west" to offer us a second chance. No such opportunity exists in the cancel culture. There, people's past becomes an albatross around their neck. No matter how long ago their offense or how sincere their apology, the cancel culture mob blinks for no one.

What an honor to serve the God who turns ashes into beauty and graves into gardens. He has never cancelled a sincere seeker or repentant sinner, and he never will. His victory over death establishes the foundation for our hope. Hope that nothing in our past can prevent us from reaching our purpose on the planet.

Our Redeemer God makes *all things new.* And that's a message the cancel culture desperately needs to hear.

Innocence Stolen

Let the children come to me; do not hinder them, for to such belongs the kingdom of God. —Mark 10:14

As I looked over the peaches in the fruit and vegetable aisle at my local grocery store, he approached me. He appeared to be around ten, maybe twelve years old. "Ma'am, could you please give me a dollar? I need it for the checkout."

I guess a part of me didn't want to be included in a skeptical world, so I followed my inclination and got out my wallet. But as I pulled out the dollar bill, I asked, "Is this really legit?"

Of course, he assured me it was as he thanked me and took off with the money. Immediately, another young boy came running by. I saw him catch up with the first boy and together they ran out the back exit.

I'd been played.

It bothered me. Not so much losing the dollar or being suckered, but I hated the idea of contributing to his deceptive success. How does a young kid learn to be so bold and brazen? I couldn't help but wonder what he told himself in order to justify his behavior. And I thought, *When was his innocence stolen?*

And when was the innocence stolen of the little girls exploited in Netflix's 2020 release of *Cuties?* Although dubbed a "coming-of-age" film, the movie depicts highly sexualized eleven-year-olds participating in a "twerking" contest. The IMBD warns parents of erotic dance scenes including one where a girl fully displays her bare breast. The law has a word for that: pedophilia. Yet Netflix prospers.

Jesus loves children. He had pretty harsh words for people who lead them astray. In fact, all three synoptic gospels record his warning

(Matthew 18:6; Luke 17:2; Mark 9:42). But without a clear moral grounding, children will go astray. They'll think it's okay to do whatever they can get away with, whether stealing from old ladies in the grocery store or prancing half-naked in front of peering eyes.

If there are children in your life, why not take every opportunity to shine your light by telling them about a God who loves them. You may not think it seems like much, but let's do all we can to keep their innocence from being stolen.

The Emperor Has No Clothes

Blessed is the one who listens to me,
watching daily at my gates,
waiting beside my doors.
For whoever finds me finds life
and obtains favor from the LORD,
but he who fails to find me injures himself;
all who hate me love death. —Proverbs 8:34–36

Wisdom.

I might get into trouble here, but it seems like our culture is producing more foolish-followers than wisdom-seekers. Time-tested wisdom is being replaced with the latest fad or fashionable thought. We're living in a world where sensitivity supersedes science and feelings trump truth. Cheap substitutes parade as the real deal. It's like *The Emperor Has No Clothes* on steroids.

What ever happened to wisdom?

Scripture tells us the "fear of the LORD is the beginning of wisdom" (Proverbs 9:10). Having a fear of God means we recognize something greater exists than our limited perceptions. It reveals an attitude of humbleness. As Proverbs 11:2 says, "with the humble is wisdom."

The man whose name is synonymous with wisdom knew this.

When Solomon was inaugurated as king of Israel, God asked him what he wanted. Solomon's response revealed his deep humility: "I am but a little child. I do not know how to go out or come in. Give your servant therefore an understanding mind to govern your people, that I may discern between good and evil, for who is able to govern this your great people?" (1 Kings 3:7, 9). Solomon realized his responsibilities called for wisdom far above his pay grade, consequently he (wisely) asked God for help.

God loved his humble request and granted him not only wisdom to a greater extent than anyone had ever known, but also honor and wealth.

So, if humility is a prerequisite to wisdom, it may explain why it's become such a scarce commodity. Pride, self-reliance, and one-upmanship dominate our culture. In this age of virtue signaling, not too many folks are signaling the virtue of humility. No wonder we're becoming a foolish people. Why seek wisdom when we think we already know it all?

But take heart. We don't have to join the foolish-followers crowd. Let's humble ourselves and ask for God's guidance. Blessing awaits those who seek wisdom. So does God's favor. Let's not be afraid to shine light on *naked emperors.*

Salty Light Bearers (Part 1): Life Preservers

You are the salt of the earth, but if salt has lost its taste, how shall its saltiness be restored? It is no longer good for anything except to be thrown out and trampled under people's feet. —Matthew 5:13

Do you know if you believe in Jesus, you are a "little Christ"? You have the honor of reflecting him to the world. Jesus describes you as the "salt of the earth." And salt consists of specific qualities.

Salt is a preserver. No one in the first century had freezers, so if you wanted to keep meat from rotting, you had to cure it with salt. Salt also symbolized preserving a promise. If two parties entered into an agreement, they would eat salt together in the presence of witnesses, and that act would bind their contract. From preserving agreements to preserving the culture, the call Jesus gives to be the salt of the earth remains as relevant today as in the past.

The church has always had a preserving influence in American culture. Christianity recognized man's fallen nature and influenced the idea of checks and balances in the constitution. Christianity helped civilize an early frontier fraught with lawlessness.

It was the Quakers who started the first abolition of slavery movement in the United States. And why wouldn't it be Christians who addressed the issue of slavery? Christianity is the most anti-racist religion on the planet. We know how God feels about racial, ethnic divisions. When Peter displayed his feelings of Jewish superiority over the Gentiles, Paul called him out on it because it was *inconsistent* with Christianity (Galatians 2:11–14). He wasn't about to watch Peter lose his saltiness and subsequently risk his own salty call.

Nothing will cause us Christians to lose our saltiness more than failing to stand up for truth. Breakpoint's John Stonestreet points out that the reason Christians must engage in culture-wide conversations is because much of the culture's viewpoint is based on a lie about the human person. If cultural pressures cause believers to be silent on basic issues, why would we be trusted to tell the truth about God?

So, don't let your salt lose its taste. Be that little Christ the world needs to see.

Salty Light Bearers (Part 2): Bring on the Taste!

You are the salt of the earth, but if salt has lost its taste, how shall its saltiness be restored? It is no longer good for anything except to be thrown out and trampled under people's feet. —Matthew 5:13

Salt serves as a preserver. But when Jesus calls us the salt of the earth, he's referring to more than using us to stave off a rotting culture. Salt also provides enhancement.

This saline substance is unique in its ability to enhance taste by intensifying certain flavors and decreasing others. Eating a chocolate salted caramel the other day, I thought, *Who in the world would have thought to put caramel and salt together and have it come out so delicious?* (By the way, I found out the man who invented that combination was Henri Le Roux, a French candymaker!)

Jesus created us to bring taste out of an increasingly tasteless world. So, what does that look like?

One person remarked that it looks like the best babysitters, who clean the dishes before the parents arrive home and leave the place better than they found it. Empowered by the Holy Spirit, salty Christians make the world better.

Countless footprints from all walks of life reflect this. Christians founded all but one of the Ivy League universities. And numerous Christian organizations today serve on the front lines of bringing education to children in third world countries. Christian benefactors founded the first hospital, and thousands of hospitals all over the world bear names including the word "Saint," pointing to their Christian beginnings. Rembrandt made the world more beautiful with his painting. Michael Jr. enhances the world today with his clean, uproarious comedy.

Salt, when properly applied, does not make everything taste the same. It's enhancing virtue brings out the true flavor of every food it lands on. It makes eggs eggier, popcorn more popcornish, steaks steakier.

When we use our gifts to enhance the world, we also stimulate the salt in our fellow image bearers. And the world exponentially becomes a more enjoyable place to live. So, let's do it. Let's bring on the taste!

God's Megaphones

Therefore, we are ambassadors for Christ, God making his appeal through us. We implore you on behalf of Christ, be reconciled to God.
—2 Corinthians 5:20

How we see ourselves affects our influence in the world. Do we view ourselves as someone through whom God makes his appeal? As envoys sent by God to represent him? As those who have access to *his Spirit* to accomplish his work? The importance of what we believe about ourselves can't be overestimated.

We have more opportunities to let him "make his appeal" through us than we think. He uses each of us differently. For example, when the Philadelphia Eagles won their first Super Bowl in 2018, many on the team were outspoken in their praise to God for bringing them to that point. Their victory provided a giant megaphone through which they could make their appeal by giving him the glory for their success. Other megaphones might not be quite that big, but whenever we quietly tell someone what God has done in our lives, we become ambassadors making his appeal. Don't let the size of the megaphone deter you.

Scripture clearly states we are ambassadors. God has called us to speak for him. He desires to make his case to an unbelieving world through us. He wants us to warn people about the consequences of not being reconciled to their Maker. Believers comprise his Plan A, Plan B, Plan C . . . you get the picture. The Church is God's means of bringing people to himself.

We amplify the voice of God every time we bring faith into our situations. I recently heard a speaker say our problem is not in what we're doing but in what we're believing. When I enter my classrooms, do I believe I am there to speak for God even though I'm evaluating speeches? When I go to my small group or the grocery store or the hairdresser do I believe the Hope of Glory walks in the door with me?

Faith-infused actions help other people hear God. We don't have to win a Super Bowl or preach on a street corner to be God's ambassador. We simply have to do what he calls us to do in faith. That faith paves the way for him to make his appeal through us and to impact the culture.

So, how about you? Are you using your megaphone for God?

Divine Setups

For I tell you, unless your righteousness exceeds that of the scribes and Pharisees, you will never enter the kingdom of heaven. —Matthew 5:20

Have you experienced divine setups by God?

You're in the middle of telling someone to forgive, and out of nowhere the name of a person you have a grudge against comes to mind. Or you're trying to teach a child to be patient and realize you're losing patience because he's not getting it. Divine setups sometimes appear like *inconvenient truths.*

The other day I was in the city, writing from my favorite coffee shop about how important it is to be generous in shining the light of Jesus. As I sat there drinking my overpriced coffee and eating my delicious lemon blueberry scone, my thoughts went to people who didn't have that same opportunity. Slowly, I began to sense the Holy Spirit convicting me. Go to the counter, buy some muffins, and give them away to people you pass on the street.

So with a bit of fear and trepidation, I bought the muffins and set out on my mission. The first person I encountered was a man with a young boy. Thinking the child would like sweets, I asked if they wanted a muffin. The man responded, "What I would like is for you to go back from where you came from!" Agitated, he said he wanted his land back. Not quite the response I was expecting, I replied, "I'm sorry, Sir. All I have are these muffins."

The next person I offered one of my muffins to also refused. So did two more people. But undeterred, I persisted until my box was empty. I prayed God would somehow use my smile and meager offering to make someone's day brighter.

In spite of the somewhat rough beginning, I knew God had challenged me to put my words into action. *You want to grow in generosity? Here's your chance.* He set me up to live out the words I was writing.

The sin of the Pharisees was that they did not practice what they preached. They told others what to do but refused to follow their own directives. And in so doing, they became blind guides. So, the next time the Holy Spirit lets your words convict you, don't hesitate to respond. Thank him for the divine setup and let the culture experience your light.

Dumbed-down Devotion

You should have struck five or six times; then you would have struck down Syria until you had made an end of it, but now you will strike down Syria only three times. —2 Kings 13:19

Beware of the mediocrity infecting our culture.

A new trend in public education is to "dumb down" curriculum in an attempt to be "fair" to all children. Some schools are ditching admission tests to gifted programs and others are dropping advanced programs altogether. Although well-intentioned, many have observed that kids will pay a steep price for being taught that competition and hard work doesn't pay. Welcome to the world of mediocrity.

It's not a world where Christians fit.

As believers, we understand the value of wholeheartedness. Jesus said the greatest commandment is to love the Lord with *all* our heart, *all* our soul and *all* our mind (Matthew 22:37). He calls us to hold nothing back. When we repent, we repent without excuse. When we succeed, we praise him fully for our success. Scripture exhorts us to work diligently, pray fervently, and give liberally. There's nothing mediocre about the Christian life.

Moreover, mediocrity invites disaster.

Israel's penchant for half-heartedness resulted in an ongoing weakening of their power and status as a country. In the thirteenth chapter of 2 Kings, Israel's King Jehoahaz finally acknowledged the nation's sin of compromise and asked God to rescue them from Syria's oppression. But their repentance of worshipping other gods was incomplete, and it resulted in partial victory. Mediocre repentance = mediocre restoration.

After Jehoash succeeded his father as king, that same spirit of mediocrity surfaced. The prophet Elisha instructed Jehoash to take some arrows and strike the ground. After three strikes, Jehoash stopped. His lack of zeal incensed Elisha. If Jehoash didn't have enough passion to fully carry out his simple command, how could he stir up enough to overcome Syria's army?

Mediocrity results in a loss of satisfaction as well as victory. The greater our devotion to Christ—no matter what anyone else is doing—the greater our contentment. Scripture exhorts us to strive toward the *high* calling, not the one in the middle.

So let's not dumb down our devotion to the Lord. Let's resist living in a mediocre world and let our light reflect wholehearted commitment to God in *all* we do. It's a "fair" response to the God who spared nothing on our behalf.

Hahahaha!

A joyful heart is good medicine,
but a crushed spirit dries up the bones. —Proverbs 17:22

I inherited a distinctive trait from my Grandma Creech (besides making good piecrusts). Sometimes she laughed so hard when something struck her funny bone that she couldn't squeeze out even one coherent word. Half the time we didn't know why she was laughing, but laughter, as you know, is contagious. So, we all joined in the guffaws and giggles.

We recently visited my brother and his family in Ohio, and I experienced a couple of those laughing jags. My brother started telling a litany of Dad jokes. And by the time he got to "What do you call somebody with no nose and no body?" "Nobody knows!" I was a goner. Every time I tried to say something, belly laughs sabotaged my words. By this time, all my brother had to do was start to snicker, and we were laughing ourselves into silliness.

Did that ever feel good.

Scripture tells us a joyful heart is good medicine. And numerous studies over the years have affirmed the emotional as well as physical benefits of a hearty laugh. Yet many believe comedy in today's culture has hit an all-time low. Comedians aren't as funny or creative as they once were. Crude jokes and bitter sarcasm have replaced the kind of humor that helps us find commonality in the absurdities of life.

I believe a culture that loses its ability to laugh will soon have nothing to laugh about.

I'm certainly not denying the sadness and grief we experience. For some, each day is a reminder of how unfair and disappointing life can be. But when we allow ourselves to dwell on all the negativity, it's like refusing the cure that could keep our bones from drying up.

Put simply, laughter is what makes life beautiful. Today I want to encourage you to embrace, as comedian Michael, Jr. would say, the *funny*. Let God's gift of laughter release you, refresh you, and invite you into new perspectives on life. Laugh so hard you can't talk. Laugh so hard you wet your pants. Laugh and let your joy lighten the load of everyone around you. Our culture is filled with people who are "crushed in spirit." Let's offer them some good medicine.

Shine Christian Shine

In the same way, let your light shine before others, so that they may see your good works and give glory to your Father who is in heaven. — Matthew 5:16

How's your light?

All those who know Christ have living within them an electromagnetic source of energy that disperses darkness, creates warmth, and reflects the source of life. Believers carry the light of God. And that light is meant to shine.

Scripture clearly shows us how to shine that light—by *doing works* of such *good report* that others *will see* and think well of Christianity. It's been said when we get to heaven the Lord will not say, "well-thought, or well-planned, good and faithful servant," but "well done." Shining the light of Christ means doing something. Something with purpose. We shine the light so those who see our good works may be brought to *glorify our Father who is in heaven*.

If we want other people to see God, the best thing we can do is turn on the light switch.

But just as different wavelengths in the light spectrum produce different colors, so each of us possess different gifts, positions, and opportunities in which to shine his light. It doesn't matter whether we have a big splashy gift or a subdued ordinary one. God expects us to use whatever he has given us, not hide it under a basket. He gifted us differently because the world needs to see the whole spectrum of the rainbow.

Satan tries to deflect the light, making us think what we have to offer has little to no significance. He wants us to emulate the steward who hid his talent, and we know how that turned out (Matthew 25:18–28). Who wants to someday stand before the Lord and hear him ask: "Why didn't you use your gift of boldness to stand up against that bully?" "Why didn't you use that gift of generosity to help a neighbor who had less than you?" "Why didn't you use that gift of intelligence to direct your co-worker to the logic of the gospel?"

I close the end of each of my college classes with the admonition from Matthew 5:16. I hope to charge up that electromagnetic energy in each of my students. And I pray as you read this that you, too, will be encouraged to let your light shine—wherever you are and in whatever you're doing.

CHAPTER SIXTEEN

We Shine the Extraordinary into the Mundane

"Your greatest regret at the end of your life will be the lions you didn't chase. You will regret the risks not taken, the opportunities not seized, and the dreams not pursued. Stop running away from what scares you most and start chasing the God-ordained opportunities that cross your path."

Mark Batterson
—In a Pit with a Lion on a Snowy Day

Nothing about the Christian life emanates boredom. God purposes us to be filled with wonder. Each day offers new opportunities for ordinary living to be transformed into something extraordinary. God invites us to take risks, dare to adventure, and discover a life more fulfilling than we could ever imagine. As we seek him and open ourselves up to ways higher than ours, we find an avenue not only to personal growth, but a place where miracles can happen. A place that reflects the power of God to a dry, skeptical world.

Risky Business

But as it is, they desire a better country, that is, a heavenly one. There-fore, God is not ashamed to be called their God, for he has prepared for them a city. —Hebrews 11:16

Do you think of yourself as a risk-taker?

Some risks are relatively harmless. One time my husband pursued aerial photography. He would rent a plane and while I tried to keep us from nose-diving, he would lean out the cockpit and snap pictures of properties. But when we tried to sell the photos to the property owners, we found out they all happened to be photographers, pilots, or had rel-atives who were. Thankfully, God shut down that risk before we literally crashed and burned.

Other risks require great courage. Eric Metaxas, in his book, *If You Can Keep It,* chronicles the tremendous risk-taking of America's found-ing fathers.[31] Nathan Hale, who was captured by the British and hung for being a spy, is most famously known for his dying words, "I regret that I have but one life to give for my country." Paul Revere risked riding like a madman through the colonies to warn his countrymen the British were coming. All the signers of the Declaration of Independence realized when they placed their signature on that document, they were signing their death warrants if the war didn't go their way. Yet they risked for something greater than themselves.

I know of an even better country born from risk.

The Bible presents a litany of risk-takers: Noah and the ark, Moses and the Exodus, Rahab and the spies. There's Peter, Paul, Stephen. Can we even have faith without a mindset of taking risks? Hebrews 11 paints a pretty clear picture of those heroes of our faith who were not afraid to lose one thing in order to gain something better. They refused to tie themselves to their reputations, comfort, or security; and they invite all believers who come after them to imitate their brave hearts.

We will never know (this side of eternity) what our lives may have been like if we had taken more risks in order to follow God's call. But we can, as did those who have gone before us, lay it all on the line in order to obtain a better country. A country where God will not be ashamed to have taken the risk to be called our God.

Ready for Adventure?

I came that they may have life and have it abundantly. —John 10:10

One morning I woke up with the word *adventure* on my mind. Since I was alone in a somewhat secluded setting by the woods for a few days of writing, it didn't seem like the optimum place for anything I would deem adventurous. I didn't even have a car!

While in the middle of my morning devotions, I heard the thunder roll. Sure enough, raindrops were beginning to fall. This was disappointing because every day I like to walk a couple miles and pray. Now here I sat—stuck—without raincoat or umbrella. So, I asked Jesus if maybe he would push the rain back for a while. I can't say I prayed with a lot of faith, but by the time I finished getting dressed, the rain had completely stopped! As I walked out the driveway, gratitude overwhelmed me. *Yes, Lord, let the adventure begin!*

I believe God intends our lives to be packed with adventure. Not necessarily the Indiana Jones kind, but the kind we can experience whether we're the richest person in America or the poorest in Sudan. Jesus said he came to give us not only life, but *abundant life.* We experience that abundance every time we open ourselves up to the leading of the Holy Spirit. It involves risk, maybe sacrifice, and a little bit of faith. And it manifests itself in more ways than we can imagine.

Adventures can be big or small. When my friend, Mary Holland, was in her early thirties, she left America to marry a man in Jamaica who ran a home for street boys. She became a wife, foreigner, and mother to ten little boys in one day! And if you think prayer can't be one of the most exciting adventures in life, you probably haven't read Mark Batterson's *The Circle Maker.*

Jesus says there's only one thing that can hold us back from this great adventure. To find the abundant life, we have to let go of the old one. The predictable, safe, we-gotta-be-in-control one. Don't you dare miss out.

So, why not tell God you're ready for an adventure?

With Intention

And when the soles of the feet of the priests bearing the ark of the LORD, the Lord of all the earth, shall rest in the waters of the Jordan, the waters of the Jordan shall be cut off from flowing, and the waters coming down from above shall stand in one heap. —Joshua 3:13

Most miracles don't just happen. God seems to like our involvement in carrying out his purposes.

When the Israelites reached the edge of Canaan, they faced an insurmountable body of water—the Jordan River. If the wandering-weary nation hoped to gain God's promise, they needed a miracle. The all-powerful God could have parted those waters without their help, but instead he gave them the opportunity to be an integral part of his plan. He directed the priests to walk right into the flood-stage waters with the ark. As they did, the surging flood would stop flowing, and the people could cross on dry land.

Before the miracle occurred, the priests first had to move with intention.

I remember a story Corrie ten Boom told after her release from the Ravensburg concentration camp in WWII. She was speaking in churches throughout Europe about God's forgiveness. One night at the end of a service, a man came up to her. Immediately, she recognized him. He had been one of the cruelest guards at the prison. As he extended his hand to her, explaining how he had become a believer, he asked for her forgiveness. She froze, paralyzed with pain from the past. Unable to feel anything but contempt for this man, she silently cried out to God. He told her to reach out and grab her former torturer's hand.

And as she took that one step—right into the waters of bitterness, pain, and grief—the floodwaters of unforgiveness receded, replaced with the swell of God's love. A miracle no less profound than when Israel crossed the Jordan occurred in that moment.[32]

But before the miracle occurred, Corrie first had to move with intention.

I believe we miss many of God's miracles because we fail to do our part. God says do something, and we don't because we don't *see* how we could make a difference. *The Jordan River is too high, Lord!* We choose to live in the dry land of unbelief rather than praise God with intention for what we don't yet see.

So, when God directs you to put your foot in the water or extend your hand, don't hesitate. A miracle might be in the making.

To the Glades!

You make known to me the path of life;
*   in your presence there is fullness of joy;*
*   at your right hand are pleasures forevermore.* —Psalm 16:11

The first thing I learned when I went to graduate school at the University of Colorado could be summed up in four words: Learn. How. To. Ski. I'm not kidding! My initial meeting with the chair of the Speech Pathology department culminated with listening to him discuss the wonders of Colorado skiing. I grew up in southern Ohio where the greatest outdoor winter sport consisted of hopping on our sleds for a fifteen second run down the hill. So, I was hooked. His enthusiasm impressed me so much, that I went straight to a ski shop after our meeting and bought skis, boots, and long johns. Grad school infused with swishing down the slopes—what a great way to get a degree!

But when Chip and I moved back East, I parked my Rossignols in the attic. Then a few years later, some of our friends picked up the sport and invited us to join them. Every winter we pooled our money and rented a chalet at Holiday Valley in western New York. Over the years we developed some catch phrases like *sad but somewhat amusing* when one of us face-planted in the snow. One of the most memorable phrases was *to the glades*!

It meant we were headed toward the forest. Off the groomed slopes, the glades offered us the opportunity to make our own trails as we traversed through the evergreens. It was exhilarating, daring, and beautiful. *To the glades* reminds me how exciting it can be to occasionally take a step off the well-worn path. To shake off the predictable patterns and embrace a new twist or turn in the day.

I think sometimes God loves to interrupt our secure boundaries and call us *to the glades*. David, in Psalm 16, writes about the delightful inheritance he has in the Lord. He knows eternal pleasures lie ahead, and such assurance gives him the freedom to explore the path of life with gusto. As long as he keeps his eyes on the Lord, he will not be shaken.

How about you? Do you hear the Lord calling you *to the glades*? Don't be afraid of a little bit of adventure. It's a great way to get a degree . . . in life.

Posture Your Day

And remember the words of the Lord Jesus, how he himself said, "It is more blessed to give than to receive." —Acts 20:35

Do you ever think about how you posture yourself for the day? I whispered a quick prayer the other morning before I left for my meeting. *Lord, please change my mindset from going to get to going to give.* I prayed this even though I wasn't convinced I had anything to offer.

When I arrived, people were already connecting. I wasn't sure what to do, but then I spotted a young teenage boy sitting off by himself. I left the adults and went over to him and struck up a conversation. He seemed pleased that an adult other than his mother (who was busy talking to someone) noticed him. We chatted until the meeting began when a woman I barely know approached me and asked if I could give her a ride home. Interesting. I said, "Sure, but I have to stop at the hardware store on the way."

"No problem," she said, "I need to go to the hardware store, too!"

The meeting ended and we headed for the store. As we waited to check out, one of the cashiers motioned for me to come to her open register. Her nametag said *Rosa*. As she checked my items, Rosa and I got into a brief conversation. Then she made a comment about enjoying the day because we never know when it might be our last.

Without thinking, I asked, "Do you know where you're going if it is?" Immediately she said she didn't know, that she used to go to church, but had fallen away. I told her she could be sure through Jesus. That he loved her enough to have me there at that very moment to tell her. Then I assured her that I would be praying for her.

It had been quite a morning. I believe it was because I postured myself in prayer for God to help me be a giver instead of a taker. Jesus said it is more blessed to give than receive. It's a mindset he wants us to cultivate. But it's rare. In fact, if we go somewhere with the intention of giving more than getting, we'll probably be different from most everyone else in the room. And yet, I believe we'll leave the most satisfied.

So, how's your posture?

The Mystery of the Lost Giraffe

Can you find out the deep things of God?
Can you find out the limit of the Almighty? —Job 11:7

When our grandson turned four years old, he spent a week visiting us in Pennsylvania. Like all good grandmas, I told Tobin he could pick out one item for himself when we went to the grocery store. He chose a stuffed baby giraffe. But when he left for home at the end of the week, he realized the giraffe was not in his suitcase. I looked under couches, chairs, and beds, all to no avail. The little critter had vanished.

It appeared the mystery of the lost giraffe would remain unsolved. And it did, until the next time Tobin came for a visit. We got out all the old Tonka trucks and tractors he likes to play with. The next morning, when I went into the room where all the cars and bulldozers lay strewn across the floor, I spotted the lost giraffe! Evidently, Tobin had stuffed it in the eighteen-wheeler carrier and forgot about it. Mystery solved!

We all love to see mysteries solved, don't we? As humans, we want to figure out the *who, what, when, where, and how's* of life. Solomon said it's the glory of God to conceal a matter and the glory of kings to search it out (Proverbs 25:2).

But I'm afraid if we're not careful, our search for answers will squeeze out the sense of mystery. Mark Buchanan writes that the Christian faith is "based on staggering mysteries—the Trinity, the Incarnation, the Cross and Resurrection, the imparting of the Spirit."[33] Rather than embracing such mysteries, we become pragmatists. We start demanding answers from God before we're willing to trust him.

Job's friend, Zophar, challenged him to consider the unfathomable mysteries of God. Although Zophar got a lot of things wrong in his assessment of Job, he was right in pointing out the importance of not limiting a limitless God to our understanding. Some things will never be grasped in this lifetime. God is infinite. We are not.

Buchannan believes the "de-mysterious-ization" of Scripture stifles our imagination. It causes us to view Christianity as a methodical duty to be obeyed rather than an ongoing adventure to be discovered.

So, although we might lose stuffed giraffes, let's not lose life's wonder. Look for the extraordinary in the ordinary.

What Are You Looking For?

You have said, "Seek my face."
My heart says to you, "Your face, LORD, do I seek." —Psalm 27:8

"One of the reasons I'm a Christian is because of all the miracles I see God doing in my life," explained one of my students. He described a series of situations, like when he received a needed amount of money at just the right time and of running into someone right after praying he would see him on campus.

One of his friends responded that he had never seen a miracle. So, my student asked his friend about the Dodge Charger he was looking to buy. His friend said, "It's amazing. Everywhere I look, I see Dodge Chargers. I never saw them before." My student wisely pointed out how maybe recognizing miracles was similar to his search for a car. He didn't see any miracles because he wasn't looking.

I agree with my student. More often than not, I think we miss God's miracles in our lives because we're not looking for them. We may believe in miracles like the virgin birth and the resurrection, but when it comes to our everyday lives, we write them off. Maybe we think God has more important things to do than help us pay bills, find a parking spot, or think of a creative idea for dinner guests. And, of course, he does, but to characterize such incidents as "luck" or "coincidence" robs us of the intimacy God desires to have with us.

So what are we looking for?

Are we viewing our circumstances as the product of natural events? Or do we see life as ripe for supernatural intervention because a supernatural God is looking out for us? The importance of seeking God in everyday life can't be overstated. He promises if we seek him with all our heart, we will find him (Jeremiah 29:13).

Let's follow David's example. When God told him to look for him, David responded wholeheartedly, "Your face, LORD, do I seek!" He looked for him in every aspect of his life, and it made him a man after God's heart.

God wants us to recognize him in all the intricacies of our lives. And discovering him is far greater than a Dodge Charger. So don't miss it.

Look for him!

Blustery Days

The wind blows where it wishes, and you hear its sound, but you do not know where it comes from or where it goes. So it is with everyone who is born of the Spirit. —John 3:8

As I looked out my window, I watched the tops of the trees dance like winsome marionettes. The wind howled, causing weak limbs to fall and loose leaves to flutter in its autumn gust. In the words of Winnie the Pooh, it was a "rather blustery day."

Since our property has a fair number of trees, blustery days can be inconvenient. They usually mean more work. Fallen branches have to be picked up. Sometimes the winds down power lines. And blustery days definitely mess up my hair.

In spite of the somewhat reckless nature of blustery days, they stir up my sense of adventure. Jesus compared the Holy Spirit to the wind. Unpredictable. Intriguing. Powerful. He says that's what lives in everyone who knows him. Pretty amazing if you think about it. The Holy Spirit—the third person of the Trinity—is born inside every believer! It makes who we are and what we do incomprehensibly significant.

Os Guinness, in his book, *Carpe Diem Redeemed*, writes, "Under the twin truths of God's sovereignty and human significance, time and history are going somewhere and each of us is not only unique and significant in ourselves, but we have a unique and significant part to play in our own lives in our own generation, and therefore in the overall sweep of history."[34]

Do you believe that?

I think a world of people drowning with feelings of insignificance, could use a few blustery days. Days when the Holy Spirit rushes in to dispose of a few dead limbs of empty philosophy and rotting fruit. Days reminding us of a force so incredible that it can sweep away the guilt of our past and kindle hope for new seasons.

Let's not resist the gales of the Holy Spirit. Let's not be afraid of those blustery days. There is One who knows where the wind blows.

One who wants us to help him write history. Open your heart to his prevailing winds.

Baby Power!

For you formed my inward parts;
you knitted me together in my mother's womb.
I praise you, for I am fearfully and wonderfully made.
Wonderful are your works;
my soul knows it very well. —Psalm 139:13–14

I felt like my heart was bursting. I could barely catch my breath when I broke out into uncontrollable sobs. But they were happy sobs. My sweet daughter-in-law said, "We can always count on you for a reaction!"

The calendar our kids create each year highlights one of my favorite Christmas gifts. Each month of the upcoming year features various pictures of the family. My daughter also marks our birthdays and anniversaries with smaller pictures on the specific dates. I was already lost in a daze of heartwarming memories when I got to August. I carefully examined each photo before my eyes moved to the dates. And what I saw ignited the near heart attack. A small picture of an ultrasound with the words "Baby Toews Due Date" graced August 4. A napalm bomb of joy suddenly exploded. Our son and his wife were having a baby.

Don't tell me the smallest among us have no significance. Far from being a mundane "glob of tissue," those little guys have the power to turn our worlds upside down! Babies are truly extraordinary.

The psalmist writes that life begins the moment God starts knitting us together in our mother's womb. He declares our Creator has written all our days before we even take our first breath. Every single one of us is a masterpiece of his creativity, designed to carry out a fearful, wonderful purpose.

A truth never to be taken lightly.

When my mother-in-law was pregnant with my husband, the doctor told her she should abort the baby. He said she might die from complications if she continued the pregnancy. But when she went to her father for advice, he responded, "Don't abort this child. God has a purpose for him." A few months later, she safely delivered a healthy baby boy. God's plan was not thwarted, and his purpose is continuing to be realized.

I think every time a baby is born, the birth should be accompanied by clashing cymbals, drum rolls, trumpets, and violins. The entrance of every new human being on the planet ushers in cause for celebration. It's magnificent, splendid, momentous, extraordinary.

It's *Baby Power!*

Every Hour of Every Day

Having said these things, he spit on the ground and made mud with the saliva. Then he anointed the man's eyes with the mud and said to him, "Go, wash in the pool of Siloam" (which means Sent). So he went and washed and came back seeing. —John 9:6–7

I remember when Peter Teague, the former president of the college where I teach, exhorted the students to persevere in their work and make the most of every opportunity. He said the time of preparation they are presently experiencing stands just as important as their end goal. I couldn't agree more. It's easy to get so focused on where we're going that we miss where we are. We forget every minute has the potential to become an earth-shaking, life-changing, awe-filled moment.

I wonder if there was ever a time in Jesus' life when he lacked this awareness. Whether he was teaching the crowds or training his disciples, it seems he never missed an opportunity to infuse life into his situations.

The man born blind described in John 9 certainly demonstrates this. Jesus was walking along with his disciples when they encountered him on the side of the road. He didn't cry out to Jesus for healing. He didn't even know who Jesus was. The disciples seized the opportunity to initiate a theological discussion on whether the man's or his parents' sin caused his blindness. They could have passed him by and left him alone to linger in his darkness. But Jesus took an ordinary minute of an ordinary day to turn ordinary dirt into a healing balm that displayed the glory of God. Light penetrated darkness Just. Like. That.

I can't help but wonder how many miracles I might be missing because I don't consider the vast potential in every hour of every day. Missionary Frank Laubach once remarked that his goal was to see if he could turn his thoughts to God even one second for every minute of the day. Not such an outlandish goal when we think of how Scripture encourages us to "pray without ceasing" (1 Thessalonians 5:17).

God wants to fill our days with his presence. And to make the most out of every hour of every day. So, let's not waste another minute. Whether we're waiting in line at Walmart, driving to our next appointment, or having coffee with a friend, let's heighten our awareness in seeking God. You never know when an ordinary moment might be transformed into something extraordinary.

CHAPTER SEVENTEEN

We Shine Comfort into Disappointment

"The road to the best things is not through the good things but through the hard things.'

Tim Keller
—Hope in Times of Fear

Adam and Eve's fall assured us we would experience one undeniable aspect of life: disappointment. Disappointment visits us in relatively minor issues as well as in situations that rip out the very threads of our security. Although God does not shield us from disappointment, he promises to use the "hard things" to bring about the "best things," as Tim Keller notes. God has a way of using the most discouraging of situations to teach us invaluable lessons about having expectations, about waiting and trusting, about knowing firsthand how it feels to be comforted by a Redeemer's love. It's a comfort we can't help but want to share with fellow travelers as they encounter this all too familiar common bond.

A Teachable Moment

Little children, keep yourselves from idols. —1 John 5:21

Have you ever noticed how disappointments can take on lives of their own? I think of young women I've counseled who have had bad breakups with their boyfriends. Their disappointment pushes them into a kind of fantasy land. The more they dwell on the relationship loss, the more exaggerated the good qualities of the ex-boyfriend become until the guy they imagine bears little resemblance to reality.

But disappointments like this are not reserved for relationships only. My recent plans to spend a few days alone with God to write, study, and pray fell through when the cottage where I planned to stay became unavailable. At first, the disappointment felt overwhelming. I had written the greater portion of both my books there and experienced the sweet presence of the Lord in almost palpable ways. How could it be his will for me not to go back?

While praying, I read from Oswald Chambers, "If we try to re-introduce the rare moments of inspiration, it is a sign that it is not God we want. We are making a fetish of the moments when God did come and speak and insisting that He must do it again; whereas what God wants us to do is to live by faith."[35] I had to ask myself if I wanted to be where God was or where I *wanted* him to be. I had planned to go away to spend time with him, but if he was closing the door, then why would I still want to go? The last thing I desired was to corrupt my time at Lakeside by turning it into an idol.

So, I let go. It was a teachable moment.

The Israelites were condemned for their idolatry. They gave human characteristics to images of wood and stone. In one of the last writings of the apostle John, he warned believers to keep themselves from idols. He knew our human tendency was to corrupt the good gifts of God by infusing them with our own imaginations.

If your disappointments are paralyzing you from moving forward, stop giving them life they were never intended to have. Ask Jesus to help you resist the lure of idolatry and embrace the comfort he wants to give you. Then trust him and, as Chambers says, "live by faith." What he has for us is far better than anything we can imagine.

Better Than a Cave in Crete

Thus says the LORD:
"Cursed is the man who trusts in man
and makes flesh his strength,
whose heart turns away from the LORD." —Jeremiah 17:5

Has someone let you down? Rejected you? Falsely accused you? Unless you've opted for living in an isolated cave in Crete, you know what it's like to be disappointed by other people. Seems to be one of the marks of a fallen world. People hurt us and as much as we try not to, we hurt other people. What was God thinking when he made us capable of inflicting so much pain on one another?

Novelist Irving Stone said that without pain, there is no love. God created us to experience the ecstasy of life but when sin entered, we became acquainted with the agony part. So, how do we respond when people we love disappoint us?

Jeremiah told the Israelites those who trusted in man were cursed. But isn't trust the foundation of any meaningful relationship? Don't we usually trust people we love? The problem lies in *how* we trust. The "trust in man" Jeremiah refers to is trust that draws its strength more from people than from God. When we trust even the "sweetest frame" more than Jesus, we set ourselves up for disappointment. And the pain of our disillusionment drags us away from the only One worthy of our full trust.

No one loved people more than Jesus. "But Jesus didn't trust them, because he knew human nature" (John 2:24, NLT). When those most dear to him dropped the ball and deserted him in his hour of greatest need, he didn't go into a corner and have a pity party. He continued to love them because he didn't have an unrealistic expectation of who they were in the first place.

Being disappointed in other people's behavior is unavoidable. But reacting to the hurt by withholding our love from them is not. When we trust the Lord to turn even our most bitter disappointments into something good in us, the pain will fade and what really matters will remain.

Yes, God knew what he was doing when he made us. He created us to engage with each other—and in the process learn how to love like he does. It's a far better option than living alone in a cave in Crete.

The Comforter

Blessed be the God and Father of our Lord Jesus Christ, the Father of mercies and God of all comfort, who comforts us in all our affliction, so that we may be able to comfort those who are in any affliction, with the comfort with which we ourselves are comforted by God. —2 Corinthians 1:3-4

Up until the sixth grade all the elementary children in my school were divided into homerooms alphabetically. My last name being *Creech*, I'd become quite comfortable with all the kids who shared my distinction of being in the first part of the alphabet. In sixth grade we landed in Miss Jackson's room. If there had been a lottery in those days, we would have felt we won it. Everyone loved Miss Jackson. She was most known for reading *Little House on the Prairie* books to her classes. She made school fun and exciting.

About midway through the first semester, the school decided to create a new class for kids with higher grades. One other student and I from Miss Jackson's class made the cut and were pulled out of Laura Ingalls Wilder bliss and thrust into a classroom of strangers. I cried unabashedly in front of my classmates, but the policy was nonnegotiable. My only comfort came through sympathetic friends who watched as I was drug away to the "A" class. It felt like the end of the world in my twelve-year-old mind.

We live in a fallen world, one where comfort is as much a necessity in life as a warm blanket on cold nights. A young mother miscarries her longed-for baby. A spouse receives a diagnosis of Alzheimer's. A company downsizes and you, along with your job, are squeezed out. What do we do in times like these where neither tears nor prayers can reverse the outcome?

We ask the Comforter to come.

He promises his presence will ease our grief and lighten our burden. Because he is the Father of compassion and God of all comfort, he is able to blunt the edge of our disappointment. He will comfort us in *all* our troubles, and I think *all* means every single one. From the relatively minor disappointments like leaving Miss Jackson to those that seem inconsolable.

We are not promised we'll be given understanding of *why* life happens the way it does. But one thing we can always count on—the Comforter will come.

Irreversible?

She said to them, "Do not call me Naomi; call me Mara, for the Almighty has dealt very bitterly with me. I went away full, and the LORD has brought me back empty." —Ruth 1:20–21

Ever feel like circumstances you face are irreversible? Think there's no way the breakthrough you long for is going to happen? You realize your faith is falling far below what it takes for a miracle. It's halftime and your team is down by double digits.

We humans face a perpetual problem of seemingly irreversible circumstances. Take the story of Ruth. If anyone had reason to be sucked into the quicksand of hopelessness, it was Ruth's mother-in-law, Naomi. Forced to leave her homeland with her husband and two sons, she faced the option of either staying in Israel and starving to death or traveling to a foreign country. But her bad situation got worse.

After a number of years in Moab, her beloved husband died. And then, the unthinkable happened. Both sons followed their father in death, leaving Naomi alone with her two Moabite daughters-in-law. When she decides to return to Israel, her one daughter-in-law, Ruth, insists on going with her.

So, the two enter Israel poor, broken, and helpless. Naomi's heart is filled with so much bitterness, she directs people to call her Mara (meaning bitter). Her circumstance has emptied her of all hope. Any prospect of leaving a legacy vanished in the Moabite desert. Naomi's desolation appeared irreversible.

But nothing is irreversible when it comes to the God with whom all things are possible (Mark 10:27). Naomi's kinsman marries Ruth, and Ruth gives birth to a son who becomes the forefather of King David, the ancestor of Jesus. Talk about a reversal!

So, to you, concerned about the poor decisions your daughter is making—her situation is not irreversible.

To you watching your son walk away from his faith—his situation is not irreversible.

To you witnessing your friends throw away their marriage—their situation is not irreversible. And to any of you facing what appears irreparably hopeless—your situation is not irreversible.

Look to God. Take comfort in knowing what he has done in the past. And watch him fill your emptiness. "Blessed be the LORD, who has not left you this day without a redeemer" (Ruth 4:14).

Satan's Victory Song

We sent Timothy, our brother and Gods coworker in the gospel of Christ, to establish and exhort you in your faith, that no one be moved by these afflictions. For you yourselves know that we are destined for this. —1 Thessalonians 3:2–3

The waiting time, that interminable period between crying out to God and receiving an answer, poses one of the greatest threats to our

Christian walk. The unknown looms ahead, fear bites at our heels, and insecurity rises within. Facts not lost on the enemy of our souls who can't wait to infuse our circumstances with his nasty little lies. Lies designed to quench the fire of our faith and extinguish the candle of hope. Discouragement is Satan's victory song.

Paul was concerned the Thessalonians would fall into that trap of discouragement as they waited after hearing about his trials. So, he sent Timothy to encourage them to stand firm. But what Timothy found when he arrived in Thessalonica was not a body of people steeped in fear. He witnessed a strong, faith-filled church whose love and trust in God was drowning out Satan's discordant melody. Paul's absence actually made them stronger. They learned to lean on God as they waited. And they flourished because of it.

Waiting times are like two-edged swords. They bring us down if we take the bait of Satan. Or they provide opportunities for us to grow stronger. Just as Paul sent Timothy, so God sends us to comfort brothers and sisters who wrestle with discouragement as they wait.

As fellow believers, we must sing louder than the enemy. In chapter 5 of 1 Thessalonians, Paul exhorts us to "encourage one another and build one another up" (v. 11). I have some friends who are experiencing pretty excruciating waiting times right now. Satan is pursuing them with relentless lyrics of hopelessness and despair. But I'm singing psalms of life over them. Psalms like "O my Strength, I will sing praises to you, for you, O God, are my fortress, the God who shows me steadfast love. (Psalm 59:17). And "But I call to God, and the LORD will save me. Evening and morning and at noon I utter my complaint and moan, and he hears my voice" (Psalm 55:16–17).

Is God asking you to encourage an "unsettled" friend? Don't hesitate. Go spoil Satan's victory song of discouragement and belt out the truth!

Reflecting on God's Faithfulness

For I know the plans I have for you, declares the LORD, plans for welfare and not for evil, to give you a future and a hope. —Jeremiah 29:11

Recalling God's faithfulness in the past has a way of sustaining us through disappointments.

A few years ago I developed sepsis. When I was rushed to the emergency room in the middle of the night, the doctor said had we gotten there twenty minutes later, I might not have survived. It was quite the scare for a girl thinking she just had a bad case of the flu! But as I think back on that time, I'm flooded with more positive feelings than negative.

From the hospital staff who cared for me, to my daughter who quickly caught a train from Rhode Island to be nearby. From friends who covered me in prayer and brought meals and strawberry kiwi lemonade, to a husband who showed me unparalleled attentiveness. It's quite humbling to be the object of such love.

Gratitude for being alive overwhelms me as I think about how each day since then might not have been. My chair at family gatherings would have been empty. A 365-day devotional book would not have been published. No beach trip to Cape Hatteras with Chip, no helping my son and daughter-in-law move into a new house, no moments of hysterical laughter watching the antics of my grandsons. It makes me view every day as a cherished gift.

When Jeremiah spoke to the exiles in Babylon, he assured them God's plans included hope and a future. With the assurance they would one day return to their homeland and be established again as a nation, they were to take heart and make the most of their less-than-ideal circumstances.

Just as the Lord had a plan for Israel, he had a plan for me, and he has a plan for you. Friend, I pray you see each day as a gift. I pray you live it to the fullest. No matter what your situation, I pray you will overflow with praise to the God who desires to give you hope and a future.

A great day of restoration is coming. Until then, let's make the most of this treasure called life.

Also the Night

Yours is the day, yours also the night. — Psalm 74:16

Have you been experiencing some troubled times? You know God is good and sovereign. He created all there is. He can do anything. The psalmist tells us he created the day, and also the night. Ah, yes. Therein lies the rub. Those dark nights.

I have to admit, the overall turmoil in the world can sidetrack me. If I'm not careful, I forget the *night also* belongs to the Lord. He created the order of the universe with cycles of day and night. And since sin entered, we all experience rounds of both light and darkness in our lives.

Psalm 74 laments the destruction taking place in Jerusalem. Their enemies have overrun them, enemies that hate them and mock God. The psalmist's brutal honesty shocks our ears. *We belong to you, God, so why are you rejecting us? Why are you letting us be crushed? How long will you allow the bad guys to keep winning?* A dark night in Israel's history indeed.

But before the psalmist gives in to total despair, he recalls God's power and faithfulness (v. 12–17. He remains Lord of all creation, the day as well as night. Through the good and the bad. No matter how deep the darkness, his faithfulness promises light will return.

When shadows of disappointment threaten to overwhelm us, we need to remain as diligent as a night watchman. Satan tries to take advantage of us when we can't see what lies ahead. He wants us to focus on the injustice, the instability, and the magnitude of defeat. The more we dwell on the darkness, the more we veer off the purposes of the Lord. Purposes that include coming out of the darkness shining a brighter light.

If you're experiencing a dark night of the soul, know you are not alone. Some giants of the faith have plummeted into the darkness and come out on the other side, people like St. John of the Cross, C. S. Lewis, Francis Schaeffer. One day we will live in the presence of the Father of Lights in a place where there will be no more night. But until then, take heart.

Stay steadfast, my friend. Morning will dawn.

Though He Slay Me

Even now, behold, my witness is in heaven,
and he who testifies for me is on high.
My friends scorn me;
my eye pours out tears to God. —Job 16:19–20

No matter how dark life becomes, within each person flickers a light of hope that cannot be extinguished . . . unless we let it.

No one knew trouble more than Job. You're familiar with his story. Life turned into one calamity after another for him. Even his wife tells him to "curse God and die" (Job 2:9). His friends falsely accuse him of sin, and God's silence thrusts him into confusion and greater despair than you or I will (hopefully) ever know. Job goes from proclaiming his unflinching trust in God to wishing he had never been born. He calls out, "where then is my hope?" (Job 17:15). Even the grave, which would put him out of his misery, offers nothing but total darkness, his decayed body a meal for the worms.

Yet reoccurring throughout his lament, we find a persistent spark of light that refuses to be completely diminished. He cries, "Even now, behold, my witness is in heaven, and he who testifies for me is on high. My friends scorn me; my eye pours out tears to God" (Job 16:19–20). Deep in Job's spirit he knows there remains someone who hears his desperate plea and speaks on his behalf. Somewhere, somehow, he knows his Redeemer lives.

God places that spark of hope in every human heart. It may be so dim we can't distinguish it. We may have fallen so far off the path we think we've gone beyond its embers of help. But it probably takes less fanning than we think to cause that hope to once again burst into flame. Don't give up. Our present suffering is not the end. Our Redeemer is our Defender. Our Intercessor is our Friend. There will come a day when all the bad will be made good. The wrongs made right. Anguishing tears made dry.

Friend, do you know your Redeemer lives? Do you know he will stand with you on that day? Don't let whatever gut-wrenching circumstance you are facing kill your hope. Your pain may be great, but your Redeemer is greater. Find comfort by putting all your hope in him.

"One Night in an Inconvenient Hotel"

Indeed, we felt that we had received the sentence of death. But that was to make us rely not on ourselves but on God who raises the dead. —2 Corinthians 1:9

What does hopelessness feel like to you? I'm sure you've been there. Every source of security—gone. All the legs supporting the table—cut off. Your faith—down for the count. Try as you might, you can't muster up the strength to fight the draw toward disappointment and depression.

To Paul, hopelessness felt like the "sentence of death." Problems and persecution had pursued him throughout his ministry in Asia. It was so severe, he despaired of life itself. But rather than giving in to it, he seized the opportunity to increase his reliance on God. The same God who raised Christ from the dead could resuscitate his waning hope.

I remember reading the story of Russian dissident Aleksander Solzhenitsyn when he was brutally thrown into the Gulag by Stalin. His imprisonment stripped him of everything near and dear to him. Yet, ironically, his confining circumstances led him to freedom. He wrote in *The Gulag Archipelago,* "Bless you prison, bless you for being in my life. For there, lying upon the rotting prison straw, I came to realize that the object of life is not prosperity as we are made to believe, but the maturity of the human soul."[36] Solzhenitsyn could bless his deplorable jail cell because it redirected him to the source of true, everlasting freedom: Jesus Christ.

The upside of desperation is waking up to what really matters.

When it seems like everyone else has abandoned us, our aloneness drives us to the One who never will. If God doesn't pull out a miracle, then we must not need what we thought we did. Isn't it interesting how surrender opens our eyes to a purpose far greater and higher than we imagined?

Theresa of Avila once wrote even a life of horrible pains will seem like "one night in an inconvenient hotel" in light of eternity's bliss.[37] If you're staying in a hotel room right now marked h-o-p-e-l-e-s-s, ask Jesus Christ for the key that unlocks the door. Like Solzhenitsyn, let God use your rotting prison straw to lead you to the freedom and comfort of what it feels like to rely on Him.

#BringYourPromises

This is my comfort in my affliction, that your promise gives me life. — Psalm 119:50

In 2014, Boko Haram abducted 276 Nigerian Christian schoolgirls. My heart was riveted to the news Maybe yours was, too. A social media campaign, #BringBackOurGirls, went viral as people across the world witnessed the horror. Although the terrorists eventually released most of the girls, a recent book chronicles the ordeal they experienced: *Bring Back Our Girls: The Untold Story of the Global Search for Nigeria's Missing Schoolgirls* by Joe Parkinson and Drew Hinshaw.

The girls who refused to deny their faith and convert to Islam faced torture, deprivation, and abuse. But they found both courage and comfort as they secretly whispered prayers together and memorized scripture from a smuggled Bible. God's promises enabled them to stand through the most unimaginable circumstances these young girls would ever face. According to the authors, "Their faith provided twin anchors of identity and hope their captors were trying to erase."[38]

Bad things happen in a fallen world. We know that, but when we see schoolgirls punished for the sin of seeking an education, we can't help but grieve. When we view innocent Ukrainians fleeing their homes, stripped of all they hold dear, we grieve. A wife sobs at a hospital in Mariupol as her husband dies from defending his war-torn country. And we cry, too.

How do we face such incomprehensible evil?

The testimony of the surviving Chibok schoolgirls reminds me of what the psalmist declared. In his affliction, he found comfort in God's promises, and it gave him life. When ungodly people derided him, he remembered the word of the Lord. When evil pressed in, he sang songs acknowledging the ways of God. Songs that reinforced God's love, power and faithfulness. Songs that brought peace to his troubled soul.

Because that's what the word of God does.

God's promises existed long before the pain and suffering inflicted by Islamist terrorists, and ruthless dictators like Vladmir Putin. The evil they unleash on the world cannot ultimately prevail against the faith believers have in God's word.

The days seem to darkening; we don't know what lies ahead. But no matter what we face, let's not let our hope be erased. Let's cry out to the God of comfort "#BringYourPromises."

CHAPTER EIGHTEEN

We Shine Hope into Doubt

"If ours is an examined faith, we should be unafraid to doubt. . .
There is no believing without some doubting, and believing is all the
stronger for understanding and resolving doubt."

Os Guinness
—The Call

Finding certainty in an uncertain world can completely upend us if we
forget the source of our assurance. When doubts flood our mind, ignor-
ing them won't cut it. But wrestling through the doubts will lead us to
a place of peace, of strength, of confidence. There's a hope the world
gives that resembles little more than wishful thinking. It will never silence our doubts. The kind of hope that sustains us through life's surges
of uncertainty comes when we remember the faithfulness of God. A
God who assures us that every circumstance we face, no matter how
hard, will make us stronger if we trust him. We conquer our doubts
when we recall God never has and never will break his promises. So,
although doubts inevitably arrive at the doorstep of our hearts, we don't
have to linger in their company. Never forget the Great Constant.

How Sure Can You Be?

Thus says the LORD: "If you can break my covenant with the day and my covenant with the night, so that day and night will not come at their appointed time, then also my covenant with David my servant may be broken." —Jeremiah 33:20–21

How sure can we be that God keeps his word? Do we believe promises like he will never leave us or forsake us (Deuteronomy 31:6)? How about his promise to come again and take us back to heaven with him (John 14:3)? And when life starts to squeeze in, do we question his pledge to work all things together for our good (Romans 8:28)?

Hope, true hope, is hard to find in a world that shifts allegiances as abruptly as a click of the remote control. We're a capricious people, aren't we? And people just like us fill the institutions where we place our hope. Maybe we need some adjustment.

When Jeremiah prophesied the coming destruction of Jerusalem, he also predicted Jerusalem's plight would be temporary. Though the devastation would be great, the restoration would be greater. The exiles would return after seventy years. The throne of David would be re-established because God had made a covenant with David that one of his descendants would always be on the throne. How likely was it that God would renege on his promise? As likely as it was that day and night would no longer exist. They could be sure restoration would happen because God said it would.

The foundation of our faith rests on knowing we can depend on God to keep his promises. When God swore to Abraham his descendants would be a great nation, then directed him to offer his only son, Isaac, as a sacrifice, it didn't make sense. But Abraham knew he could be sure the God he served kept his promises, even if it meant raising Isaac from the dead. His complete trust in God produced radical obedience.

We know if we have hope for this life only, we are to be most pitied. True hope reaches beyond the confines of the natural world. It assures us that nothing, nothing, nothing, can cause God to break his promises

to us. In this unreliable world of vacillating people and broken promises, we can be completely sure of that one thing.

It Could Be Worse

For to you have I committed my cause. —Jeremiah 20:12

It was one of my most embarrassing moments in front of an audience.
I was speaking to a group of college students at a local university. It
was my first time speaking there, and suddenly anxiety got the best of
me. My nervousness manifested itself in a dry mouth. A very dry
mouth. In fact, my mouth became so dry that my upper lip *stuck* to my
front teeth! Do you know how hard it is to speak when your lip is attached to your tooth? Not a pretty sight. Thankfully, someone finally
brought me a bottle of water. And I continued my talk.

I like to tell that story to my Public Speaking students to illustrate
how there is life on the other side of public speaking mishaps. I ask
them, "What's the worst thing that could happen if you mess up?"
Things could always be worse.

For example, what if we were in Jeremiah's situation? If ever anyone was between a rock and a hard place, it was Jeremiah. He felt bitter
because God had called him to do a job that brought him shame, ridicule, and no observable success. The people turned on him when he
warned them about the coming disaster God was sending. On the other
hand, the "fire of God was in his bones" and he couldn't stop preaching.
A combination of the irreversibility of the impending doom, the betrayal of friends, the relentless pursuit of his enemies, and the negative
nature of his message, pushed him to despondency. He cursed the day
he was born. It doesn't seem like life could have gotten any worse for
this prophet of God.

But actually, it could have been worse. He could have turned away
from God. He could have thrown his lot in with the rebels and denied

his call. He could have refused to "commit his cause" to the Lord. But he didn't. He opted for life on the other side of his suffering.

Whether our pain comes in the form of social embarrassment or in a deluge of rejection, always remember it could be worse. As long as you remain faithful to God and keep pressing ahead, you will land in a better place. A place that is an eternity away from the worst thing that could happen.

Why We Remember

For whatever was written in former days was written for our instruction, that through endurance and through the encouragement of the Scriptures we might have hope. —Romans 15:4

You're probably familiar with the saying, "Those who cannot remember the past are condemned to repeat it." Knowledge of the past not only helps us avoid making the same mistakes, it also prepares us for future battles.

When Winston Churchill stood almost as a singular voice against the Nazis, he was in the process of writing a history of England. As he recalled Britain's former victories—like defeating the Saxons in the eleventh century and the indominable Spanish Armada in 1588—he found courage to defy Hitler's onslaught. Churchill's stand indisputably saved the free world.

As believers, the importance of remembering our past carries no less weight. Moses spent the last months of his life preparing Israel for victory in the promised land. How? By reviewing their history and reminding them of God's call to them as a nation. His words infused them with courage to face the upcoming battles.

Bible stories, according to the apostle Paul, were not recorded for us to put in lockboxes and sit on our mantles. They were written to teach us how to endure through difficulties, be encouraged through problems, and cultivate hope.

Do you ever feel like you're facing a pit of hungry lions? People ready to pounce on your every word to devour your influence? I have some friends in politics who find courage to stand against their opponents when they remember how God closed the mouths of lions surrounding Daniel.

Or maybe you're tempted to throw in the towel. You've prayed and prayed with no apparent results. Then you remember the parable Jesus told about the persistent friend, so you discard your weariness and keep knocking.

Perhaps you face a coalition of troubles in your family, your checkbook, your workplace. You think you could never have victory over this "vast army" arrayed against you. Then you remember Jehoshaphat when he cried out to God, "We don't know what to do, but our eyes are on you" (2 Chronicles 20:12) and you gain faith for another day.

And so, draw strength from the Scriptures. God's Word was written to help you endure, to overcome your doubt, and to rest in his sweet assurance.

It's why we remember.

From Rocks to Rolls

Or which one of you, if his son asks him for bread, will give him a stone? Or if he asks for a fish, will give him a serpent? If you then, who are evil, know how to give good gifts to your children, how much more will your Father who is in heaven give good things to those who ask him! — Matthew 7:9–11

I was talking with a friend the other day. Hopelessness and confusion threatened to turn her faith upside down. She had prayed long and hard over a particular issue, but the answer to her cries turned out to be the exact opposite of what she was asking. She said, "I feel like I asked God for bread, and he gave me a stone."

I could relate to her pain, and I suspect some of you can too. It's hard to keep going when reality seems to contradict Scripture promises.

But the more I thought about her dilemma, the more I realized God hadn't given her a stone. Satan had. No, he didn't appear in red tights with a pitchfork. He made his arrival through fallen people. People he managed to manipulate into bringing great harm.

God never promised the stones of a fallen world wouldn't be hurled in our direction. What he did promise was to take all the evil Satan intends and work it for our good (Romans 8:28). He will transform those stones into bread. He'll make biscuits out of those boulders. Pebbles into pita. Granite into multigrain. There is nothing we experience he cannot redeem for higher purposes. And redemption (wait for it) . . . rocks!

There's one time in Scripture, however, when Jesus refused to turn stones into bread (Matthew 4:1–4). After fasting forty days in the wilderness, Satan tempted him to use his power to satisfy himself. Jesus would have none of it. In no uncertain terms Jesus declared he relied more on the Word of God to sustain him than physical food. He knew God had a higher purpose than meeting his momentary hunger.

So the next time you get hit by a stone storm, don't get caught in the moment. Remember the Word of God. He is a good father who delights in giving *good gifts* to his children. Wait on him. Trust him. In time, he will turn those rocks into rolls.

Be Hope Strong

Be strong, and let your heart take courage, all you who wait for the LORD! —Psalm 31:24

How's your hope tank these days? A little depleted? I think the coronavirus left us all feeling more vulnerable and less secure than we were when life was normal. (Was that decades ago?) The security we experienced in our health, a stable job, even relationships was shaken. One woman tweeted she finally got up the nerve to look at her 401K and discovered she can't retire until she's 105!

The problem with dwindling hope is that it flashes like a neon sign to the enemy of our souls. I can almost hear Screwtape (in *Screwtape Letters*) commanding his nephew, "Go get 'em while they're down!" So, he creeps into the fog of our confusion and discontent to sow further havoc. Old issues appear seemingly out of nowhere to deliver a gut punch that knocks us off our already unsteady feet.

Make no mistake. Satan wants to use every crisis we face to infect us with far greater viruses than COVID–19. He wants to strip away our faith and make us immune to hope. We can't let him.

Bob Goff writes, "Hope doesn't go to sleep just because it's dark outside; it lights a candle and stays up waiting for the rest of the story."[39] Hope recognizes the darkness; in fact, hope that doesn't disappoint begins with suffering (Romans 5:3–4). Every time we decide to light that candle of hope, Satan's power withers.

The psalmist admonishes all those who hope in the Lord to be strong and take heart. Although the times might be uncertain, God's love and faithfulness are not. The power of hope proves strong enough to overcome whatever the enemy hurls our way.

In recent years cities that have experienced terror attacks have adopted phrases like "Boston Strong" or "El Paso Strong" or "Dayton Strong." The idea behind the slogans indicates the community will end up stronger as they come through the crisis. How about we followers of Christ express the same aspiration in our days of challenge. How about we choose to be "Hope Strong."

However

So I will throw you out of this land into a land neither you nor your ancestors have known, and there you will serve other gods day and night, for I will show you no favor. However, the days are coming . . . [when] I will restore them to the land I gave their ancestors. —Jeremiah 16:13–15 (NIV)

Doom loomed over Israel. They consistently rebelled against God, choosing instead to follow their own "evil hearts." Their worship of false gods and blatant disregard for his moral standards had reached the tipping point. Jeremiah prophesied the astronomical consequence of their sin would be imminent exile from their homeland to a godless foreign nation. Even though they deserved such punishment, Jeremiah inserts an unexpected word in his discourse—however—to show them their fate was not permanent.

Their time in exile was going to lead them to repentance and re-acknowledgement of the Lord as their God. They would once again find rest in Zion. The restoration would be so significant that it would serve as a new mile marker in their relationship with him. Before, the nation marked the exodus from Egypt as the sign of God's faithfulness. Soon, they'd refer to their return from Babylon as the mark of his renewed favor.

However. That seven-letter word made the difference between *I-give-up* disappointment and *I-dare-you-to-believe* hope. It intersected a path headed for destruction and redirected it to a road of restoration. It hailed the good news of redemption. Of sovereign love.

Of inevitability undone.

I admit it's hard for me to look for the silver lining when things don't turn out the way I'd imagined. I was the girl who thought if I didn't marry my high school sweetheart, God must be calling me to be a nun (even though I wasn't Catholic). *However,* the Lord had far better plans for my life. Some sentences aren't ready for a period. Sometimes I need to trust him for a semicolon followed with a *however.*

Praise God for giving us *howevers.* Life might be squeezing in on us; *however,* God has a plan to bring good from our grief. You don't see a way out; *however,* our way-making God has already laid a new path. Life in a fallen world will always be hard; *however,* nothing is too difficult for God.

So don't give up, child of God. A *however* might be right around the next sentence.

Hope or Hype?

But I will hope continually and will praise you yet more and more. —
Psalm 71:14

The culture tries to paint a picture of hope, but I'm afraid it often seems
more like hype. How many times we've been at a Penn State football
game, we're behind, and the band starts to play, "Don't Stop Be-
lievin'." As much as I love Penn State football, and as much as I hope
they will win, I really don't think my believing they will win makes one
bit of difference. My hope is wishful thinking. Strong wishful thinking,
but it isn't based on anything solid.

Or often on social media, people who are facing some difficulty ask
for "good thoughts," or "good vibes." I have to wonder, how can simply
thinking fondly about someone affect the outcome of his or her doctor's
appointment or open-heart surgery? It seems to me a poor substitute for
prayer. Prayer has a basis for hope because it directs our *good thoughts*
and *good vibes* to the One who can actually affect the outcome.

King David declares in Psalm 71 he will always have hope. To appreciate his frame of mind, it's important to understand his
circumstances. Old age has crept up on him. His strength is waning, and
his enemies are taking full advantage. They conspire against him, they
mock him, they taunt him with lies, saying God has left him. David
laments his troubles as "many and bitter." Yet instead of giving in to
despair, he steadfastly asserts he will not stop hoping in God.

Neither w*ishful thinking* nor *good vibes* from the universe provide
the foundation for his hope. His hope is built upon what he knows about
the character of God. He recalls God's faithfulness in the past. God has
come through for David his whole life, and he will not forsake him now
when he is "old and gray."

This is what I call "true hope" because it's anchored in the unchang-
ing character of hope's author.

If you are a follower of Christ, you have access to true hope. A hope
"built on nothing less than Jesus' blood and righteousness." Nothing

stands stronger. No matter what trial you might be facing, you have reason to hope. And that's not hype, my friend.

Not So Fast

But if we hope for what we do not see, we wait for it with patience. — Romans 8:25

"Don't worry, Grandma." Those were the wise words Mason, my then three-year-old grandson, spoke when his milk splattered across the table. In fact, encouraging the people around him not to worry turns out to be a staple in his vocabulary. Whenever he senses distress on any level, his empathy kicks into gear.

I couldn't help but think of his advice a few days later when my computer asked me if I wanted it to correct a corrupted file. I clicked "agree." And just like that, over thirty thousand words from a recent project vanished from my USB. Evidently "correcting" meant deleting the file completely. I couldn't retrieve it, no matter how hard I tried. So, I called my son (Josiah is my go-to with tech problems). Unfortunately, three of his friends were waiting for him to begin a round of golf.

I had no other recourse than to wait. The loss hung over me all day. So did worry. And regret. And resignation that I would have to start all over again from the beginning.

Then late afternoon my son called to see if I had made any progress. He installed an app that enabled him to dig deeper into my files, and sure enough he located the missing work. Relief washed over me in waves of gratitude. What seemed impossible turned into reality. The lost was found. Hope restored.

It taught me something about the importance of not being so quick to give up hope.

In Romans 8, Paul exhorts the Church to live by the Spirit, not the flesh. He knew of their sufferings and didn't want them to lose hope. He assured them all they endured served a purpose. It prepared them for participating in the glory of God (v. 17). A certainty yet to come, one they would have to wait for, one that required patience.

So much of life involves patience. When interruptions invade our time, our default leans toward worry, doubt, and frustration. I believe God wants us to adopt a better way. Learn to resist impatience and trust in the God who never stops working for our good. Whether spilled milk or missing computer files, let's not be so quick to dismiss hope. Heed my grandson's words:

"Don't worry."

Don't Be Ashamed. Don't Be Ashamed. Don't Be Ashamed.

But I am not ashamed, for I know whom I have believed, and I am convinced that he is able to guard until that Day what has been entrusted to me. —2 Timothy 1:12

I was talking with a woman the other day who has trouble remembering who she is as a child of the Most High God. Oh, she doesn't experience amnesia when it comes to recalling all her mess-ups. Consequently, she finds herself locked into a prison of shame rather than walking in the freedom Christ died to give her.

The problem with shame is that it leads to self-pity, and self-pity drains us of every whit of confidence. Satan uses it to hinder us from pursuing God's plan. So, giving into shame detours us from the end goal. We spend all our energy thinking about our unworthiness rather than letting God use us—although we are poor broken vessels—to advance his kingdom.

A dank, stinky cell imprisoned Paul. Yet he never let himself fall into the doldrums of shame. In fact, in the first chapter of his second letter to Timothy, he refers to *not being ashamed* three times. He exhorts Timothy *not to be ashamed* of the gospel or of him (v. 8). He's *not ashamed* of his status as a prisoner (v. 12), and he commends Onesiphorus for *not being ashamed* of his chains (v. 16).

A lot of our shame stems from a sense of not living up to expectations, from ourselves or from others. But perfect behavior from fallen creatures will never be attainable in this life. Thankfully, God provides a way out. "No one whose hope is in you will ever be put to shame" (Psalm 25:3, NIV).

Paul wasn't ashamed because he knew the One in whom he believed, and he put his hope fully in him. He recognized his life consisted of more than his accomplishments or failures. He lived for a purpose so high only God could help him pull it off.

And so do we.

Do you ever forget you are a child of the Most High God? His plan for you includes your mistakes, faults, and outright defeats. Don't let the devil use shame to detour you from hoping in the one in whom you believe.

You Make Me Feel Like a *Super*natural Woman

Jesus stood up and said to her, "Woman, where are they? Has no one condemned you?" She said, "No one, Lord." And Jesus said, "Neither do I condemn you; go, and from now on sin no more." —John 8:10–11

I can't imagine how hopeless this adulterous woman must have felt. Dragged from her literal bed of sin, the scribes and Pharisees deposited her in front of Jesus and the crowd of people who had gathered to hear his teaching. The Pharisees cared nothing about her. They humiliated her in order to trap Jesus. If she was stoned to death in the process, so what?

But their pride and hypocrisy didn't last long. Jesus, of course, knew their motives. When he asked for the one with no sin to cast the first stone, they begrudgingly dropped their bludgeons of death and retreated into the shadows. It seems significant that Jesus wrote in the sand two times during the exchange. According to tradition, he wrote the sins of her accusers. Can anyone say huge backfire?

They had exploited this woman before the wrong man. When she looked into the eyes of Jesus she saw, probably for the first time in her broken life, pure, unconditional love. Enough love to say, "I don't condemn you." But also enough to warn her to "stop sinning." Score 0 for the hypocrites and 1 formerly lost woman for the kingdom of God.

It makes me think of songwriter Carole King's song, "You Make Me Feel Like a Natural Woman. " I think the woman in the story knew quite a bit about being a *natural woman*. But Jesus went further. He made her feel like a *supernatural woman*. His love restored her sense of dignity and worth. After that encounter she would never look at herself through natural eyes only.

And if you're a follower of Jesus, neither should you. As women, we expect a lot of ourselves these days. We fail. Many of us live with deep regrets. If you're a man, you may have a wife, a sister, a friend who lets the past define her. Tell her the good news. Jesus offers hope for a clean slate each day. He protects us from being knocked over by stones of shame. Not only will he make us feel like a *supernatural woman*, he will transform us into one! That's hope!

Part Six

When Do We Shine the Light?

CHAPTER NINETEEN

When We Trust in the Face of Fear

"Fear nothing but the loss of Him. Nothing."

Peter Kreeft
—Before I Go

FEAR. I write it in all caps because it's an intimidating word. An emotion wielding far too much power for children of God.

David asks in Psalm 27:1 "of whom shall I be afraid?" In these days of uncertainty, most of us could hand him a list. We fear the crumbling of our culture and the destruction of our country. We worry about the IRS, the CDC, and an alphabet of crooked elitists. And we're anxious that the world might succeed in enticing the Church to settle for an "appearance of godliness" while denying the power of Christ. And that doesn't count the personal concerns we bear for those we love.

Yet David declares he has *nothing* to be afraid of if the Lord is his stronghold—not an evil man, not a coalition of slanderous enemies, not a whole army arrayed against him. He will not fear even if his mother and father reject him or if it seems like God is hiding his face. He remains confident God's goodness will prevail. Because the Lord is the source of his light and salvation, he has nothing to fear. Neither do we. Whenever fear lands on our doorstep, we have the opportunity to push it back by maintaining our trust in God. He will decapitalize every FEAR. And we will shine the steady light of confident trust.

A Pandemic of . . . Fear

For a day in your courts is better
than a thousand elsewhere.
I would rather be a doorkeeper in the house of my God
than dwell in the tents of wickedness. —Psalm 84:10

I think one of the biggest blights the coronavirus spawned included a pandemic of fear. It made us fear getting sick and making other people sick. We feared the consequences of wearing masks, of not wearing masks, of opening schools, of not opening schools. Of course, fear has been around much longer than COVID-19. But living in an atmosphere saturated with fear tends to wake up the boogeyman hiding in us all.

I don't consider myself a fearful person. I lean more toward worry than full-blown panic. But I've been peeling through some layers, looking for the root of why I recently reacted so negatively in a particular situation. Guess what I found. A puny giant inside me yelling through a megaphone of fear: FAILURE. FAILURE. FAILURE.

One of my biggest fears is that of failing. It makes me want to *distance* my fragile ego from people who make me feel like I'm falling short. It *masks* my pride by tempting me to stay within the confines of what I can control. And perhaps worst of all, it messes with my mind, throwing me into a *fever* pitch of shame and *coughing spasms* of hopelessness. I feel like I will never succeed at anything again.

But we can never truly fail if obedience to God remains our highest priority. For in him, even our failures are used for good. He desires to take every mistake, every shame, every humiliation and use it to achieve his purpose of making us better humans. Humans more like him. So, I can either feed my fear of failure by measuring my "success" on what other people think, or on what's important to God.

I want to cultivate the psalmist's mindset when he declared nothing compares to being close to God. He would rather live one day near him than a thousand without him. He would rather serve in a menial position (a doorkeeper) than thrive in a world devoid of his presence. The psalmist understood life is not about what we achieve, but about knowing God's love.

And God's love casts out all fear. That's a pretty powerful *vaccine*.

Uncertain Times

Why should I fear in times of trouble,
when the iniquity of those who cheat me surrounds me. —Psalm 49:5

Uncertain times. I've heard that phrase periodically during my short stint on the earth. But probably more so in the last few years than ever before. Actress Patricia Heaton recently tweeted, "If you're a commonsense person, you probably don't feel you have a home in this world right now. If you're a Christian, you know you were never meant to."[40]

Although we don't look for comfort in the world, how should we respond in these *uncertain times?* It's tempting to withdraw into safe cocoons where we think trouble can't reach us. We kinda' like those words of David in Psalm 11, "Flee like a bird to your mountain, for behold, the wicked bend the bow" (vv. 1–2).

God never intended for *uncertain times* to transform his children into escape artists. We are not *of* the world, but we remain *in* it. Are you still breathing? Then you have purpose. On the other hand, what if we obsess over the pain, confusion, and chaos erupting all around us? We are no better off than the avoiders if we view *uncertain times* through the prism of the *now*. Psalm 49 warns us not to let temporary perceptions sway us. No matter how powerful, wealthy, or successful the wicked deceivers appear to be, their influence will fade. Rather than doubting God with groans of where are you, we trust him to lead us through these times and beyond—right into eternity.

So, the more I think about these *uncertain times*, the more convinced I am that God made us for them. When the foundations are shaking, when false idols are crumbling, when accusatory tongues are wagging, we should be acting like the Lord's first responders and throwing out life jackets to those drowning in seas of uncertainty

The Prayer of St Francis comes to mind:

> *Where there is hatred, let me sow love;*
> *Where there is injury, pardon;*
> *Where there is doubt, faith;*
> *Where there is despair, hope;*
> *Where there is darkness, light*
> *Where there is sadness, joy*[41]

A prayer not just for *uncertain times*, but for all times.

Runnin' on Trustin'

To you they cried and were rescued; in you they trusted and were not put to shame. —Psalm 22:5

If you believe the Dunkin Donuts' advertisement, you would think "America runs on Dunkin." I'm not so sure I agree with their clever slogan, but just about everything runs on something. Including Christianity.

Christianity runs on trustin.' Everyone who wants to grow in their faith, knows (yet sometimes forgets) that trusting God fuels every aspect of life. Without trust, we have no way of connecting to God. Trust helps us keep that connection even in the depth of our fears. In fact, sometimes it's through the fearful circumstances we encounter that our trust grows strongest.

Trust involves surrender. A. J. Swoboda writes, "Nothing builds trust like facing all your unsolved problems and unresolved struggles by getting down on your knees and not trying to fix them."[42] I've found this to be so true. It seems every time I reach the end of my rope, I find trust waiting right there whispering, "What took you so long?"

The psalmist's trust in God took him from despairing fear to unshakeable confidence. He begins Psalm 22 with the desperate words of "My God, my God, why have you forsaken me?" Isolated from human comfort, he's unable to raise himself up from the "dust of death" (v. 15). But then, in the midst of his excruciating pain, he recalls who God is and what he has done in the past. And as he begins to praise God, trust ignites his faith. In the last verse of Psalm 22, he shouts with confidence of how future generations "will proclaim his righteousness, declaring to a people yet unborn: He has done it! (v. 31, NIV).

Friend, we belong to that future generation. And we have opportunity to proclaim and declare his righteousness right smack dab in the thick of our fears. Have you experienced anxieties? Me too. But I know nothing can block the Holy Spirit from leading me to a deeper level of trust.

As we look forward to days filled with who-knows-what, let's not forget the One who controls it all. Remember *who he is* and *what he has done* in the past. Then, let's keep runnin' on trustin.'

School of Trust

By the waters of Babylon,
there we sat down and wept,
when we remembered Zion. —Psalm 137:1

Educational facilities from daycares to universities cancel classes and activities for one reason or another (from weather to pandemics). Yet there's one school, as my husband recently noted, that never closes its doors. This school remains open through every imaginable crisis . . .

The school of trust. Whether we wanted to enroll or not, it's a school we are all thrust into during troubled times.

Of course, trusting God in fearful times is not new curriculum for believers. We became students of trust the moment we confessed Jesus as Lord. What many of us didn't realize was how the Holy Spirit would keep signing us up for advanced classes. He keeps presenting us with new opportunities to learn and to grow. And slacking off in the face of challenges appears nowhere on the syllabus.

But when Israel met the opportunity to advance in trust, I'm afraid that's exactly what they did. They slacked. Their lack of trust had landed them as prisoners in a foreign land. As a nation, they had compromised their allegiance to God by diluting their trust with idols. As a result, they soon lost their sensitivity to God. Now, they sat by the rivers of Babylon and wept when they remembered what they lost.

I'm not begrudging their grief. I'd cry too. It's calloused to look at the suffering and pain surrounding us and not grieve. And it's tempting, like Israel, to focus on revenge toward our enemies. But bitterness and calls for revenge only increase our despair. The choice to trust God leads us out of our grief and restores our hope.

I recently learned a new word: *opsimath*. It refers to a person who began to learn or study late in life. In the confines of Babylon, God offered Israel a new opportunity to become *opsimaths* in the field of trust. Maybe he is doing the same for us in our crises. Will we choose to open ourselves to learning new ways to trust God or will we stubbornly cling to our disappointments?

Some day we will all graduate. May it be with the high distinction as *summa cum lades* of trust.

How Do We Deal with Fear?

For God gave us a spirit not of fear but of power and love and self-control. —2 Timothy 1:7

Sometimes, even in a season of relative calm, when I'm relishing in all the goodness of God, fear sneaks into the edges of my mind. *What if something bad is about to happen to my husband? To one of my kids?*

Maybe that racing pulse rate indicates I'm headed toward a heart attack. There. I said it. Just exposing fears to the light helps dissipate them to some extent.

How do we deal with fear?

It plagues our human existence. Scripture affirms its predominance. Did you know there are 365 references in the Bible telling us not to fear or be afraid? That's one a day! The Bible describes how even giants in the faith like Daniel experienced tremendous fear. When an angel appeared to explain the meaning of the apocalyptic vision Daniel had received, his whole body trembled (Daniel 10:11). The angel calmed his fears by telling him not to be afraid—twice! (vv. 12, 19).

Whether our fears stem from dangers real or irrational, we must not entertain them. Fear doesn't come from God. Instead of fear, he gives us power, love, and self-control as weapons to fight against it. The three work in tandem in our fearful wrestling.

Power—more power than we will ever need. We have access to the strength of our Sovereign God, and it's far greater than fear. Love—sacrificial, death-defying love. Our situation fills God with compassion that surpasses anything we've known. Self-control enables us to act on the truth of what we know about God's power and love for us. It helps us kick fear out by the seat of its pants. Remember that the next time fear tries to invade the margins of your thoughts.

Life is unpredictable; pain is inevitable. We have no assurances bad things won't happen. But we don't have to fear what lies ahead. God promises to use the difficulties we experience for something good. No matter what.

Friend, don't let fear dominate even one day of your precious life. Strengthen the gateway to your mind and don't let fear slip in. Shine with confidence and trust in our powerful, loving God.

Overwhelmed?

Come to me, all you who labor and heavy laden, and I will give you rest. —Matthew 11:28

Overwhelmed! It seems like being overwhelmed has become a staple of our culture.

We're akin to border agents trying to cope with thousands of migrants rushing the southern border of the United States. We exhaust ourselves as we seek to manage a caravan of responsibilities demanding our immediate attention. A friend recently said in a two-week period her family faced an $1,100 car repair, an unexpected $250 eye doctor bill for their daughter, and reoccurring nightmares from their youngest son resulting in substantial sleep loss for everyone. Add to that a whole weekend of migraines. My goodness, just thinking about her circumstances inundates me.

How do we deal with this mental overload?

It's hard. When our duties at home, school, or work are all screaming, "Pick me," and our relationships are crying out not to be neglected—weariness sets in. Our sense of security and safety crumbles when an ongoing flood of worries, fears, and guilt for not "doing enough" breaches the borders of our mind. What's a person to do?

Remember we have a place of refuge.

Jesus called all of us weary and burdened ones to come to him. And he knew a few things about carrying the weights of the world. He promised if we bring our onslaught of troubles to him, he would help us carry the load. He would lead us to the same place of refuge that sustained him. Jesus committed everything to his Father. He never let the demands of the world define his responsibilities so world-induced pressures could never wear him down. He found confidence in knowing he was doing just what the Father called him to do . . . nothing more, nothing less. He wants us to do the same.

So, the next time you feel overwhelmed, don't be afraid. Your circumstances cannot possibly overwhelm the One who wants to walk with you. Jesus meant it when he said, "Come to me." Take him at his word. Lay your burdens on his shoulders and find that sweet place of confident trust.

The Fear Factor

The LORD is on my side; I will not fear.
What can man do to me? —Psalm 118:6

"Do you see many students who struggle with fear?" asked the girl who was interviewing me for a school publication. Considering I teach Public Speaking—the number one fear of most Americans—I didn't have to think twice.

Fear comes in all sizes and packages. Some fears are best dealt with by refusing to give them more power than they already have. When Satan plagues our mind with a backpack of scenarios in hopes of provoking us to fear, we must ignore them or command them to leave. Any thought that pulls us into fear is not a thought authored by the God of peace.

Other types of fears must be faced head-on. If you want to pass the class, you have to give the speech. If you want to visit London, you have to get on the airplane. If you want to be more like Jesus, you have to stand up for truth, even if it means rejection. We overcome these fears by trusting the Source of our peace.

When Scripture admonishes us not to fear, it often includes the reason why: the incredibly powerful promise *for I am with you.* When hard pressed, the psalmist remembered his God—more powerful than all his enemies—stood as his helper (Psalm 118:5–7). Such was the case when God commanded Joshua to lead Israel into the promised land (Joshua 1:9), when David instructed Solomon to take on the massive task of building the temple (1 Chronicles 28:20), and when any of us face the valley of the shadow of death (Psalm 23:4). Fear loses its grip when we realize we're not in this alone.

Oh, friend, don't let the isolating lies of fear be a factor in your life. A factor that tries to extinguish your light.

The Antidote to Worry

Therefore I tell you, do not worry. —Matthew 6:25 (NIV)

It is not harmless. It bears unsuspecting consequences. It sucks the life out of hope and stops faith in its tracks. It's often the first sign of unfaithfulness. Jesus said not to do it. Yet most of us don't think of *worry* as lethal.

Everyone has concerns. Lack of concern for ourselves and others indicates indifference, irresponsibility, and a callous disregard for the world around us. But what do we do with those concerns? Do we feed them until they become life-consuming worries, or do we let our concerns drive us to a deeper dependence on God?

Jesus displayed unremitting compassion to all those around him: to the two blind men who begged him for sight. To the crowds who followed him because they had no shepherd. To the young rich man who wanted to follow him but wanted to follow his wealth more. To the city of Jerusalem because he knew they would reject the truth. Yet his concerns never resulted in hand-wringing despair. Instead, he *entrusted* all these situations to the Father of love.

Trust is the antidote to worry. I believe God wants to use all our concerns to move us to new depths of trust. The kind of trust we experience with a good friend. Maybe that's what Joseph Scriven was thinking of when he wrote the familiar hymn, "What a Friend We Have in Jesus." It echoes a heart who has learned to ask—then trust the most loyal, reliable, faithful friend anyone could have.

I'm pretty consistent about taking my concerns to the Lord in prayer. Not so consistent about leaving them there. All too often I ask-then-worry rather than ask-then-trust. I short-circuit the process and maybe miss a miracle. How about you? What do you do after you ask? Do you trust God to take care of your concerns, or do you persist in needless worry?

I can't think of a better time than now to empty your bag of concerns and believe Jesus will take care of each one. Ask—then trust.

Rolling with the Punches

You who fear the LORD, trust in the LORD! He is their help and their shield. —Psalm 115:11

I've recently noticed a significant change in my life. When things don't work out the way I expected, it doesn't bother me as much as it used to. Disappointments don't hang on me like they have in the past. The Lord's patience with me in my tendency to worry rather than trust seems to be paying off. He is teaching me to "roll with the punches," to turn disturbing situations over to him rather than trying to work them out myself.

When the psalmist exhorted the Israelites to trust the Lord in Psalm 115, he urged them at the same time to steer clear of idols. He said we become like what we trust, so if we trust in anything or anyone more than God, our lives inevitably become stunted.

So, one thing is essential in learning to roll with the punches. We have to deal with our idols.

Idols, even those whose makeup have an uncanny resemblance to us, will always betray us. You know the kind of idols I mean—success, acceptance, money, good works. We have to knock 'em out before they strike us with a fatal blow. Dodge the temptation, as it says in Psalm 146, to put our trust in mere human beings who have no more power to save than all of Marvel's superheroes put together. Remember how God has promised to be our help and shield? He can protect us against anything the world, our flesh, or devils hurl against us. When our trust is transferred from idols to God, we're ready to roll with the punches.

The God who created me and who knows me better than I know myself is worthy of my trust. The God who authors love, forgiveness, and redemption is worthy of my trust. The God who has a plan that exceeds my disappointments and extends beyond my expectations is worthy of my trust.

He is worthy of yours as well. Friend, find rest in trusting God. Let him help you learn to roll with the punches launched at you from a fallen world. He's got you covered. If you let him.

Golden Calf Christians

When the people saw that Moses was so long in coming down from the mountain, they gathered around Aaron and said, "Come, make us gods who will go before us. As for this fellow Moses who brought us up out of Egypt, we don't know what has happened to him." —Exodus 32:1 (NIV)

Have you ever engaged in Golden Calf Christianity? That's when you're tired of waiting on God. You crave answers, but all you hear is crickets. You're afraid of being stranded and stuck in the wilderness. And you feel the pressure to do something—ANYTHING—to get you moving forward. Because you can't see God, you don't trust he's still there.

So, you build a golden calf. A golden calf of your own ideas and thoughts. Rather than continuing to wait on the Lord, you push ahead, leaning on the idolatry of your own understanding to lead you. Not unlike Israel after their exodus from Egypt.

You know the story. God delivered his people from 400 years of oppression under Egyptian slavery. The plagues, the blood on their doorposts sparing their firstborn, and the miraculous parting of the Red Sea seemed like a distant past. Their leader, "this fellow Moses," had supposedly gone up Mt. Sinai to meet with God. But after forty days, he was still nowhere in sight. Their conclusion: no Moses, no God, no vision. Their hopes of a promised land lay as burnt as the desert sand. They reacted exactly the way Scripture warns us people without vision respond. They threw off all restraint (Proverbs 29:18) and created a golden calf to worship.

The consequences were devastating. Not only did they become the laughingstock of their enemies, three thousand people died on the spot. Had it not been for Moses' intercession, God would have annihilated the whole nation.

There's no doubt about it. Waiting on God can be tough stuff. It requires us to trust him when we don't see him. It means we choose to believe his Word because *he said it,* not because we understand our circumstances. And when we feel like we can't hold on any longer, we have to lean hard on the Holy Spirit, rather than creating a golden calf to save us.

So, if you're waiting for direction from God right now, don't become fearful and fall into Golden Calf Christianity. Because Golden Calf Christianity isn't Christianity at all. It's idolatry.

"Mock On"

Bear with me while I speak, and after I have spoken, mock on. —Job 21:3 (NIV)

You're probably familiar with the pop expression, "rock on." Well, how about "mock on"?

After Job suffered the loss of family, fortune, and physical well-being, his three friends came to comfort him. But they ended up making his pain even more excruciating by falsely accusing him of hidden wickedness. They mistakenly believed his suffering was due to unrepentant sin in his life.

So how did Job respond to their condemnation? He told them to "mock on!" Such was Job's confidence. When accused of things he knew were untrue, he didn't melt like a marshmallow. He stood firm in his integrity. "Far be it from me to say that you are right; till I die I will not put away my integrity from me. I hold fast my righteousness and will not let it go; my heart does not reproach me for any of my days" (Job 27:5–6).

Job never wavered in his assessment of his own character. Why? Because he never wavered in his assessment of God's character. Oh, he questioned God. He didn't understand why God was allowing him to suffer. But his confidence in God's character of goodness and justness remained unshakeable. He believed if he could just present his case before God, he would be vindicated. He looked for God's judgment, not people's. That's why Job could tell his accusers to "mock on."

When we have confidence in who God says he is, we will have confidence in who he says we are.

It's not a conspiracy to say followers of Jesus are facing some strong headwinds from our culture today. Winds that give no indication of slowing down. One journalist recently reported it's becoming cool to mock Christianity. If we hope to exude the same kind of confidence Job displayed, it rests on the unwavering assurance of God's credentials, not ours. We are imperfect people, but we serve a perfect God. One who always has our back no matter what the crowd says.

I pray you and I will know who we are in Christ. That we won't let whatever false accusations that come our way fill us with fear. I guess if Jesus was mocked, we should expect no less. And he knows how to bravely lead us through.

An Incubator of Trust

Be still before the LORD and wait patiently for him. —Psalm 37:7

Waiting. For most of us, waiting is not our favorite pastime. We rarely see it as valuable or instrumental in our spiritual growth. We're more likely to view it as something to endure, a harbinger for worry and fear. Waiting from God's viewpoint, however, offers a completely different picture.

Scripture admonishes us to wait. The psalmist encourages us to silence our worried minds and wait patiently. I think of waiting as an incubator for trust. If there was no time gap between God's promises and his fulfillment of those promises, how would we ever develop trust? Only after we have had to wait upon God and experience him pulling us through, does our trust start to deepen.

A friend of mine recently faced a huge dilemma. Her decision would literally alter the course of her life. She made her lists of pros and cons, she pursued advice from respected friends, and she sought the Lord, and sought the Lord, and sought the Lord. But nothing. Although she was doing everything she could to figure out God's direction, she remained on the fence.

God was taking her to a deeper level of trust.

I encouraged her to just stop. Stop asking, stop searching, stop trying so hard. Put her confidence in who God says he is—her protector, her guide, her Father. If she could release all her expectations of how God would speak and simply *trust* that he would, not only would she find which way to go, she would have developed something even more valuable than the direction.

My friend never got the handwriting in the sky she was looking for. But as she continued to move forward, she sensed one overriding message from the Lord, "Do you trust me?" Each time she answered yes, she moved a step closer to the answer. The waiting period proved to be exactly what she needed.

God could have given her clarity from the beginning, but he knew she was ready for something more. Maybe you are too. I pray the next time you find yourself on hold, you will let your waiting be an incubator of trust. We shine a pretty big light when we trust the Lord as we wait.

CHAPTER TWENTY

When We're Happy Because of God's Goodness

"The world and the church once agreed that happiness was good and that all people seek it. We desperately need holiness, but it's happiness we long for, and the church shouldn't retreat from such an important word."

Randy Alcorn
—*Happiness*

Although happiness isn't the highest goal of Christians, it proves to be one of God's desires for his children. He enjoys seeing us recognize his gifts, from puppies to beauty and laughter to heartfelt friendships. All too often we miss his goodness by relegating our good fortune to coincidence. Only as we peer behind the curtain and realize a Father who loves us is orchestrating all our "happy places" do we begin to grasp the extent of his goodness. And how can we not help but shine that happiness upon every remembrance?

Good Little Gifts

If you, then, though you are evil, know how to give good gifts to your children, how much more will your Father in heaven give good gifts to those who ask him! —Matthew 7:11 (NIV)

Sometimes I get overwhelmed with God's good gifts.

About seventeen years ago, a friend asked if our son would take their little shih poo puppy. What kind of dog is that? Definitely not the Labrador, German Shorthair, or Dachshund he (or his dad) would have wanted. But in spite of mismatched expectations, Beaumont became a part of our family. I can't imagine a sweeter dog. When Josiah left for college, Beau would actually sleep in front of the door to his empty bedroom!

I've heard seventeen years is a long time for a dog to live, and the last few years took a toll on Beau. His vision, hearing, and smell all started to decline. Even his tail started going bald. He began having minor strokes, which left him disoriented. He stopped following me from room to room and no longer ran up to the car to greet me when I got home. His back legs became so unsteady that we had to carry him up and down the stairs. But because he didn't seem to be in physical pain, I just couldn't put him down.

So we prayed God would let him die naturally. He would have a bad day, but then the next day bounce back (relatively speaking), as I kept crying out to God. "Lord please don't have us make the decision."

Then came the morning when he barely moved as I lifted him out of his crate. I carried him downstairs and laid him down on his rug before leaving the house. When I got home a few hours later, he was laying still, but managed to lift his head when I walked in the door. I picked him up and within minutes, Beau breathed his last. Not only did God answer our prayers for Beau to die naturally, he went even further. He let me get home and hold him as he died. What sweet, tender comfort from a Father who cares about even the little parts of our lives.

There's plenty of unlovely things going on in the world right now. But we serve a God who still gives good gifts to those who ask him. Ahhhhh, let's never forget it.

It Had to Be You

I had heard of you by the hearing of the ear, but now my eye sees you.
—Job 42:5

One of my friends works with teenage girls. She recently said she was trying to *train* them to recognize God in their circumstances. I couldn't help but think what an apt word: *train.* Realizing God in the day-to-day doesn't come naturally. We have to train ourselves (or others) in how to connect the dots. Elizabeth Barrett Browning penned,

> *Earth's crammed with heaven,*
> *And every common bush afire with God;*
> *But only he who sees takes off his shoes,*
> *The rest sit round it and pluck blackberries*[43]

Seeing God working in everyday life makes everyday life exponentially better. My husband and I recently attended a production at Lancaster's Sight and Sound Theatre where one of my former students was performing. Our seats were located close to the wall in the upper level of the 2,047-seat auditorium. As the show opened, we searched intently to find Richard. He was a "swing" actor, meaning he didn't know from performance to performance which part he would play. Then we spotted him on the part of the stage right next to us. We figured he must have arranged us to sit there so we would be sure not to miss him. But when we talked with him after the show, we found out he didn't! Our seats were "randomly" chosen at the ticket booth. And we realized only a sovereign God could arrange such a "coincidence."

All too often we get stuck looking at our circumstances solely through natural lenses. Take Job. Job had heard about God. But before he could truly see him, he had to remove his own way of looking at things. Only then would he recognize the God he had heard about. And, boy, did he! It transformed him into a new man.

As long as we view life by what's immediately in front of us, we will miss the beauty and glory of God. We'll be like those in Browning's poem, content to pluck blackberries, oblivious to God's presence.

Recently, I've been singing "It Had to Be You" every time I identify God's divine orchestration in my life. No one else could thread my circumstances into a thing of purpose and beauty. Only a loving sovereign God can infuse the everyday with such holy joy. With something that makes me take off my shoes.

How about you?

Little Mercies

The steadfast love of the LORD never ceases; his mercies never come to an end; they are new every morning; great is your faithfulness. — Lamentations 3:22–23

Right after Chip and I were married, we moved to Florida where he and his brother bought a lot, cleared the land, and built a spec house to sell. Since at that time I had no job, I got up early every morning and went with him to work. Did I mention it was August—the absolute hottest time of the year in Florida? Sometimes while I was mixing mud or carrying a concrete block, I would literally pray for a breeze. I still remember my quiet praise when small gusts of wind found their way to Killarney Street. The Lord's little mercies.

Those unwarranted little mercies go beyond our daily bread. As gifts from a generous God, they can put a smile on our face, cause a tear in our eye, and refresh our soul. They interrupt a stumbling, weary world and remind us of an unfaltering, tireless love. A personal, one-on-one kind of affection.

Cool morning breezes in summer still make me think of God's mercies. So do sightings of a hummer at my birdfeeder, a pleasant conversation, or a mocha crème donut from Beiler's. To some people, these things may seem insignificant, but to me they serve as connectors to a great, faithful Lord whose love "never ceases" for his children.

Often those little mercies arrive in less subtle ways.

A friend of mine was going through a very difficult, heart-wrenching season of life. But it seemed every time she turned on the radio, "His Eye Is on the Sparrow" was playing. After about the third time, all thoughts of coincidence faded. She recognized God's mercy was peeking through her clouds of confusion, reminding her he was still there.

Our world seems to be getting increasingly dark. Jeremiah's memorable words in Lamentations 3 proclaim God's mercies in similar dark days. But he didn't let the dust of the world or the injustice of man shade the unshakable truth that God provides new mercies—even little ones—each day to help us get through.

I pray you take the time to recognize God's little mercies for you. May you drink in his great faithfulness and steadfast love. Every morning.

Too Good Not to Be True

For we know in part and we prophesy in part, but when the perfect comes, the partial will pass away. —1 Corinthians 13:9–10

Theologians have written how Christianity is too good not to be true. But when I accepted Jesus as Savior, I had no idea how good or how true.

Growing up in the church, one of my favorite hymns was "Love Lifted Me."[44] I remember belting out the chorus with gusto. "When nothing else could help, love lifted me!" The problem was I hadn't actually tried anything else and had no idea "I was far from the peaceful shore sinking deep in sin." My understanding of the good news reached about as far as escaping hell and getting a ticket to heaven. It would be years later, while in grad school at the University of Colorado, before I took a deeper look inside myself and realized how much I needed that ticket. I became certain nothing else could help because I'd tried a few of those "nothings." The gospel proclaims not just good news, but the best news ever.

And it's not fake news. It's true! I remember flying back to the States in 1977 after my husband and I studied at L'Abri in Switzerland. The apologetics taught by Francis Schaeffer and others opened up a new universe of understanding how faith fits in the world. I remarked to Chip, "I always knew Christianity was true, but not *this* true!" As Schaeffer would often say, "Christianity is *true truth*."

I'm still learning how good and how true.

It's too good not to be true to realize the little girl who didn't understand how she needed to be lifted by love would someday be rescued by the Master of the Sea. It's too good not to be true that love as described in 1 Corinthians 13 will in the end prevail. Patience, kindness, humility, and forgiveness will triumph over selfishness, cruelty, pride, and hatred. It's too good not to be true that our longing to be fully known and fully loved will be fulfilled in each of our futures. That all our partial understanding and unfulfilled prophesies will find completeness.

Refuse to be discouraged because you don't yet see or understand how things so good could really be true. Take God at his Word. Keep pressing in and leave childish ways of thinking behind.

Amazing Intimacy

Why, even the hairs of your head are all numbered. Fear not; you are of more value than many sparrows. —Luke 12:7

It's almost too outrageous to believe. Too profound to understand. Yet the Bible says it's true. The Creator of the Universe, Maker of all that is and ever has been, concerns himself with the intricate details of our lives. He can even identify the number of hairs on our head! Clearly, he knows more about us than we know ourselves. This should address any fear we have as to whether our life holds significance. We have been called to relate—up close and personal—to the God who understands us and loves us.

But do we recognize him?

Oswald Chambers writes, "The things that make God dear to us are not so much His great big blessings as the tiny things because they show us His amazing intimacy with us."[45] I think we sometimes misappropriate those "tiny things" as coincidences, maybe even luck. We then miss the opportunity to cultivate the intimacy he desires.

I once took some fruit to a woman, who after a year in our country remained foreign to both the culture and the language. She spent most of her days alone tending three small children while her husband worked. Before I left her home, I asked (via *Google Translate*) if she needed anything. She indicated she could use some detergent. I immediately left in search of Tide pods. But a funny thing happened on my way to the grocery store. It struck me that I wasn't just doing a "good deed." God was allowing me to participate in showing someone his kindness.

It proved to be one of those "tiny things," but the gratitude I felt loomed large. I was grateful I could help my friend, but even more grateful for the honor of being God's vessel. God had designed a tailor-made circumstance to usher me into a deeper awareness of his love for both of us. It spoke to me of his amazing intimacy.

Don't miss those tender moments, my friend. God wants to have an intimate relationship with you. He wants you to know you are "worth more than many sparrows." Let him speak to you in the small crevices of life. Ask him to bring you in to his amazing intimacy as you recognize his goodness.

Something Beautiful Happened

And a man lame from birth was being carried, whom they laid daily at the gate of the temple that is called the Beautiful Gate to ask alms of those entering the temple. —Acts 3:2

Something beautiful happened at the Gate Beautiful in Jerusalem. A crippled man—a man who had never walked in his whole life—received new legs. He sat at the temple every day, hand outstretched, hoping for a few charitable crumbs in order to simply exist. He had no idea when he asked Peter and John for money that he was going to receive a bank vault! Peter's transforming words: "I have no silver and gold, but what I do have I give to you. In the name of Jesus Christ of Nazareth, rise up and walk!" (Acts 3:6).

And he did! Right there in front of Peter, John, and the whole crowd, that poor man got new legs. Legs that took him off the beggar list. Legs that would restore his sense of dignity as a member of society. Once completely flaccid legs could now not only walk but jump up and down. And that's exactly what happened on this beautiful day. A poster boy for the power of Jesus Christ was born.

I believe something beautiful happens every time heaven touches earth. Sometimes it comes in dramatic fashion like the lame man walking. Other times the supernatural seems almost natural. But no matter how it happens, it's a beautiful thing.

A decoupage of my husband and me hangs in our foyer. My aunt captured the picture right after we were married. We're waving and laughing, the epitome of newly married bliss. She penned "Something Beautiful Happened" across the frame. There's no question in my mind that heaven intervened in bringing us together. How else can you explain a Pennsylvania boy fresh out of Vietnam picking up a University of Colorado grad student when she was hitchhiking at the Grand Canyon? Almost fifty years later, and it's still beautiful.

Beauty is one of God's good gifts. And he delights in making beautiful things happen. So, why not ask him to let us be carriers of his beauty? Maybe he would use us to cause a smile to light the face of someone weighed down by the ugliness in the world. Let's not miss one opportunity to shine what *we* have and bring heaven to earth.

An Angelic Lift

Are not all angels ministering spirits sent to serve those who will inherit salvation? —Hebrews 1:14 (NIV)

I'm not sure whether I've ever seen an angel, but one experience has caused me to wonder.

Chip and I were students in Switzerland at L'Abri studying under Francis Schaeffer. We didn't have much money, so we decided to hitchhike to Lausanne on our day off to explore the city. But as we stood by the side of the road with our thumbs out, the clouds darkened and a storm started to break through. Right then, an older woman pulled off the road and motioned for us to get in her car. She spoke French; we spoke English, but somehow, she understood where we were going. We traveled with her a short distance when she took a turn in the road and pulled up to a train station. She indicated we should catch a train to avoid the downpour. She then handed us money for the fare. It was the exact amount we would need, not only for the ticket to Lausanne, but also for the trip back.

We stood dumbfounded. *What just happened?* Our hearts full of gratitude, we continued our journey. But as we looked back at the unusual circumstance, we both wondered if it was possible our benefactor was an angel in disguise. (And this was before *Touched by an Angel* popularized angelic visitations as somewhat common.)

The author of Hebrews describes angels as alive and active in human activity. These heavenly beings are sent by God to minister to us. The psalmist calls angels the mighty ones who do God's bidding (Psalm 103:20).

The early church fathers readily acknowledged the presence of angels in daily their lives. More contemporary authors like Billy Graham, Tim Keller, Joel Miller, Judith McNutt, and many others verify the nearness and importance of angels.

So, how are we to think about angels? Although we shouldn't become obsessed with either angels or demons, I wonder if God wants us to be more aware of them. It might help us to realize our supernatural

God sends supernatural agents to help us. Maybe they even come in the form of an elderly woman driving a car.

For a Few Laughs

A time to weep, and a time to laugh; a time to mourn, and a time to dance; —Ecclesiastes 3:4

Who doesn't like to laugh? Everyone enjoys a good chuckle. As it turns out, laughter is more powerful than what we might think. The book of Ecclesiastes points out laughter as one of those "time to's." It's an essential part of the cycle of life. Studies show laughter improves our immune system, helps reduce stress, and increases circulation. One study even found people with a strong sense of humor outlived those who didn't laugh as much. Laughter is yet another sign of God's goodness.

So humor is an essential part of a healthy life. But I'm afraid the positive qualities of humor are being twisted today. Instead of building people up, the sharp knives of sarcasm are ripping them to shreds. All boundaries of decency and respect for those who disagree with certain comedians' viewpoints have been removed. "Funny" is being replaced with mockery and ridicule, which is anything but funny. All for a few laughs.

I'll never forget when I was first convicted of using humor in a hurtful manner. We were at a party, having a good ole time. Laughter flowed. As sometimes happens in those settings, one person emerged as the butt of the jokes. I hate to admit it, but I was on a roll. I missed the warning signs my humor was going too far. When my friend told me days later how much my joking had affected him, I was stunned. I had no *intention* of hurting him. But that didn't make me innocent. That incident happened over forty years ago. I still cringe when I think of it. All for a few laughs.

I don't think Jesus likes it when we use his gifts to hurt other people. People made in his image, just like us. Is getting a few laughs really worth belittling someone's dignity? Even if we think a person needs to be taken down a notch or two, has God assigned us to do it? We must not fall into the trap of using humor to replace the need for a direct conversation.

Humor used to hurt people is humor robbed of its medicinal qualities. In fact, it turns humor into poison. Let's not do that. Let's refuse to denigrate others and not laugh at those who do. A few laughs aren't worth it.

Beauty's Invitation

He has made everything beautiful in its time. —Ecclesiastes 3:11

I had opportunity to write one spring from a spot surrounded by beauty. The heavily wooded village of Mt. Gretna, Pennsylvania, housed cozy cottages with names like *Happinest, St. Augustine's Tavern, Wanderlust.* The lovely porches, renowned for their pots of geraniums, tiny twinkling lights, and wicker furniture, seem to say, "Come on up and sit a spell."

Physical beauty is a gift from a Creator God who makes everything beautiful. It offers us a much-needed reprieve from the wear and tear of daily life. It invites us to unplug, to disengage, at least for a while, from worry and responsibility and unattractive thoughts. As I walked on the rail trail a short distance from my cottage, I discovered a world embedded in a canopy of evergreens that restored my soul. Only the Author of beauty could do that.

God also gives us beauty to help us escape from some of the world's ugliness. And there's a lot of ugliness these days, isn't there? From the bombed-out cities in Ukraine, to raging wildfires in California, to the horrific aftermath of Midwest tornadoes, the loveliness once evidenced in those places has been chased away, replaced with harsh sceneries of devastation.

But beauty pushes back against despair. It instills within us hope that God will in time turn the ashes into beauty once again (Isaiah 61:3).

So, if beauty can be seen in natural creation, how about in God's highest form? Beauty in you. In me. How can beauty erase the scars of ugly words like "I don't love you anymore" or "You're worthless" or "We've decided to let you go"? How can it bring renewal from bombs of lies, wildfires of false accusations, and storms of unkind actions that have spattered holes on our landscape? I don't know how, but I know God works through beautiful words like redemption, grace, and forgiveness to paint new canvases.

So, the next time beauty invites you to "Come on up and sit a spell," why not go for it? Light a candle at your dinner table, splurge on some flowers, take a walk in the woods, enjoy a sunset, compliment the beauty you see in someone else. As you take the time to accept beauty's invitation, you just might discover how much you needed it.

You Got A Friend?

Oil and perfume make the heart glad, and the sweetness of a friend comes from his earnest counsel. —Proverbs 27:9

It's hard to overestimate God's gift of friendship.

When I think of friendships, I go back to the first ones. The school days ones. The West Portsmouth, Ohio ones. Memories of those friends remain dear to me because of our common roots. No one in my circle of friends today knows about Slab Run or Dreamland Pool or River Days. But my fellow West-siders do, and I love them for it. The West Side remains our common ground even though our connections are limited to occasional reunions.

Most all friendships form around a commonality. People we work with, ski with, read books with, volunteer with. We experience a camaraderie when we like the same things.

And that brings me to spiritual friends. Friends whose commonality rests on believing in Jesus. Friends who bow before the same God. Who seek to live according to his principles of love, integrity, justice, and mercy. We don't look the same. We come with different levels of education, different life experiences, different economic statuses. But we share an unbreakable bond that extends to eternity.

Spiritual friendships not only serve to keep us accountable; they lessen our loads. My spiritual friendships embrace the kind of loyalty that shares my burdens in prayer. They inspire me with their courage and faithfulness to God. They stand as lampposts of grace in my dark times, directing me to the Light ahead. Some call them "pit friends." I think of them as my "Sam Gamgees" (*The Hobbit*).

If I could encourage you with one thing today, it would be this. Cultivate spiritual friendships. I know, it takes time. But don't let busyness crowd out your friendships. Jesus certainly poured into his friends, and he challenges us to follow his lead. Enjoy the sweetness of friends. God's goodness to you.

Happy Places

Go, eat your bread with joy, and drink your wine with a merry heart, for God has already approved what you do. —Ecclesiastes 9:7

One of my happy places takes the form of the local bookstore. I love it when I get the chance to sit at a little table by the window and pull out my laptop. I eat my multigrain bagel with gladness and drink my latte with a joyful heart. It may sound strange, but I feel God's approval as I click on the blank Word document and try to write down his thoughts. Maybe it's somewhat akin to Eric Liddell sensing God's delight when he ran. God has always intended for the highest form of his creation to be happy.

Yet happy places can be elusive in a world occupied with a surplus of suspicion, anger, and disappointment. Only one third of Americans report being happy. It seems like there has never been so many expecting so much yet receiving so little. And all too often we squander the little joy we do manage to find.

So, what are the culprits draining our happiness bucket? Too often we let other people poke holes in our joy. Max Lucado writes in *How Happiness Happens*, that we've got to stop "petting our peeves" if we hope to be happy.[46] Don't let other people's quirks, mistakes, and insensitivities take center stage in our thinking. Instead, make an intentional decision to patiently bear with one another in love (Ephesians 4:2). Funny how a little grace dissipates toxic environments and rebounds right back in our court.

It's also hard to be happy when we don't see our short span on the earth as a gift from our Creator. When Solomon offered his sage advice to enjoy the little things in life, he was thinking about life's brevity. "Anyone who is among the living has hope—even a live dog is better off than a dead lion!" (Ecclesiastes 9:4, NIV). Although he didn't have a clear perspective on eternity, he knew the wisdom in making each moment count in everything from relationships to work.

So, friend, I hope you discover a happy place, a place where you feel God's pleasure, a place that lifts you—even temporarily—out of the world's sorrows. Enjoy God's gift of life. Don't waste it.

All in the Family

For you did not receive the spirit of slavery to fall back into fear, but you have received the Spirit of adoption as sons, by whom we cry, "Abba! Father!" —Romans 8:15

Family stands as one of the greatest reflections of God's goodness.

My heart turned somersaults of joy as I watched our daughter and son-in-law raise their right hands and swear to become legal parents of the little guy who had been in their foster care for the past two years. God had answered their prayers through Mason. Their *Gotcha Day* had finally come. Both heaven and earth must have rejoiced as they answered *we will* to the judge's questions.

I know "earth" did its part. We celebrated for the next three days! Grandparents, aunts, uncles, cousins, and friends all traveled to be a part of the momentous occasion. Of course, our new grandson had no idea as to why all the fuss. And as far as his new older brother's awareness? "We're having junk food at the party!" Tobin exclaimed. Clearly the high point for a four-year- old. What could be better than hotdogs, hamburgers, and cupcakes?

Someday the significance of what happened in the courthouse will dawn on them. But it makes me think about our adoption into the family of God. Are we just as oblivious?

Paul's letter to the early Roman church explains our adoption as children of God. Before Christ, we lived under condemnation. We belonged to the *Sin* family, bound and marked by that surname. We were slaves to fear, without hope of rescue. But when God sent his Son, everything changed. Jesus paid the debt we owed to our *Sin* family and opened the door to a new family, a new name, a new spirit . . . the Holy Spirit.

I sometimes take that transaction for granted. Like my grandson, I'm busy enjoying the hamburgers and cupcakes and I forget the deeper significance. There is nothing more important than knowing the Holy Spirit lives in me. He empowers me to overcome temptation. He enables me to draw close to God. And he entrusts me with all the treasures of the *Family business.*

How about you? If you are a believer, you've been adopted as God's child and your *Abba, Father* loves you more than you can imagine. Brother, sister, maybe it's time to go ahead, and enjoy this incredible gift of being *all in the family.*

CHAPTER TWENTY-ONE

When We Celebrate Traditions

"Oh come let us adore Him"

—Adeste Fideles

Holidays can be a major stressor for many people. Yet celebrating traditions is important to God. In both the Old and New Testaments, he calls us to remember what he has done. Holidays provide a way to both remember and appreciate what we so easily forget. Christmas especially invites us to commemorate the day that gives the other 364.242199 days meaning. But the treasures of Christmas extend far beyond December 25. From Jesus' supernatural birth, Mary and Joseph's humility, shepherds, and wise men, to Christmas trees, carols, and gift-giving, we discover crucial life-lessons. Lessons that enable us to shine as brightly as the star the magi witnessed so long ago.

Why Traditions?

Now I commend you because you remember me in everything and maintain the traditions even as I delivered them to you. —1 Corinthians 11:2

When it comes to Christmas traditions, I'm a bit of a memory-making machine.

Ornaments on our tree remind me of special friends, special places, and special events like "Baby's First Christmas" and "New York" from when Mom and I took a bus trip to the Big Apple. I think of candlelit Christmas Eve services. Of eggnog in my coffee. Of Bing Crosby belting out "White Christmas" on the video we watch every Christmas morning. Of gift opening that begins with reading Luke 2. The sights, smells, sounds, and stories of Christmas are embedded in my mind as deeply as the English language. Traditions.

I recently asked my students about their Christmas traditions. Their responses ranged from eating cinnamon rolls to father and son dressing up in Santa suits. Some spoke of extended family members gathering each year to buy gifts for needy families. Others recalled their tradition of getting new pj's every Christmas Eve. One thing was clear. Traditions left a deposit of security and good feelings in those who experienced them.

I know some of us can go a bit overboard with traditions. Scripture warns us not to let our traditions take the place of God (Mark 7:9), but I believe God likes them. I think that's why he lashed out at the Pharisees who abused traditions by making them more about their legalistic system than about him. They short-circuited the noble purpose of traditions and set them up as the end, not the means, to spiritual growth. Remember how they committed gifts to God as an excuse not to care for parents (Mark 7:11–13)? And how they set such strict laws for the Sabbath that they could deny mercy to a person in need (Matthew 12:1–13)?

The enemy always works that way. He tries to subvert God's good gifts into distractions at best, idolatry at worst. God wants us to take moments and remember where we've come from to help us not forget where we're going. Traditions serve as signposts on the journey.

Satan will seek to infuse our Christmas traditions with anything he can to take our eyes off the goodwill associated with the birth of God's

Son. Let's not let him do that. Let's allow God to cement our memories with the good-will and pleasantries of Christmas traditions. Let's pass them on to our children to remind them of God's gift.

Come, All Ye Faithful

To the saints who are in Ephesus, and are faithful in Christ Jesus. — Ephesians 1:1

When Paul addresses the church in Ephesus, he calls them faithful. That's quite the designation. But what does it mean to be faithful?

Maybe it's believing in God even when it doesn't make sense. Like when an angel appears and says you are favored by God and will bear his Son. Rather than resisting with question after question, you respond with divine simplicity, "Behold, I am the servant of the Lord" (Luke 1:38). Or maybe it's finding out your fiancé is pregnant, and because you are *faithful to the Law* you plan to divorce her quietly so she won't be disgraced. But then an angel comes to you in a dream and tells you to marry her because the child is conceived by the Holy Spirit. Your original plan takes a back seat as you do what the angel of the Lord commands (Matthew 1:24). Neither Mary nor Joseph understood how, why, or what was happening—but instead of resisting, doubting, and refusing, they trusted in God. They are among the faithful.

Faithfulness gave birth to Christianity.

Maybe being faithful means choosing to please God more than ourselves. The early church certainly demonstrated that mindset. They faced torture, ridicule, imprisonment, even martyrdom. They knew it was impossible to please God without faith, so when it came down to a choice between comfort and devotion to God, they went with God. They are among the faithful.

Faithfulness sustains Christianity.

So where are you this Christmas? Are you struggling to keep the fire of your love for God burning? Are you wavering in your faith because things you hoped for turned out differently? Are you choosing to rely on yourself or other people to help you make decisions rather than wait-ing for answers from him? Maybe sin is enticing you to be untrue to the One who will always be true to you. Are you among the faithful?

God is calling us to shine faithfulness smack dab in the middle of our holiday.

I pray for you, and for me, as we hear the strains of "O Come, All Ye Faithful" this season, we'll be able to say with abandon, "Count me in." I pray we will be among the faithful who come. Who come and adore him—Christ the King.

So It Was Thought

Now Jesus himself was about thirty years old when he began his minis-try. He was the son, so it was thought, of Joseph. —Luke 3:23 (NIV)

I love the little caveat Luke inserts into the genealogy of Jesus. Every-one *thought* Jesus to be the son of Joseph. Why wouldn't they? As Mary's husband, Joseph raised Jesus as if he were his own son. Per-fectly natural thinking. But Joseph knew better. So did Mary. They readily accepted their part in God's supernatural plan. A plan that ex-tended far beyond their understanding and surpassed anything anyone could have imagined.

The gospel of Luke challenges each of us in how we think. Will we limit our thoughts to what is perfectly natural, or open up our minds to things that can only be explained through a supernatural God? The birth, life, and resurrection of Jesus provide ample evidence for us to rise above thinking like everyone else thinks.

Jesus' birth was like any other man's . . . *so it was thought.*

Peter had been fishing all night with no success; there were no fish to be caught . . . *so it was thought.*

The man covered from head to toe with leprosy would live a life of isolation . . . *so it was thought.*

The paralytic would never walk again . . . *so it was thought.*

The tax collector lived beyond redemption . . . *so it was thought.*

Jesus died; it was over . . . *so it was thought.*

Old wineskins of thought have no room for miracles. Jesus offers us both new wine and new wineskins empowering us to soar beyond the limitations of our natural way of thinking. We can't let our faith become comfortable with dismissing God's supernatural working as something in the past. "Jesus is the same yesterday and today and forever (Hebrews 13:8).

So, are you entertaining any *so it was thoughts* today?

This marriage can't be saved . . . *so it was thought.*

My teenager is a lost cause . . . *so it was thought.*

My life has no worth . . . *so it was thought.*

Revival will never come to our nation . . . *so it was thought.*

Don't buy into what everyone else thinks. If your thought-life conforms to "perfectly natural," it's time to rethink. As a child of God, take up a new wineskin. The same power that raised Christ from the dead, lives in you.

Think like it!

And Wonders of His Love

Show me the wonders of your great love,
you who save by your right hand
those who take refuge in you from their foes. —Psalm 17:7 (NIV)

We sing about it. We read about it. It's so familiar we almost trivialize it. Yet I can't think of a better time of year to ponder and proclaim the wonders of God's love than Christmas.

Some Christmases are harder than others. Like Christmas 2020. It came at the close of a year marked with lots of loss, uncertainty, riots, and regrets. People grew weary of lockdowns, politics, and an ongoing flood of vitriol. Many of us felt helpless and hopeless. We yearned for Christmas to remind us of better days. I found myself asking, like the psalmist, *Lord, help us see the wonders of your love.*

A few weeks before Christmas, one of our neighbors rang the doorbell. A package intended for us had mistakenly landed in his mailbox. When we asked about his family, we were shocked to hear his wife had pancreatic cancer and was undergoing chemo.

After he left, I told my husband I wanted to get her a card. He said he'd thought about taking her a bouquet of holly from our holly tree. A small gesture, but sometimes tiny acts of kindness point to something bigger, maybe something full of wonder. So, a couple of days later, we knocked on their door, card and holly in hand. "I walk by your house every day," I said, "and I want you to know I will pray for you as I go by." I've kept that commitment by asking God—daily—to show them the wonders of his love.

When David was in a hard place, he cried out to God, asking him to reveal the wonders of his great love and rescue him. God answered David's prayer again and again. He will answer ours, too, as we intercede for ourselves and those around us. People need to know more than ever about this God whose love compelled him to come to earth and save us. He has given us the job of proclaiming it, no matter what the season. Let's remember that as we sing the timeless refrain:

He rules the world with truth and grace,
And makes the nations prove
The glories of His righteousness,
And wonders of His love,
And wonders of His love,
And wonders, wonders, of His love.[47]

Not So Silent

And the angel said to them, "FEAR not, for behold, I bring you good news of great joy that will be for all the people. For unto you is born this day in the city of David a Savior, who is Christ the Lord." —Luke 2:10–11

Silent night; holy night,

All is calm; all is bright.[48]

Clamorous protests continue to flood our country from its border walls to the halls of Congress and beyond. Harsh words of anger and acrimony fill our airwaves. *Our world is far from silent.*

We no longer look to God for our standard of living and consequently, an insidious "creep of cruelty" has invaded our culture says a prominent columnist. *Our world is not holy.*

Conflicts, floods, fires, and hurricanes rob people of stability as well as their earthly goods. *Our world is neither calm nor bright for many.*

And life expectancy in the United States has dropped significantly in the last few years, due in large part to the alarming increase in suicide and substance abuse. *Our world is not resting in heavenly peace.*

I have a feeling there's never been a century, a decade, or a year when the world has not needed to hear about *the dawn of redeeming grace.* "Today a Savior has been born to you . . . the Messiah, the Lord."

Christmas tells us two thousand years ago one silent night spoke—and continues to speak—louder than all the voices of malice and disruption. The holiness contained in one helpless baby proves strong enough to defeat every evil, unrighteous act that would ever exist on the face of the earth. It reminds us that hope comes in unlikely ways to those seeking truth. And peace can happen on the inside no matter what is happening on the outside.

I don't know your circumstances. But I do know our not so silent world will drown out this marvelous message of hope if we let it. So, as we recall the strains of beloved Christmas carols, let's remember how Jesus came *one silent, holy night* so we could enter into a lifetime of *God's pure light.* Bask in those *radiant beams. Christ the Savior is born!*

The Gift of Anticipation

For to us a child is born,
to us a son is given;

and the government shall be upon his shoulder,
  and his name shall be called
Wonderful Counselor, Mighty God,
  Everlasting Father, Prince of Peace. —*Isaiah 9:6*

As I read the observation by *World* columnist Andree Seu, I almost yelled out loud, *Yes. Yes. Yes. That's me!* She wrote, "Anticipation is in our nature, and our Maker wants it that way." She says human nature is wired so that we need to have things to look forward to.[49]

Sometimes I feel like the anticipator-in-chief. I anticipate everything from my morning coffee and devotions when I wake up to reading a chapter or two in a book before going to sleep. I look forward to writing in the coziness of my favorite coffee shop. To meeting with my small group of ladies on Monday afternoons. Or spending a Sunday evening watching a British mystery with my husband. In fact, there's almost no part of my day that I don't anticipate in one way or another.

And the holidays? Oh my goodness! Anticipation on steroids.

Of course, not all anticipation is positive. Fear of what might happen distorts anticipation and spells it as d-r-e-a-d. As many of you know, I teach Public Speaking—not the most anticipated class on the curriculum. In fact, one student confessed when she found out she had to take Public Speaking, she prayed for the rapture! But she made it through and said how, in spite of her fears, the class turned out to be one of her favorites. So much of what we dread does not come from the Father of hope. But from an enemy who wants to steal from us the gift of anticipation.

God gifts us with anticipation to release joy as well as provide hope in dark times. No wonder Satan wants to take it away.

As we approach celebrating the most anticipated event in human history—with its fifty-five Old Testament prophecies about Jesus' birth—let's not miss it. Every year the Christmas season offers us an opportunity to remember the God who keeps his promises and gives us reason to hope. To trust. To anticipate.

So, I pray you release that God-wired gift this year, no matter what your circumstances. May you let the Wonderful Counselor, Mighty God, Everlasting Father, Prince of Peace assure you he comes to make all things new.

I Wonder as I Wander

Behold, the virgin shall conceive and bear a son,
and they shall call his name Immanuel. —Matthew 1:23

I've always liked the Christmas carol, "I Wonder as I Wander."

> *I wonder as I wander out under the sky,*
> *How Jesus, the Savior, did come for to die.*
> *For poor onerry people like you and like I*
> *I wonder as I wander*
> *Out under the sky.[50]*

Its clever wordplay and moving melody remind me of someone who is, well, wandering. Wandering can be exciting and adventurous, not necessarily meaning that we're aimlessly lost. But some wandering can be a symptom of independence. The psalmist cries out for God to help him not wander from his commands (Psalm 119:10). Maybe it's what we're wondering about when we wander that determines where we stand.

The exciting kind of wandering comes when birthed from a sense God is with us. Knowing the Almighty God directs us to new places to complete new purposes has a way of filling us with awestruck wonder. *God, why would you let me experience such vitality, such beauty, such fulfillment?* My friend who obeyed the nudge of the Lord and made a six-month commitment to Youth With A Mission can tell you about this kind of wandering (A wandering that culminated in finding the love of her life).

The troublesome kind of wandering comes when we fail to consider what God thinks about it. We don't seek him in our decision making. Maybe we're afraid if we take our plans to the Lord, he'll nix what we want to do. Or maybe we get impatient waiting for him to speak, so we choose to move on our own understanding. That's what happened to Israel after leaving Egypt. How did forty years of wandering in the desert work out for them?

For most of us, Christmastime brings with it a bevy of activity. We wander from mall sales to website specials. From baking cookies to attending festive parties. From decorating Christmas trees to family gatherings. We know how vital it is not to forget "the reason for the season," but pausing to ponder how Jesus came can seem as distant as Bethlehem.

So, I pray in all your wandering during the Christmas season, you will take time to wonder about the son born by a virgin called Immanuel. About the Savior who came to earth for poor onery people like you and like I.

Oh Christmas Tree

The people who walked in darkness
*   have seen a great light;*
those who dwelt in a land of deep darkness,
*   on them has light shone. —Isaiah 9:2*

Several years ago my husband and I decided to plant Blue Spruce Christmas trees. We had high hopes that selling them would help pay for our daughter's college tuition. In the end, we probably made enough money to pay for about two semesters' worth of books. Not the best business venture. But I don't regret it.

Although by now the trees have either grown too tall for most living rooms or taken on a pretty straggly appearance, a couple folks still come every year looking for something to make the yuletide bright. And it's become a special tradition for us to trek up the hill and pick one for ourselves.

One year the pickings were especially slim. We looked and looked, but nothing seemed suitable. Finally, we found one that might work.

Although a bit misshapen, full branches covered one side. The problem occurred on the backside. Lots of branches, but no needles! A look only Charlie Brown could appreciate. Since it was the best option, we chopped it down, brought it into the family room, and started to decorate. By the time my husband finished finessing the lights, I was stunned. Something truly beautiful now stood in the place of what started as a somewhat ugly, skinny, half-barren tree.

Kind of like my life. Sometimes I feel full and blessed. But other days, the "backside" takes center stage. Branches of disappointment, sadness, and worry create holes that drain me of vitality and mar my appearance. I feel as needy as our little tree, desperate for someone to come and cover my emptiness with lights.

Christmas reminds me Someone has. When Isaiah prophesied about the coming Messiah, he said "a light has dawned." That Light rearranges my misshapen heart and fills the voids of my darkness. Just like our Christmas tree, I will always be imperfect, but the light of Jesus covers me in a way that reflects his beauty. He'll do the same for you.

Amazing what a half-Charlie Brown Christmas tree can show you. *Oh Christmas tree, oh Christmas tree, much pleasure doth thou bring me.*

The Great Light Has Come

For at one time you were darkness, but now you are light in the Lord. Walk as children of light. —Ephesians 5:8

Sometimes I forget that I *was* darkness. In the pre-Christ days when I worshipped myself instead of my Creator, I didn't realize how much I needed someone to save me from the dark. You would think I'd always remember how darkness used to define me, but I suspect I'm not the only one who comes to take the light we walk in for granted. *Wasn't I always this forgiving, this compassionate, this honest and true?*

Uh . . . no.

I watched some of the Kyle Rittenhouse trial on television. He was the seventeen-year-old who shot two and wounded one of the rioters during a Black Lives Matter protest in Kenosha, Wisconsin. Portrayed by the prosecutor (and the press) as a white supremist, they accused him of "crossing state lines to come and kill black people." Turns out, they were wrong. He actually worked in Kenosha and went to help the business owners whose businesses had been destroyed and to care for the wounded. He carried his gun for protection. The men he shot were all white. And a video of the incident proved he acted in self-defense.

As Rittenhouse stood before the judge, the jury rendered their verdict on all five counts. On the first count, *not guilty*. On the second count, *not guilty*. And on the third, fourth, and fifth counts, *not guilty!* Emotion overcame Rittenhouse, and he collapsed when he realized he was fully exonerated.

As I watched his emotion, I started thinking about standing before the Lord on judgment day. All my sins, mistakes, accusations leveled against me—both true and false—will be exposed. But after every count, I'll hear the Lord pronounce me *not guilty, not guilty, not guilty!* I am completely acquitted because of the blood of Jesus. I think the full realization will cause me to collapse too.

The prophet Isaiah foretold that the Messiah would come as a great light (Isaiah 9:2). "The people who walked in darkness have seen a great light; those who dwelt in a land of deep darkness, on them has light shone." The trial of Kyle Rittenhouse reminded me of the great light that declares me innocent. The light that delivered me from darkness and lives in me now.

I pray that this Christmas the great light has found a home in you as well.

Go Tell It on the Mountain

Preach the word; be ready in season and out of season. —2 Timothy 4:2

Are you telling the good news about Jesus Christ as the Christmas carol admonishes us to do?

Statistics reveal 96 percent of believers will never lead another person to Christ. We seem to lack either the conviction or compassion to engage in spiritual conversations. We can get so focused on ourselves, that we become oblivious to the needs around us.

Not only do we fail to initiate discussions about the gospel with those outside the Church who may be headed to hell, we stop sharing what God has done in our lives with fellow believers. I was talking with someone the other day who told me when he first became a Christian and started attending church, he was surprised about how many conversations revolved around football and food. He was a young believer, hungry for stories about God. Now, thirty years later, he finds himself going to church talking about football and food.

Of course, there's nothing wrong with talking about football and food, or the news, or work, or family. But I had to ask myself, *What do I think about most?* My thoughts inevitably determine my conversations. So, if I never talk about Jesus, maybe it's because I'm not thinking about him.

My husband met a new hygienist at his dental appointment the other day. As they talked, she admitted how inadequate she felt about using the practice's computer system. My husband jumped on it. He asked her if she believed God had led her to the job. "Yes," she responded. He reminded her of God's faithfulness, assuring her that if God was leading, he would equip her to do the job. It may seem like a small incident, but when he left, she couldn't stop thanking him for what he said.

Paul exhorted Timothy to preach the word in season and out of season, whether convenient or inconvenient. I think Christmas offers us a pretty convenient season to remind folks about what the birth of Jesus means. If we don't tell people about God, who will?

The people in your sphere need to hear the good news about God. So, go tell them. Tell them who he is and what he's done in your life.

Tell them at home, at work, at church. Tell them from the *mountain, hills, and everywhere.*

Wrong-Covering Love

Hatred stirs up conflict, but love covers over all wrongs. —Proverbs 10:12 (NIV)

How can I describe *wrong-covering love*? It's the God kind of love. It's not repulsed by the baser parts of our human nature. It covers all our pettiness, failures, doubts, and blatant sins. It hangs around when we try to push it away. It continues to love us even when it fully knows who we are.

Once we receive it, we can't help but want to extend it to those who wrong us. Because that's what love does. It refuses to hold grudges. Like Teflon, it covers our hearts with a substance capable of deflecting all the anger-tipped arrows of hatred we encounter in a fallen world. When you have the privilege of seeing wrong-covering love in action, you won't forget it.

I witnessed this love in one of my friends when she was snubbed by a family member. Rather than withdrawing in rejection, she chose to proactively pursue the one who hurt her. And our creative God gave her creative ways to break through. In the end, the power of God's love kept the relationship from being derailed. In fact, it grew stronger than ever. Love won. It always does when we give it a chance.

Solomon, the wisest man who ever lived, contrasted the effects of hate and love. Hatred causes conflict. It stirs up the stinky pot of divisiveness. Love, on the other hand, refuses to dwell on what's wrong. It focuses on what's right. It births truth, security, hope, and peace. Wouldn't you rather give up that nasty unforgiveness in exchange for all the goodness love brings about?

Christmas resounds with no stronger message than that of love. You, like me, will probably be exchanging gifts with loved ones this year. Maybe you will extend special blessings to those less fortunate. Or you might be gathering with friends or family members you find hard to love. I pray you will remember that the same love covering the Son of God in swaddling cloths wants to cover you in all your weaknesses, all your nakedness. Then he wants you to extend that wrong-covering love to everyone you meet, as the title of one of Bob Goff's books declares, to *Everybody Always*.

The Power of Christmas

Now the birth of Jesus Christ took place in this way. When his mother Mary had been betrothed to Joseph, before they came together she was found to be with child from the Holy Spirit. —Matthew 1:18

I once spotted a sign on a marquee: "The gift of Christmas isn't found in the mall." Although we know Jesus can't be contained in gift exchanges, traditions, or Christmas Eve services, it's easy to miss the depth, breadth, and extent of the power of Christmas.

Imagine . . .

Seeing in Mary's yieldedness, our own opportunities to respond to the Holy Spirit when he whispers our name. "Let it be to me according to your word" (Luke 1:38).

Seeing in Joseph's willingness to accept logic-defying truth, a challenge to let go of our own life-crushing defensiveness. Of choosing to lean on the Lord rather than our own understanding. "When Joseph woke from sleep, he did as the angel of the Lord commanded him" (Matthew 1:24).

Seeing in the shepherds' reaction to the angelic proclamation a renewed mindset to abandon our own "fields" to find the only "field" that matters. "And they went with haste and found Mary and Joseph, and the baby lying in a manger" (Luke 2:16).

Seeing in the magi who "traveled afar" in search of the King of Kings, to go anywhere and do anything to find the truth. "Wise men from the east came to Jerusalem, saying, 'Where is he who has been born king of the Jews? For we saw his star when it rose and have come to worship him'" (Matthew 2:1–2).

And finally, seeing in Jesus' birth the shocking triumph of humility, as we opt to nurture our own hearts with humbleness. "And she gave birth to her firstborn son and wrapped him in swaddling cloths and laid him in a manger, because there was no place for them in the inn" (Luke 2:7).

The story of God's love never gets old. Let's pause to let it soak in. We might just rediscover that the good news of great joy is for you and for me today.

In the power of Christmas.

Concluding Thoughts

I've read reports of people trapped in underground caves or mines. They experience pitch darkness. They have zero exposure to any light at all. No moon. No stars. No first rays of dawn. The blackness surrounds them like a weighted blanket. Their only hope lies in the flickering lantern of a rescuer. Once that appears, they have one option: follow the light. No matter how disoriented or confused, if they want to find safety, they have to follow the light.

I hope you realize by now that you, friend and child of God, are the light this increasingly dark world needs. The Lord has given you and me the responsibility to illuminate the way through tunnels of despair and caves of oblivion. We can't do that unless we keep our own lamps filled with oil.

In the book of Revelation, Jesus is shown in the throne room of heaven with eyes a flame of fire and feet burnished with bronze. He stands in the midst of seven lampstands that represent the seven churches (Revelation 1:12–15). John warns one of the seven, the Ephesian church, that although they have excelled in works, have endured many trials, and have walked in truth, they have lost their first love. If they do not repent and return to him, he will *remove* their lampstand (Revelation 2:2–5).

Kind of like the five virgins Jesus never knew.

I pray this book has encouraged you to not fall into the same fate as the five virgins or the "Ephesian" crowd. Keep your lamp filled with oil, burning with love for Jesus. Burning brightly. Fiercely. Eternally.

For the Great Feast is about to begin.

Acknowledgements

Where I write is kind of a big deal to me. So, I want to thank my brother-in-law, Dick Toews, for so generously letting me use his cabin as an oasis where I could pray, study and put down my thoughts. All the in-between times, you could find me with a cup of coffee and a pastry at one of my favorite haunts—Barnes & Noble, Panera, and Starbucks. Also, a special shout out to Beiler's Donuts and New Holland Coffee Company in Lancaster. Thank you for making my writing more enjoyable.

A big thank you to Marlene Bagnall for her excellent editing. You have made my book a better one. And I can't begin to express my gratitude for all the support I've received from my family. Josiah, had you not retrieved my missing pages, there might not even be a book! Thanks to my community at New Covenant Christian Church. I can't imagine doing life without you.

Chip, no one inspires me more than you to keep my lamp burning. With each passing year, the light of Jesus increasingly shines through you. You spark ideas, listen to ideas, refine ideas and serve as a constant sounding board. Your encouragement in writing this book has been immeasurable. I guess God knew what he was doing all those years ago in Flagstaff, Arizona. Thank you for continuing to *pick me up.*

Jesus, you are the light of my life. That you choose to shine through such a poor imperfect vessel remains a wondrous, humbling mystery. *Solo Deo Gloria!*

Endnotes

Chapter One: Followers of Jesus Shine Worth into Wandering Hearts

[1] Bob Goff, *Everybody Always* (Nashville: Thomas Nelson, 2018), 146.

[2] Emily Pearson, *Ordinary Mary's Extraordinary Deed* (Layton, Utah: Gibbs Smith, 2002).

[3] Barbara Bush, *Barbara Bush: A Memoir* (New York: Simon & Schuster, 1994), 153.

Chapter Two: We Shine Faithfulness to the Fickle

[4] Timothy Keller, *Hope in Times of Fear* (New York Penguin, 2021), 74.

Chapter Three: We Shine the Way Home to the Lost

[5] A.J. Swoboda, *The Dusty Ones: Why Wandering Deepens Your Faith* (Grand Rapids: Baker, 2016), 164-174.

Chapter Four: It Brings Love into Isolation

[6] Quoted in *Pearls of Wisdom: A Harvest of Quotations from All Ages,* (compiled by Jerome Agel and Walter D. Glanze, Perennial Library, (New York: Harper & Row, 1987). 143.
[7] Timothy Keller, *Prayer: Experiencing Awe and Intimacy with God* (New York: Penguin, 2014), 118.

Chapter Five: It Prepares Us for Eternity

[8] C. S. Lewis, *The Last Battle* (New York: Macmillan, 1956), 184.
[9] Pamela Meyer, "How to Spot a Liar" https://www.ted.com/talks/pamela_meyer_how_to_spot_a_liar (July 2011).
[10] C. S. Lewis, *The Great Divorce* (New York: HarperCollins, 1973), viii.
[11] Timothy Keller, *Hope in Times of Fear: The Resurrection and the Meaning of Easter* (New York: Penguin Random House, 2021), 204.

Chapter Six: The Oil Provides Gratitude and Praise in a Thankless World

[12] Viktor Frankl, *Man's Search for Meaning* (Boston: Beacon Press, 2006), 66.
[13] C. S. Lewis, *The Great Divorce* (New York: HarperCollins, 1973), 78.

Chapter Seven: The Oil Provides Holiness for Broken Lives

[14] Mark Buchannan, *Your God Is Too Safe* (Colorado Springs: Multnomah, 2001), 144.
[15] C. S. Lewis, *Screwtape Letters* (New York: Macmillan, 1962), 9.

Chapter Eight: The Oil Provides Truth Over Deception

[16] Lara Bazelon, "Divorce Can Be an Act of Radical Self-Love," https://www.nytimes.com/2021/09/30/opinion/divorce-children.html, accessed 7/22/22.
[17] Oswald Chambers, *My Utmost for His Highest* (New York: Dodd, Mead & Company, 1935), 183.

[18] J. R. R. Tolkien, *Fellowship of the Ring* (New York: Ballentine, 1965), 81.

Chapter Nine: The Oil Provides Faith In Lieu of Unbelief

[19] Mark Batterson, *The Circle Maker* (Grand Rapids: Zondervan, 2016), 15.

Chapter Eleven: With Dependence on God's Strength in Our Needs

[20] Matin Luther, "A Mighty Fortress Is Our God." https://hymnary.org/text/a_mighty_fortress_is_our_god_a_bulwark, accessed 9/9/21.
[21] Oswald Chambers, *My Utmost for His Highest* (New York: Dodd, Mead & Company, 1935), 146.
[22] Lysa Terkeurst, *It's Not Supposed to Be This Way* (Nashville: Thomas Nelson, 2018).
[23] C. S. Lewis, *The Weight of Glory* (New York: HarperCollins, 1980), 140.

Chapter Twelve: With Mercy in a World of Offenses

[24] John Bevere, *The Bait of Satan* (Lake Mary, Florida: Charisma House, 2004).
[25] Chuck Colson, *My Final Word* (Grand Rapids: Zondervan, 2015), 219.
[26] Leonardo Blair, "Most Adult US Christians Don't Believe Holy Spirit Is Real: Study," *The Christian Post*, September 10, 2021. https://www.christianpost.com/news/most-us-christians-dont-believe-holy-spirit-is-real-study.html, accessed 7/22/22.

Chapter Fourteen: With Persistence in Prayer, Problems, and Tight Places

[27] Peter Kreeft, *I Burned for Your Peace: Augustine's Confessions Unpacked* (San Francisco: Ignatius Press, 2016), 97.
[28] C. S. Lewis, *The Weight of Glory* (New York: HarperCollins, 1980), 26.
[29] Mark Buchannan, *Your God Is Too Safe* (Colorado Springs: Multnomah, 2001).

[30] J. R. R. Tolkien, *The Two Towers,*
https://www.youtube.com/watch?v=k6C8SX0mWP0, accessed 8/3/21.

Chapter Sixteen: We Shine the Extraordinary into the Mundane

[31] Eric Metaxas, *If You Can Keep It: The Forgotten Promise of American Liberty* (New York: Penguin, 2016).
[32] Corrie ten Boom, *Guideposts Classics: Corrie ten Boom on Forgiveness,* https://www.guideposts.org/better-living/positive-living/guideposts-classics-corrie-ten-boom-forgiveness, accessed 4/5/21.
[33] Mark Buchannan, *Your God Is Too Safe* (Colorado Springs: Multnomah, 2001), 56.
[34] Os Guinness, *Carpe Diem Redeemed: Seizing the Day, Discerning the Times* (IL: InterVarsity Press, 2019), 18.

Chapter Seventeen: We Shine Comfort into Disappointment

[35] Oswald Chambers, *My Utmost for His Highest* (New York: Dodd, Mead & Company, 1935), 122.
[36] Aleksandr Solzhenitsyn, *The Gulag Archipelago: 1918-19656, Volume 2* (New York: Harper Perennial Modern Classics; Reissue edition, 2007), 615-617.
[37] Teresa of Avila, https://aleteia.org/2017/07/07/in-light-of-heaven-the-worst-suffering-on-earth-will-be-seen-to-be-no-more-serious-than-one-night-in-an-inconvenient-hotel/, accessed 1/26/22.
[38] Joe Parkinson and Drew Hinshaw *Bring Back Our Girls: The Untold Story of the Global Search for Nigeria's Missing Schoolgirls* (New York: Harper, 2021)

Chapter Eighteen: We Shine Hope into Doubt

[39] Bob Goff, *Live in Grace, Walk in Love: A 365-Day Journey* (Nashville: Thomas Nelson, 2019), 137.

Chapter Nineteen: When We Trust in the Face of Fear

[40] Patricia Heaton, posted on https://www.dailywire.com/news/patricia-heaton-after-riots-if-youre-a-common-sense-person-you-probably-dont-feel-you-have-a-home-in-this-world-right-now, accessed 6/22/22.

[41] "Prayer of St. Francis," full prayer at https://www.cathe-dralstm.org/about-our-catholic-faith/expressing-our-faith/treasury-catholic-prayers/prayer-st-francis-assisi-prayer-peace/, accessed 7/22/22.

[42] A.J. Swoboda, *Messy: God Likes It That Way* (Grand Rapids: Kregel, 2012), 64.

Chapter Twenty: When We're Happy Because of God's Goodness

[43] Elizabeth Barrett Browning, From "Aurora Leigh." http://www.learning-living.com/2015/05/elizabeth-barrett-browning-earths.html, accessed 3/14/22.

[44] James Rowe, "Love Lifted Me," https://hymnary.org/text/i_was_sinking_deep_in_sin_far_from_the, accessed 7.22.22.

[45] Oswald Chambers, *My Utmost for His Highest* (New York: Dodd, Mead & Company, 1935), 155.

[46] Max Lucado, *How Happiness Happens: Finding Lasting Joy in a World of Comparison, Disappointment, and Unmet Expectations* (Nashville: Thomas Nelson, 2019), 27-40.

Chapter Twenty-One: When We Celebration Traditions

[47] Isaac Watts, "Joy to the World," 1719. *Heavenly Highway Hymns,* https://hymnary.org/text/joy_to_the_world_the_lord_is_come, accessed 7/22/22.

[48] Joseph Mohr, lyrics; Franz Gruber, composer, "Silent Night" 1833. https://hymnary.org/text/silent_night_holy_night_all_is_dark_save, accessed 7/22/22.

[49] Andre Seu, "Looking Forward," *World Magazine*, November 21, 2019.

[50] John Jacob Niles, "I Wonder as I Wander," https://hymnary.org/text/i_wonder_as_i_wander_out_under_the_sky, accessed 7/22/22.

About the Author

Becky Toews lives in Lancaster, Pennsylvania, with her husband, Chip. They have served in ministry for over forty-five years after studying under Francis Schaeffer at L'Abri in Switzerland. They have two children and three grandsons. Becky also teaches Public Speaking at Lancaster Bible College and is the author of *Virgin Snow: Leaving Your Mark in the World* and *Between the Lamp Posts: 365 Devotions for God-Seekers.*

You can visit her website @ beckytoews.com where she posts weekly devotional thoughts. You can also connect with her on Facebook @ www.facebook/authorbeckytoews/ and on Twitter @Becky_Toews and Instagram @beckytoews.

Becky's Books

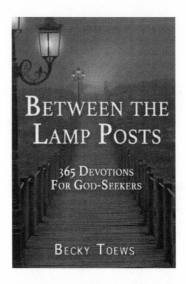

Between the Lamp Posts: 365 Devotions for God-Seekers

Looking to add substance to your daily bread?

You know the need for a regular devotional life. But you're busy. You want something to intensify the light of Scripture that lasts through the day. Something that adds substance to your daily bread. *Between the Lamp Posts* offers relevant, contemporary insight to enrich your walk with God. Illustrations from everyday life will help you apply the Scripture in practical ways. You'll find how principles of faith can be found in Screamo concerts, Bonsai trees, and Swiss chocolate bars. And how titles like "Stubbornness of Hope," "What Do You Do with Doubt?" and "Not Your Typical Messiah" illuminate your steps. The 365 devotionals will stretch your thoughts, stir your passion, and challenge you to go the next mile.

Available in print or kindle at Amazon.com or you can order a copy directly from Becky at beckytoews@newcovcc.us.

Virgin Snow: Leaving Your Mark in the World

Fresh tracks moving through unchartered territory saying, "I was here—identifiably here." Like leaving footprints in fresh snow, we all leave marks in life. *Virgin Snow* shares a biblical perspective of how to develop marks that last. In our pursuit of fulfillment, only the character of Christ, distinctly engraved on us and shared with others, will produce the meaning we long for.

Virgin Snow offers a fresh outlook concerning the everyday challenges we face and does so in an understandable, practical way that is ideal for personal or group study.

Available in print or kindle at Amazon.com or you can order a copy directly from Becky at beckytoews@newcovcc.us.

Made in the USA
Middletown, DE
03 October 2022

11798254R00205